Special Educational Needs Review

**Books are to be returned on or before
the last date below.**

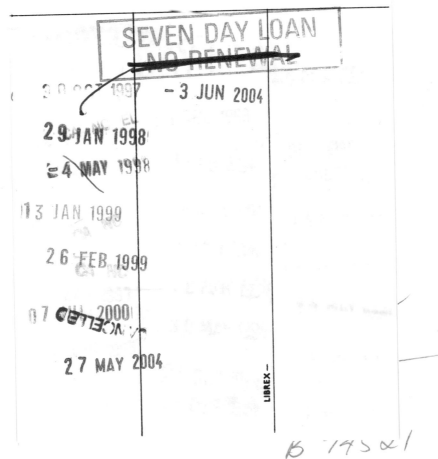

Education and Alienation Series

Series editor: Neville Jones, Principal Educational Psychologist, Oxfordshire

Special Educational Needs Review
Volume 2

Edited by

Neville Jones

 The Falmer Press

(A member of the Taylor & Francis Group)
London, New York and Philadelphia

UK   The Falmer Press, Falmer House, Barcombe, Lewes,
            East Sussex, BN8 5DL

USA   The Falmer Press, Taylor & Francis Inc., 242 Cherry Street,
            Philadelphia, PA 19106–1906

© Selection and editorial material copyright N. Jones 1989

First published 1989

British Library Cataloguing in Publication Data

Special educational needs review.—(Education
    & alienation series).
    Vol. 2
    1. Great Britain. Special education
    I. Jones, Neville. 1930–   II. Series
    371.9′0941

ISBN 1-85000-490-0
ISBN 1-85000-491-9 Pbk

**Library of Congress Cataloging in Publication Data is available on
request**

Jacket design by Caroline Archer

Typeset in 10/12 Garamond by
Chapterhouse, The Cloisters, Formby L37 3PX

*Printed in Great Britain by
Redwood Burn Limited, Trowbridge, Wiltshire*

Contents

Abbreviations

ACE	Aids for Communication in Education
ACSET	Advisory Committee on the Supply and Education of Teachers
BAGA	British Amateur Gymnastics Association
BRIB	Birmingham Royal Institute for the Blind
CDT	Craft, Design and Technology
CNAA	Council for National Academic Awards
CSF	Cerebrospinal fluid
DES	Department of Education and Science
DTI	Department of Trade and Industry
EDY	Education of the Developmentally Young
ESG	Education Support Grant
FE	Further Education
GERBIL	Great Education Reform Bill
GRIST	Grant Related In-Service Training
HMI	Her Majesty's Inspectorate
ILEA	Inner London Education Authority
INSET	In-Service Training
IT	Information Technology
LAPP	Lower Attaining Pupils Programme
LEAs	Local Education Authorities
MEP	Microelectronics Education Programme
MESU	Microelectronics Education Support Unit
NAPCE	National Association for Pastoral Care in Education
NFER	National Foundation for Educational Research
PSUs	Professional Study Units
RACE	Rapid Action for Conductive Education
RNIB	Royal National Institute for the Blind
SEMERCs	Special Education Microelectronic Resource Centres
SEN	Special Educational Needs
SENIOS	Special Educational Needs in Ordinary Schools
SLDs	Severe Learning Difficulties
SNAP	Special Needs Action Programme
SNSC	Special Needs Software Centre
TRIST	TVEI Related In-Service Training
TVEI	Technical and Vocational Education Initiative

Preface

Oxfordshire Disaffected Pupil Programme

The positive approach of the Oxfordshire Disaffected Pupil Programme (DPP) draws attention to what can and is being achieved in our schools to improve the experience of pupils who are, or who may feel, alienated in school. The focus of the Programme is towards the kind of good teaching and effective management for all pupils, which in themselves prevent disaffection, and which can actively engage in the processes of restitution and re-engagement for those pupils who are already alienated. This is to recognize that in spite of ideas for individual pupils, and education as a whole, such ideals cannot always be reached and regularly maintained. No matter how effective and skilled teachers are in their teaching and the management of their schools, there will always be some pupils who are more than a little disaffected with their school experience, and some who as a consequence become actively alienated.

The Programme, however, is essentially about the prevention of disaffection. This can be achieved through curriculum innovation, the ethos and values of schools, effective leadership, through teachers refining their teaching skills together with effective classroom management — all within a context of positive teacher-pupil relationships, by the involvement of parents and others from the local community — and indeed, through organizational planning within schools which can in itself so easily marginalize pupils and their learning.

Disaffection is a normal human sentiment but it has connotations that are both positive and damaging. Disaffection can be a spur to re-evaluating personal goals and a motivating force to achieve these: it can damage self-esteem, confidence and worthwhileness, when it becomes expressed in severe, complex and persisting forms. It is when pupils feel they cannot resolve their dissatisfactions, or feel they are not receiving help to do so, that they are then at risk of becoming educationally alienated. The Disaffected Pupil Programme, as part of its enquiry, liaison, and dissemination aspect, is engaged in bringing attention, through publications, to the innovatory work now being carried out throughout the education service in Britain. This volume is part of that work.

The Review is part of a new series of publications, bringing together a collective knowledge and expertise from known authorities in their respective fields, both in this country and overseas. The aim in this book is to provide a forum for the dissemination of current thinking and ideas about the education of pupils with special educational needs.

This Preface provides an opportunity to express an appreciation to many colleagues in the field of education in general, and special education in particular, for their advice and counselling as to the style and emphasis that would be enhancing for a book series of this kind. In particular I wish to express my warm thanks to Christine Cox, my Editor at Falmer Press, for her positive guidance in the planning of this and other volumes, and for support on every occasion to secure this second volume in the series in print.

Neville Jones
Director, Disaffected Pupil Programme
Oxfordshire.

Introduction

Ronald Davie

At the invitation of the Editor I shall not attempt to draw together the contributions by a distinguished and experienced panel of authors in this second review on special educational needs. Rather, what follows will comprise a brief overview of the special needs field, as we enter the 1990s. It focuses inevitably on the two major pieces of educational legislation which have so dramatically transformed the framework within which services for children with special needs operate, namely, the 1981 Act and the 1988 Education Reform Act. The particular issues which currently occupy centre stage are integration, partnership with parents, inter-agency cooperation, open enrolment, grant-maintained status, local management of schools and the National Curriculum. This rather crowded cast-list inevitably raises questions about the script and, in particular, whether the stage direction has been properly thought through.

The first three issues mentioned above are most obviously linked to the 1981 Act and yet the reciprocity between this and the 1988 Act should never be forgotten. Indeed, there have been dangers (Davie, 1989), not yet entirely dispelled, that the two Acts may have some areas of incompatibility — in spirit, if not in law.

The integration of pupils with special educational needs into mainstream schools was the flagship of the 1981 Act. Much progress has been made on this front, although a great deal remains to be achieved. The arrival of the 1988 Act, some fear, may slow down progress and even reverse this trend. This is a particular source of concern in inner London, where the disappearance of ILEA may be followed by a period of uncertainty in some of the newly autonomous borough education departments.

There are twin dangers in this context. Such uncertainty may result in some return to segregation, because the latter offers the security of a known system. On the other hand, there could be a temptation to seize this opportunity to close down special provision either simply to save money, or because of a simplistic equating of mainstreaming with integration.

Outside of London, the threat to continuing progress on integration seems to come from two main directions. First, given finite resources, the energy and commitment which the 1988 Act will demand is almost certain to diminish the drive on other education fronts. Integration may fall into this backwash. The second danger for integration may lie in the implementation of the National Curriculum. I shall return to this aspect later.

The other major thrust of the 1981 Act was, of course, the concept of a partnership with parents. Research findings on the implementation of the Act (Goacher *et al.*, 1988) indicates that there is some way to go before this goal nears realization. Whilst it seemed clear that the principle of partnership was in general recognized and accepted, 'Changed practice had yet to begin in many areas of the LEA procedures. Previous patterns of working, sets of beliefs about parents and their willingness and capacity to play a larger part in decisions about their children, professional uncertainty and paternalism all had a part to play in the process'. The small sample of parents interviewed as part of this national study were by no means completely happy about the way they had been treated.

On the other hand, a local investigation carried out by the National Children's Bureau for one London borough suggested a fair measure of satisfaction by parents with the services for their children with special educational needs (Berridge and Russell, 1988).

The need for effective collaboration between education, health and social services was more implicit than explicit in the 1981 Act and in the consequential guidance and circulars. Perhaps partly as a result, this collaboration leaves much to be desired. A significant minority of local education departments failed entirely to consult or involve health or social services in the formulation of their policy and procedures under the Act (Goacher *et al.*, op. cit.). Predictably, there is now no sense of ownership or commitment in many of these health or social services authorities. The successful implementation of the procedures across departments can thus depend upon the goodwill, interest or personal affinity of individual professionals. This is clearly not an acceptable situation.

Turning now to the 1988 Education Reform Act, we have a piece of legislation which many have compared to the 1944 Act in its importance and scope. As far as schools are concerned, there is much to commend in the new Act. The need for increased accountability and for a continuing search for higher standards is largely accepted; and the principle of a National Curriculum is agreed by the major political parties and by most within education, not least those concerned with special needs. The reservations about the 1988 Act and about the speed and manner of its introduction cannot concern us here. However, two fundamental features of the legislation are especially relevant to the special needs field in ways which call for careful and continuing scrutiny.

First, although open enrolment, grant maintained status and the local management of schools are separate concepts, they have in common that they are designed to expose schools to the market forces of parental demand and public scrutiny. The costs and benefits of this approach for the education service as a whole are a debatable issue but the potential dangers for pupils with special educational needs are clear.

The pressure on schools to monitor and wherever possible improve their educational standards, whilst laudable in itself, may result in children with significant learning difficulties being seen by some as a millstone. As a group they will depress the published academic results of the individual school and, of course, they make heavy demands on resources. If schools come to see themselves increasingly as small businesses, courting their actual and potential shareholders (parents) with their balance sheets (GCSE and other results), the temptation to discontinue unprofitable lines (pupils with poor results and high costs) may become irresistible for some. Of course, it would be unthinkable and unacceptable to do this openly or ruthlessly. Nevertheless, a school which convinces itself that its major strengths and thrust lie in catering for pupils with good academic achievements, may quickly give out messages — most of them non-verbal — to parents of low achieving children (and to the children themselves) that at worst they are unwelcome and at best that their needs will be better met elsewhere. One of the tragedies of such a scenario is that the latter message will probably be self-fulfilling.

I sketch this chilling projection into the future partly to pinpoint the dangers but also to signal the difficulties of avoiding such tendencies. For example, any Secretary of State for Education will insist that a school which opts out of local authority control should maintain its present character in serving the local community for a prescribed period at least. However, any monitoring of a school's compliance with such a stipulation must be somewhat crude and the subtleties of attitude and ethos in a school are the most likely factors to be at play here. Furthermore, if as a result of such factors, that minority of parents whose children find learning difficult *choose* to take their offspring elsewhere, could a future Secretary of State deny them that choice?

In such ways might the character of schools change beyond the control of any local or central legislation or bureaucracy. Indeed, the underlying philosophy requires that they do change in response to demand. However, popular appeal and majority-led decisions can be hard on minorities; and when the minority, as in this case, comprises children who are handicapped in some way, the well known public ambivalence towards disability could result in some rejection of these pupils.

What is true for schools who have opted out of local authority control applies equally to the principle of open enrolment. The end result of the above tendencies could at worst be the creation of ghetto schools, which largely contain pupils whom other schools do not want, which have low standards but which cannot be closed down because there is nowhere else for them to go. Of course, low achievement cannot be equated with special educational needs. Nevertheless, the possibility of pupils with learning difficulties of any kind being concentrated in particular schools, whether mainstream or special, is contrary to the spirit of the 1981 Act.

The potential problems created for pupils with special educational needs by the local financial management of schools derive from a similar root. Such children are expensive to teach because of the high pupil/teacher ratio often required and, occasionally, special equipment. In addition, they need more support services from educational psychologists, from advisors, from peripatetic teachers and others than does the average child. At present the position on support services seems unclear but if schools managing their own financial affairs are free to buy in such services or not, the temptation to economise might work to the disadvantage of pupils with special needs. It might well be possible to construct formulae in an attempt to control the situation somewhat and reduce this danger. Nevertheless, if the implicit value system of a school were to give low priority to pupils with special needs, there is a myriad of ways, including financial ones, in which this can find expression.

Enough has been said to illustrate the nature of the concerns in this area. The fundamental issue is the extent of the compatibility between, on the one hand, a demand-led service with schools competing for pupils, being judged by their published academic results and having a considerable degree of financial autonomy with which to reinforce their priorities; and, on the other hand, the special needs of a sizeable minority of pupils who are expensive to resource, who will depress a school's competitive performance but whose interests must be safeguarded, thus reducing the school's autonomy and placing constraints upon its priorities.

At the present time, this substantive issue is overlaid with uncertainty and anxiety about the eventual outcome.

The second major feature of the Education Reform Act which must claim our attention in any overview of the current and likely future situation is the National Curriculum. As mentioned earlier, the general principle of a National Curriculum is widely accepted, although caution has been expressed about the danger of over-prescription; and the framework of ten 'subjects' seems out of keeping with some of the exciting cross-curricular work developed in many of the best schools in recent years.

Amongst other objectives, the National Curriculum aims to assist schools in monitoring progress made by individual pupils, in a way which will be helpful to, and shared by, teachers, parents and pupils alike. The aim of stretching pupils — all pupils — to their best achievements must be universally shared.

For many, though by no means all, pupils with special educational needs these achievements will be somewhat or very limited but the principle of realizing their full potential remains. Most teachers in this field will accept that the scope for improving standards amongst pupils with special needs is at least as great as amongst the rest of the school population, so that the National Curriculum should be applied with the same rigour. 'Soft options' and inappropriately low aspirations do a disservice to these pupils, as to any others. They have an entitlement to the curriculum and a right to be challenged and extended intellectually.

On the other hand, their special needs may at times require a flexible approach which enables them to gain access to the programmes of study, or to have their progress assessed, by alternative means than those which are appropriate for the majority. Thus, practical work may present problems for some with a physical disability; and oral work will be difficult for those with a communication disorder, including deaf children. In addition, the pacing of some pupils through particular programmes of study, and even the definition of a 'balanced' curriculum, may differ between pupils.

It remains to be seen how far it will be possible to combine the necessary rigour with the necessary flexibility. The twin evils to be avoided are, on the one hand, excessively prescriptive curricula, which thus require that sizeable minorities of pupils have to be opted out, in part or in whole, merely in order that schools may comply with the over-legalistic requirements of statutory orders. This route would doubtless lead to increased numbers of 'statements' and some re-appearance of the categorization which the 1981 Act was designed to dispel. The other evil is a system so flexible as to have no real bite and which in its own way would deny the undoubted benefits and entitlements of the National Curriculum for children with special educational needs.

I hope and believe that these twin evils can be avoided. Furthermore, the detailed thought and guidance which will need to go into such avoidance will benefit not only those pupils conventionally described as having special educational needs, but also any pupil whose particular case may require such a combination of rigour and flexibility to meet his/her individual circumstances.

References

BERRIDGE, D. and RUSSELL, P. (1988) *A Red Bus Next Year?* (Consumer perceptions of special education in the London Borough of Haringey), Haringey Education Dept., 48 Station Rd., London N22 4TY.

DAVIE, R. (1989) 'Special education needs: Policy into practice', in: EVANS, R. (Ed.) *Response to Special Educational Need*, Oxford: Basil Blackwell.

GOACHER, B., EVANS, J., WELTON, J. and WEDELL, K. (1988) *The 1981 Education Act: Policy and Provision for Special Educational Needs*, London: Cassell.

1
Towards Special Needs Training for All?

Peter Mittler

Unless the present favourable opportunity is taken to improve the professional qualifications of teachers in special education, and hence the
quality of special education itself, we fear that the next twenty years may
yet again be a period of unfulfilled hope (Warnock Report, DES 1978,
para 19. 32).

Warnock to Baker: Or back to the future?

In the ten years since the publication of the Warnock Report, we have begun to
understand that the training of teachers in special education is inseparable from the
training of all other teachers. The dividing line between special and ordinary
education and hence between special and ordinary teacher education has all but
disappeared. If every teacher is a teacher of children with special educational needs,
it follows that the concepts and practices of special education must be an integral
element of each and every aspect of teacher education. By the same token, any
changes in the curriculum and organization of schools is bound to affect children
with special needs, either for better or worse.

During the last decade, the school curriculum has been undergoing a major reappraisal, with an emphasis on questions of access and relevance to all pupils in the
school, including those from socially disadvantaged backgrounds, children from
ethnic and linguistic minorities, as well as those with special needs of all kinds. For
example, some fundamental curricular reforms were outlined in a series of challenging reports from the Inner London Education Authority (1984, 1985). These
reports proposed a shift from the 'cognitive-academic', examination-dominated
curriculum towards one influenced by personal, social and aesthetic education
(Hargreaves, 1982), as well as changes in teaching style and in the organization and
management of schools (Sayer, 1987).

Although the imminent abolition of the ILEA now makes it unlikely that
these reports will be implemented, a number of curriculum initiatives, particularly
in secondary schools, could greatly improve the access of children with special needs

to the mainstream curriculum. These include profiles and records of achievement, criterion-referenced assessment, developments in personal and social education, alternative curricular strategies, the Technical and Vocational Education Initiative, as well as the process of teaching and assessment leading to the General Certificate of Secondary Education (Mittler, 1987). Above all, the establishment of special needs departments in secondary schools and the appointment of designated special needs support staff in primary schools has led to attempts to define and implement 'whole school approaches' to meeting special needs. These include in-class support rather than withdrawal, and an examination of curriculum access in each subject area, in partnership with subject and class teachers, in terms of readability of texts, clarity of worksheets, the language of instruction and the organization of the classroom during individual lessons (Galloway and Goodwin, 1987; Hinson, 1987; Mittler, 1987; Thomas and Feiler, 1988).

Staff development is therefore an integral element of policy, planning and implementation. At the same time, teacher training will have to respond and perhaps to provide leadership with equally radical matching initiatives. Courses in special needs will need to permeate all aspects of teacher education, rather than being grafted on as an optional extra.

Clearly, a national or local strategy of teacher education is needed, one that involves a working partnership between higher education, the DES and LEAs, including Teachers' Centres and resource centres, as well as individual schools and teachers. Unfortunately, there are few signs of such national or local strategies emerging. Teacher education is not given the priority or the resources which it deserves at any level. LEAs are preoccupied with their changing responsibilities, especially with the Education Reform Act; many advisers have left LEAs, ground down first by GRIST and then by GERBIL, their posts either frozen, absorbed or lost altogether. The DES seems to have lost all direction where special needs are concerned and there is little evidence that the advice and experience of HMI is heeded by Ministers or the senior civil service.

The 1988 Education Act

The implications of the 1988 Education Reform Act call for an even more radical re-appraisal of the whole basis of teacher education than anything that could have been foreseen by the Warnock Committee. The concerns voiced by the special needs constituency can be summarized as follows:

1. How will the national curriculum and regular testing affect children with special needs already in ordinary schools? Is there a risk that too many of these children will be unnecessarily 'exempted' from some or all of the national curriculum? Will more of them be given the 'protection of a statement' and sent to special schools? Will there be two groups of children — those on and those not on the national curriculum, or, alternatively, statemented and non-statemented children?

2. Conversely, are ordinary schools less likely to accept children from special schools in future, since they demand extra resources of time, staff and equipment?

3. Because the national curriculum is conceived largely in terms of traditional subject boundaries, what will be the place of cross-curricular initiatives, such as personal and social education, careers education, health education, domestic science, the low-attaining pupils programmes, TVEI? Will the 'whole child — whole school' approaches of special needs survive a more subject-oriented, assessment-driven curriculum?

4. What priority can children with special needs expect once schools have a greater degree of financial delegation and much more autonomy in setting their own priorities?

5. Will initiatives which have up to now been taken by Local Education Authorities in the field of special needs survive the considerably weakened role of LEAs envisaged in the future? These initiatives have included a wide range of duties arising from the 1981 Education Act, including identification and assessment, staffing and deployment of LEA support and advisory services; the organization of multi-disciplinary assessment; working with parents; staff development.

6. Will special needs really be met in the new grant-maintained schools, given their nature and the circumstances in which they have been created? Although a clause was at the last minute inserted indicating that such schools were subject to the 1981 Education Act, there are fears that other priorities will prevail. Furthermore, it would not be surprising if LEAs gave priority to their own schools when requests for special needs support services were made by a grant-maintained school or City Technical College.

Grant Related In-Service Training (GRIST)

The Education Act, together with the fundamental changes already introduced into the control and funding of in-service education, demand a reappraisal of the whole basis of INSET work for all teachers, as well as of the relative contribution of teachers, schools, advisers, LEAs and higher education.

The government have already introduced wide-ranging changes in the planning and funding of in-service courses — partly by selecting nineteen national priority areas at the centre and partly by allowing LEAs to spend their INSET funds without further central monitoring. In theory, this should mean that teachers should be being helped to identify their needs for further training and that LEAs should be expressing a commitment to meet those needs. Whether this will happen remains to be seen. Even more uncertain is the role of universities, polytechnics and colleges in working in partnership with teachers, schools and LEAs. As things look at the moment, LEAs can no longer afford to second teachers for longer courses.

The future of special needs work in higher education needs to be rethought from first principles. The traditional one-year full-time course leading to advanced diplomas and M.Eds is under threat and may not survive. Secondments for research leading to M.Phil and Ph.D will be rare or non-existent, except for overseas students. Part-time, half-day or evening courses, organized largely along modular lines, are likely to survive, but LEAs are increasingly calling for these to be skill-based and school-focused.

Given the small teaching force in higher education, how should they best deploy their resources? Should they continue to offer courses on site or should they travel to LEAs, to Teachers' Centres and to schools themselves? How can courses be funded, given the cutbacks and early retirements in higher education? How can skilled and highly qualified teachers be offered part-time tutorships, as encouraged by government policy, when they cannot be spared by their LEAs, under current GRIST funding patterns? Who should have greater priority: teachers in special schools retraining for a new role as support teachers or teachers in ordinary schools on the verge of assuming new responsibilities for pupils with special needs? Which has greater priority: initial teacher training, the training of specialist, advisory and resource teachers or the training of all teachers to become teachers of children with special needs?

There are those who argue against giving priority to training support and advisory teachers, on the grounds that by their very presence they deskill and deprofessionalize the ordinary classroom teacher. On this argument, the more we train specialists, the more we risk segregating teachers from one another and from the children they teach (e.g. Potts, 1985, and other chapters in Sayer and Jones, 1985). The counter-argument is that until we reach the Utopia in which 'every teacher is a special needs teacher', we require a transitional stage where a small well-trained cadre of specialists work with their colleagues in mainstream education, supporting and advising them to the extent that they wish and in response to the needs of the children they teach.

Initial teacher training

The compulsory special educational element in initial teacher training which is now being enforced by HMI and the Council for the Accreditation of Teacher Education (CATE) is clearly a step in the right direction and a foundation stone for later INSET. But it remains to be seen whether this requirement can be implemented. Indeed, the most recent HMI report on initial teacher training singles out special needs as an area to which too little attention is paid in initial training (HMI, 1988).

Such special needs training as exists in higher education in Britain is carried out by a very small number of staff — sometimes by a single token special educator, sometimes by staff with no training and little first-hand experience in this field. Even with a small but powerful team, real progress in influencing the initial training of teachers can only come about through a total infiltration and permeation of the whole of the mainstream teacher training curriculum both for primary teachers and for secondary subject specialists.

The reappraisal of the initial teacher training curriculum that this involves is so radical and fundamental that it is difficult to see how it can be achieved within the present restrictions on teacher training. Needless to say, no funds have been made available to enable higher education to recruit additional special needs teacher trainers, or even to protect existing staff from redeployment or from the temptations of early retirement schemes. Consequently, there has been a reduction of special needs tutors in higher education, rather than the expansion called for by Warnock.

Training for a whole-school approach

If a whole-school approach to special needs is to be developed, all teachers in all schools will need to be involved at some level. The immensity of such a task seems overwhelming.

There is now a growing recognition that every teacher has the right to a positive plan for professional development, and that the school itself must in future play a more active role in mobilizing the resources needed to provide this.

In the past, professional development has largely been seen in terms of opportunities to attend advanced courses, often in distant (in every sense) colleges and universities. Although there is still a key role for higher education within a total training strategy, the emphasis now is more on school-based or school-focused in-service training, supplemented by local courses organized through Teachers' Centres or provided through the support services. Such courses are clearly well placed to identify and meet local needs, whether within a single school, a network or cluster of schools, or a local community.

But will the new GRIST arrangements meet these needs? In theory, GRIST provides a framework in which LEAs can negotiate a staff development strategy for each school and each teacher, as well as for the LEA as a whole. Training to meet special needs in schools and Further Education Colleges are two of nineteen priority areas which will attract 70 per cent financial support from the DES.

Evidence available so far suggests that the total amount of money now available to LEAs is considerably less than under the earlier pooling arrangement, despite the fact that the new scheme was announced by Ministers as 'a new £200 million initiative'. Whatever the true facts, it is clear that few LEAs feel able to continue to second staff for full-time courses of advanced study in institutions of higher education. Even the future of one-term courses is in doubt. The emphasis seems to be largely on short, skill-based school-based courses, planned and delivered by advisers and by other LEA staff. In the field of teacher education as a whole, there is evidence of a two-thirds reduction in the number of teachers seconded for one-year full-time courses in 1987/1988. Indeed, the essence of GRIST is that LEAs have the freedom to choose not to use higher education.

The increased emphasis on school-based INSET is in many ways welcome, for many reasons. But few teachers seem to have realized that opportunities to study for award-bearing diplomas and degrees have been greatly reduced. Contracture or closure of longer courses will remove opportunities to undertake more detailed, in-depth study and reflection and to train for positions of leadership in schools and LEAs.

One-term full-time courses for 'designated' teachers

Although helping all teachers in all schools to modify attitudes and practice to include the whole range of abilities and needs within the ordinary school is the only proper long-term strategy, an essential intermediate step involves the designation and training of a core team in each school to assume particular responsibility for meeting special needs.

Since 1983, funds have been earmarked for one-term full-time courses to permit the release of teachers with designated responsibility for special needs in ordinary schools. Twenty-five courses were in operation in 1986; although the intro-duction of GRIST initially undermined recruitment, these courses are likely to continue in one form or another. Circular 1/88 makes it clear that DES expects designated teachers in ordinary schools to be trained by this route.

Teachers are selected by their employers and not by the training institutions on the understanding that they will become change agents in their own schools and sometimes, in the case of primary schools, for a consortium of neighbourhood schools. A contractual arrangement is developed between the seconded teacher, the headteacher, an LEA adviser and the higher education tutor which aims to facilitate the implementation of change in the school.

These courses have now been evaluated by the NFER (Hegarty and Hodgson, 1988). Based on in-depth interviews with people involved in four courses and ques-tionnaire studies of the remaining twenty-one, it was clear that the courses had a considerable impact on schools and on the knowledge and skills of participants, many of whom were able to implement at least some degree of change for the better in planning and provision for pupils with special educational needs. In addition to the national evaluation, Jeffs (1988) has provided a thoughtful analysis of such one-term courses at Bristol Polytechnic, emphasizing ways in which the planning, organization and content of such courses can contribute to better practice in schools.

In considering the impact of these courses, several factors seemed important. These included the course member's status, seniority and personal qualities, a readiness within the school to change and develop and above all support from the head of the school.

> Just as a supportive head can facilitate change, so an indifferent one can inhibit it (Hegarty and Hodgson, 1988, p. 95).

It is clear that these one-term courses are well designed and taught and meet the needs of schools in improving their special needs provision. But with 23,000 primary schools and over 4,000 secondary schools, many more courses will be needed, particularly for teachers who do not live or work within easy access to a training institution.

Courses for teachers in special schools

Whatever the pace of progress towards integration, teachers now working in special schools and classes are also in need of retraining not only in relation to the needs of the children in their school but also to prepare them to play a wider role in the community, with parents and with colleagues in mainstream schools.

Many special schools are now acting as 'resource centres' for their neighbourhood schools (Jowett and Hegarty, 1988). There is often a systematic programme of exchange of both staff and pupils. Teachers from the special school may teach in an ordinary school or act in an advisory capacity while teachers from the ordinary school gain experience in the special school. These 'clusters' or 'networks' were beginning to be introduced in London, following the implementation of the Fish report (ILEA, 1985).

Teachers from special schools who are spending increasing amounts of time teaching in mainstream schools have a valuable contribution to make in a number of fields, for example microtechnology, direct instruction, behavioural methods, working with parents, using community resources, particularly the new training initiatives being developed for school leavers by the Manpower Services Commission. But their knowledge of developments in these fields will need to be recent and relevant to the needs of their colleagues in ordinary schools. Furthermore, they will need to acquire some of the skills of the adult educator, including skills of consultancy and negotiation. Above all, they will need to be well informed about curriculum development and implementation issues in ordinary schools.

Despite the potential value of their contribution, teachers in special schools have been excluded from most of the recent initiatives in training. First, they were specifically barred from the one-term courses developed since 1983. Since the publication of the report by the Advisory Committee on the Supply and Education of Teachers (ACSET, 1984), all initial specialist training for teachers wishing to work with children with severe learning difficulties or sensory impairments is being phased out. In future, specialist training will only be available on an in-service basis after a period of experience in ordinary schools.

So far, LEAs do not seem to be seconding teachers to these courses in large numbers, though this may be due as much to the uncertainties and confusions of GRIST as to any deliberate policy. In response to continued representations from special needs interest groups, the DES issued circulars reminding LEAs that 70 per cent funding is available and that they expect training for teachers of pupils with sensory impairments and severe learning difficulties to be provided in institutions of higher education by means of one-year full-time courses or their part-time equivalents (Circular 1/88). No national figures are available to assess the extent of the LEAs' response.

Further confusion was created by earlier circulars which had indicated that such training would be limited to teachers working in ordinary schools, thus excluding at a stroke all teachers working in special schools for children with severe learning difficulties or sensory impairments from acquiring a recognized qualification in their chosen field of specialization. Although this extraordinary restriction was explained as 'an unfortunate drafting error', it still reappeared in the next version of the circular before it was finally withdrawn in an explanatory letter to LEAs. Such uncertainty at the centre does not inspire confidence that officials at the DES have grasped basic issues in the field of special education, and reinforces the case for a Special Needs Advisory Council, repeatedly rejected by the government.

Courses for teachers working with other groups of children in special schools, such as those for children with moderate learning difficulties, emotional and behavioural difficulties, language and communication or physical difficulties are regarded as local priorities, and will therefore only attract 50 per cent funding. This seems a short-sighted policy and seems to reflect a low priority on the part of the DES for the retraining of these teachers to play a role more in keeping with the 1981 Education Act.

Advanced courses

In the session 1984/1985, an NFER research team made a special study of all full-time and part-time diploma courses in the field of special needs. Since this study was carried out a year after the implementation of the 1981 Education Act and some two years before GRIST, it provides a useful overview of the INSET scene at that time. Four courses were studied by personal visits and interviews with tutors and students and the remainder by means of a detailed questionnaire (Dust, 1988). The study did not include taught M.Eds or research degrees leading to M.Phil or Ph.D. Some of the principal findings are summarized below.

1. Forty-six institutions of Higher Education were offering seventy-four advanced diploma courses in special needs. These were mounted in nine universities, ten polytechnics and twenty-seven colleges. Half of these courses were full-time and the other half part-time or mixed-mode. Information was available from 102 tutors and 636 students, divided almost equally between part-time and full-time.

2. Fifty-nine of the seventy-four courses covered two or three areas of special need, usually the whole range of mild, moderate, severe and specific learning difficulties, as well as children with emotional and behavioural difficulties.

3. Half the students worked in special schools and a small number were working in units attached to ordinary schools. Twenty-two per cent came from secondary schools, 13 per cent from primary or middle schools, 6 per cent from support services, and 4 per cent from Further or Higher Education. Half the teachers from ordinary schools already had special needs responsibilities. Teachers from secondary schools included many who were subject specialists; PE teachers were particularly prominent. The whole range of seniority was represented, with Scale One and Two teachers accounting for 32 and 43 per cent of the total and heads or deputies another 7 per cent. Surprisingly few of the students envisaged a change of

role or responsibilities after completing the course, in contrast to students on one-term full-time SENIOS courses where such a change of role was a key factor in the selection of staff for these courses by the schools and LEAs (Hegarty and Hodgson, 1988).

4. Of the 102 tutors surveyed, 99 had classroom teaching experience; in all but ten cases this school experience was in primary or secondary schools. A quarter had previously worked as educational psychologists and many others had a first degree in psychology, reflecting the dominant influence of psychology on special education. Most tutors are involved in other courses — especially initial training and other advanced work.

5. More than half the part-time courses were run only in the evenings (often twice a week) but these had the highest drop-out rate. A common combination was half-day release followed by an evening session, though this often involved having to give up a free period. More courses were developing mixed-mode patterns of attendance; for example, one term full time followed by a day a week for the second term and evening study for two further terms.

6. A strong preference for one-year full-time courses was expressed by both students and tutors, as these provide opportunities for in-depth study and preparation for new roles, as well as allowing students to broaden their experience by visiting and working in a range of schools and agencies. Such opportunities were considered to be one of the most valuable features of a full-time course.

Content of courses

Dust's (1988) NFER survey of diploma courses summarizes a number of common elements in course content. These are broadly similar to the content of one-term full-time SENIOS courses as reported in a parallel NFER study by Hegarty and Hodgson (1988) and can be summarized as follows:

1. *A critical study of current provision*, including an analysis of the Warnock Report, the 1981 Act and a range of issues concerned with non-categorical and needs-driven approaches and the problems of moving towards mainstream provision. Special attention is paid in most courses to the rapidly changing nature of advisory and school-based support services, the use of resource bases and resource centres in ordinary and special schools and the changing nature of relationships with parents and with other service providers and agencies.

2. *Theoretical components*, including various conceptual frameworks which are currently under discussion, including those deriving from curriculum theory, psychology (particularly learning theory and its derivatives), sociology and social administration and theories concerned with organization and management of change. Most courses discussed changing concepts of impairment, disability and handicap and emphasized the

limitations of a defect model which ignored environmental influences on the development of special needs.

3. *Curriculum development and adaptation*, including the design, delivery and implementation of the curriculum. Dust noted that surprisingly little reference was made in course handbooks to material concerned with modifications to the mainstream curriculum, though this aspect features strongly in the one-term SENIOS courses. Most courses included material on the use of microtechnology in the curriculum for pupils with special needs.

4. *Professional skills*, particularly assessment, intervention and individual programme planning. Many courses taught students how to use and interpret tests, make systematic observations and keep records, as well as about referral and statementing procedures. Several courses gave particular emphasis to consultancy and negotiating skills as well as to the management and evaluation of change. Most students had to prepare a detailed child study.

5. *Research components*, usually involving a school-based or school-focused project requiring observation and data collection and interpretation, using simple statistics where appropriate. Most of the courses included a dissertation.

6. *Placements* were a feature of most full-time but not of part-time courses and required a substantial element of teaching or observation in schools and support services, usually different from those familiar to the student. These placements were designed to extent the students' professional experience and skills.

In summary, the diploma courses which were available shortly before the introduction of GRIST seemed to be meeting the needs of teachers, schools and LEAs by providing opportunities for a fairly detailed study of changing provision and practice in the field of special needs. All courses aimed to provide a working integration between theory and practice and to extend the existing professional skills and experience of teachers in the light of new developments, particularly in assessment, intervention and individual programme planning.

The future of full-time courses has been thrown in doubt by the dramatic reduction in full-time secondments, as well as by the lower priority attached to part-time courses provided by institutions of higher education and the difficulty experienced by teachers in being released even for one afternoon a week.

Requirements for a new curriculum?

Will the course content summarized in the NFER studies still be appropriate in the light of the rapid changes being introduced by the Education Reform Act and other changes in provision?

Although all the areas of course content are important, the harsher climate of the 1990s may make it necessary to revise course content and to change areas of emphasis in award-bearing courses at diploma and M.Ed level. A number of examples suggest themselves.

1. Much greater emphasis on assessment, including both norm-referenced and criterion-referenced tests, the use and abuse of tests, sources of bias and under-achievement, problems of selecting tests that are culturally and linguistically appropriate to the population.
2. Promotion and maintenance of attitude change and awareness among decision-makers, inside and outside schools, including elected and appointed members of LEAs, members of governing bodies and community representatives, including parents of children without special needs in ordinary schools.
3. Organization and management of change, particularly when teachers are of relatively low status within their schools. Such skills may need to include determined advocacy on behalf of children with special needs and their families, including where necessary the mobilization of support based on civil rights.
4. An understanding of obstacles to policy planning and provision at both national and local level, including questions of decision-making and priorities, resource allocation and implementation, as well as an understanding of resistance to change.
5. Work with families and community agencies.
6. Work with children themselves to help them to understand and work for their rights and to develop skills of self-advocacy and assertiveness.
7. Setting work in the field of special needs in the wider framework of equal opportunity issues and exploring similarities and parallels with other minority groups and interests.

Jeffs' (1988) analysis of one-term SENIOS courses emphasizes the following areas of skill and knowledge as essential to staff wishing to work towards as whole-school approach.

Knowledge

Legislation; implications of disability; classroom techniques; remedial techniques; developmental stages; materials; concepts; support structures; support agencies.

Skills

Matching pupil to task; objective setting; curriculum modification; adapting resources; assessment/record keeping; classroom modifications; evaluating materials; task analysis.

Organizational knowledge

How organizations work — staff, resources, timetable, parents, pupils; group dynamics; negotiating frameworks; inter-professional barriers; forms of liaison with outside agencies; group problem-solving techniques.

Organizational skills

Liaison/consultation skills — teachers, support personnel, parents; advisory skills; in-service skills; co-teaching skills; development/presentation of policy; presentation of an argument; negotiation skills; running a meeting.

The Special Needs Action Programme (SNAP)

Apart from nationally disseminated courses such as the Special Needs Action Programme (SNAP), little published information is available on how LEAs as a whole have responded to the challenge of developing a coherent local strategy which includes the retraining of all serving teachers. Nevertheless, the work of a few LEAs has been so innovative and imaginative as to have exerted a national influence.

The SNAP programme has been under development in Coventry since 1981 but is now being used or adapted in more than half the LEAs in the country. Organizationally, SNAP is based on the same cascade or pyramid principle as the EDY course, namely that one person is trained as a trainer and accepts a contractual commitment to train others in turn. In the case of EDY (Foxen and McBrien, 1981; Farrell, 1985; Robson, 1988) one person from each LEA (usually an educational psychologist) received an intensive one-week, school-based, ten-unit course on behavioural methods of teaching on condition that they ran similar workshops in special schools in their own LEAs. Since the training of the first 100 trainers, over 4,000 trainees have successfully met the objective criteria for the award of an EDY certificate.

The SNAP course was designed to reach all teachers in all primary schools in Coventry by training a coordinator from each school in a six-unit course based directly on Precision Teaching and including materials and exercises on assessment by means of a Basic Skills Checklist, setting objectives, task analysis and record-keeping. Like EDY, the course also concentrates on ways in which these approaches can be fitted into the daily life of the classroom and also on difficulties which might be encountered in dissemination and on ways in which these might be overcome. The 'Small Steps' course on learning difficulties was followed by other modules on visual and hearing difficulties and on behaviour problems but these have not been as well supported.

As part of a series of NFER studies on INSET, Moses (1988) reported a follow-up carried out in 1985 of eleven schools which had taken part in the early SNAP courses two years earlier. Although the schools had undergone many changes and half the coordinators had left the schools on promotion, 'virtually all the teachers who were interviewed knew about SNAP and had an accurate conception of what it entailed . . . ' and 'every school but one had children on the Small Steps programme' (Moses, 1988, p. 150).

Regional collaboration

The past five years have seen increasing evidence of collaboration between Institutes of Higher Education (IHEs) in designing and teaching INSET courses. Indeed, the evidence suggests that such collaboration has been pioneered in the field of special education.

The North West regional modular diploma in special educational needs has been described in some detail in the IMPACT companion volume (Robson *et al.*, 1988 and also by Robson and Sebba, 1988). In its earliest form, the diploma was designed and taught collaboratively by Manchester University and Manchester Polytechnic but the scheme has now been strengthened by the addition of Crewe and Alsager College, North Cheshire College of Higher Education and Liverpool Polytechnic. The diploma is validated in parallel by Manchester University and the CNAA but a number of units are also contributed by LEAs. The structure of the twelve-unit diploma enables students to develop areas of specialization but without losing sight of foundation and contextual elements.

The first three units, known as Contextual Studies, aim to help students to gain a critical understanding of current developments in special needs provision, including the 1981 and 1988 Education Acts. Following this, students select six Professional Study Units from a range of some sixty courses available in several different institutions. Each module has been submitted to joint validation procedures to ensure level and coherence. Tutorial guidance ensures that students' choice of units is not only professionally and academically coherent but also helps them with the Case Study and Major Assignment through which these units are assessed. Finally, students undertake a school-focused, or agency-focused, study which takes the form of an evaluated intervention in their own work setting.

The design of the course as a whole and of the PSUs in particular reflects the very wide range of interests and needs of professionals working with pupils with special educational needs. These range from work with profoundly and multiply impaired children to work with children in ordinary schools with temporary learning or behaviour difficulties. For example, the Diploma provides a framework for new INSET specialized courses for teachers of children with sensory impairments and severe learning difficulties and also gives credit to students who have taken the one-term full-time SENIOS courses and relevant Open University courses such as Special Needs in Education and the Handicapped Person in the Community.

Similar collaborative frameworks have been developed in other regions, particularly in Scotland where a national diploma has been designed by a number of colleges (Blythman, 1985). Other regions where collaborative links have been established include London, the South-West and Yorkshire and Humberside.

Courses for staff in colleges of further education

The story of special needs in Further Education is one of confusion and uncertainty, lit by flashes of brilliant innovation. It is not surprising, therefore, that provision for the training needs of staff reflects this state of affairs.

The FE sector represents the typical British patchwork quilt — islands of excellence and innovation on show to visitors and constantly in the news but enormous variation from college to college even within one LEA. For a long time, national leadership and guidance have been sadly lacking. There has been confusion and uncertainty about the 'legal basis of further education', with court action threatened by parents in several areas but never quite materializing and the government breaking a clear commitment at the time of the 1981 Act that legislation would be forthcoming. The report of a series of HMI visits was shrouded in secrecy and never published and pressure on DES to provide guidance was invariably met by the information that a new committee was in the process of examining the issue.

The Warnock Committee's clear recommendations for FE colleges and for the training needs of their staff led to little action. The ACSET (1984) working party on special needs reaffirmed these recommendations in stronger language, again with little effect. Inexplicably, training for staff with special needs responsibilities in FE was not one of the DES priorities under GRIST, though strong pressure ensured that this omission was rectified the following year. Whether LEAs took advantage of this priority is not known at national level but experience in one region was not encouraging. Despite a detailed market survey of the needs of college staff conducted by questionnaire and personal visits (Whelan, 1986), followed by the offer of a one-term full-time course specifically designed to meet identified needs, take-up by LEAs and college staff was disappointing. It was apparent that the combination of FE and Special Needs fell between two advisory stools, with the result that no clear responsibilities had been allocated at LEA level.

Despite these difficulties, two positive developments should be celebrated. The first arises from the outstanding work of the Further Education Unit which has produced a long series of excellent publications and curriculum guides, specifically concerned with ways in which special needs can be met in FE Colleges. These are almost uniformly of very high quality; indeed, it is ironic that the quality of curriculum guidance produced for the FE sector is considerably better than that available to staff working with pupils of school age. These publications, which are mostly available free from the FEU, include a staff development programme, 'From Coping to Confidence', which seems to have had a considerable impact.

The second closely related initiative is the report of the FE Special Needs Teacher Training Working Group *A Special Professionalism* (DES, 1987). This is a most impressive document, since it outlines in some detail a framework for eight levels of training, ranging from awareness training for managers, and for staff with various levels of involvement with special needs students, through to in-depth advanced training, culminating in advanced courses leading to certificate, diploma or M.Ed awards. A great deal of thought has clearly been given to the content, mode of delivery, length and academic standards required by each of these levels, such that the framework outlined by this report could provide a firm foundation for a national and regional strategy. Here again, no comparable framework for staff development has been developed by the DES or any other official body for teachers working with school-age pupils.

As against these positive developments, the series of consultation documents leading to the Education Reform Act appeared to have entirely overlooked students with special needs and seem to have been written without any reference to the 1981 Education Act or the recommendations of the Warnock Committee. Concerted parliamentary pressure and lobbying by professional and voluntary organizations, helped perhaps by an influential document from the Prince of Wales Advisory Group on Disability (1988), finally resulted in a minor but perhaps symbolic concession in the final hours of Parliamentary debate in the House of Lords, to the effect that governors of FE colleges 'should have regard to students with learning difficulties'. This may be a useful reminder to new governors, drawn largely from business and industry, particularly since the government rejected an amendment which would have required the governing body to have included one person with personal or professional experience of special needs.

Does INSET have any impact?

At a time when issues of accountability and value for money are at a premium, it is necessary to justify investment of resources in almost any educational activity, INSET included. However essential special needs INSET is thought to be, it is not unreasonable to ask for evidence of effectiveness.

Although such evidence is not easy to obtain, an attempt to do so was made by Project IMPACT, a DES funded project which was concerned to assess the impact of inservice courses on teachers and other professionals working with pupils with special educational needs. The results are reported in full in Robson, Sebba, Mittler and Davies (1988).

Project IMPACT designed and implemented evaluations of a range of courses, including a series of short courses (Sebba and Robson, 1987), the North West Regional Modular Diploma in Special Needs (Robson and Sebba, this volume) and the self-instructional Education of Developmentally Young (EDY) materials on behavioural methods of teaching children with severe learning difficulties (Robson 1988).

As a result of these studies, the project team suggested that the following questions could be asked for any course. These questions were thoroughly explored with particular reference to the EDY course.

What is the course trying to do?
How is it trying to do it?
Does it fulfil its intentions?
Does it affect practice?
Whom does it benefit?
How much of a priority is it?

In addition, the IMPACT team developed some general and specific *Guidelines for Effective INSET*. The following are a few examples of relevant items from the General Guidelines (adapted from Robson *et al.*, 1988). More detailed specific checklists were also developed:

Identifying the Needs;
Initial Development of the Course;
Pre-Course Considerations;
During the Course;
After the Course.

General guidelines

1. The starting point is a need. A course may not be the best way of meeting the need (see stage 1 checklist).
2. The need should be seen and expressed by participants who should contribute to the planning of objectives and content.
3. A one-off course is unlikely to be effective. A course should be an integral element of policy and planning.
4. A course is effective if it leads to change in practice. This calls for management support and action from the Local Authority and from senior management, especially the headteacher.
5. Courses on management of change must have regard to the wide range of different work settings in which people work.

Conclusions: an agenda for change

(adapted from Robson *et al.*, 1988).

The traditions of staff training which we have inherited have served us badly and are largely irrelevant for the future. Although there are now some encouraging signs that staff development is beginning to be taken seriously, staff training simply has not kept up with the changing needs of the children and adults with whom we work, nor with rapidly changing legislation and service delivery. Because the field of special needs is changing so rapidly, we are all out of date in relation to the tasks that face us.

1. Everyone working in services for children and adults with special needs should be receiving continuous on-the-job updating. To this end, there should be a national and local strategic plan of staff development for all, from the most senior to the most junior members.
2. The curriculum content of most staff training courses requires reappraisal and constant review. There needs to be local discussion and decision-making on the knowledge and skills which are considered essential or desirable in staff working with students of all ages with special needs.

3. The training of teachers working in special education has too long been segregated from the training of other teachers. Consequently, other teachers have seen special education as someone else's responsibility.

4. The training of teachers has too long been isolated from that of other professionals. Each locality could set up a coordinating mechanism to try to develop more joint training, whether award-bearing or not, or at the least to ensure that different professional groups had access to one anothers' in-service and updating courses.

5. Most courses in the past have trained staff to work in segregated or institutional settings — special schools, day centres, residential homes, etc. In future, we need, in addition, to train staff to work in community settings — with parents in their own homes, with children and young people too young or too old to attend schools, in youth clubs and leisure and recreational settings — indeed, wherever people with special needs are living and working.

6. The role of specialist staff is increasingly one of providing direct support for people with special needs in ordinary settings, as well as supporting staff in ordinary services where necessary. In future, specialist training should aim to equip staff to pass on their knowledge and skills to their colleagues, to families and volunteers and to the students themselves.

7. Course providers and trainers in colleges and universities will in future need to negotiate with potential students and their employers concerning course content and mode rather than continue to offer courses according to their own interpretation of what is needed. This may mean that staff of higher education institutions will in future need to find ways of encouraging and supporting on-the-job training in schools, day and residential centres and other work settings.

8. All staff need regular opportunities to visit and work in other services in their locality or further afield and to discuss with colleagues and managers the relevance of what they have seen, heard and read to the practice of their own school or service. Such visits should be part of the normal staff development policy of each school and should form a major element of all training courses.

9. All schools or services should have a small library of relevant books, periodicals and training materials, as well as access to a larger resource centre which contains videotapes and audiotapes illustrating various approaches to working with students or families.

10. In the longer term, the education service must accept responsibility for meeting the continuing special educational needs of adults of all ages and levels of ability and provide assistance, training and support to the adult education service in extending its role to this wider population.

References

ADVISORY COUNCIL FOR THE SUPPLY AND EDUCATION OF TEACHERS (1984) *Teacher Training and Special Educational Needs*, London, Department of Education and Science.

BLYTHMAN, M. (1985) 'National initiatives: The Scottish experience', in Sayer and Jones, *op. cit.*

DEPARTMENT OF EDUCATION AND SCIENCE (1978) *Special Educational Needs* (The Warnock Report), London, HMSO.

DEPARTMENT OF EDUCATION AND SCIENCE (1987) *A Special Professionalism: Report of the FE Special Needs Teacher Training Working Group*, London, HMSO.

DUST, K. (1988) 'The diploma courses', in Hegarty and Moses, *op. cit.*

FARRELL, P. (Ed) (1985) *EDY: Its Impact on Staff Training in Mental Handicap*, Manchester, Manchester University Press.

FOXEN, T., and MCBRIEN J. (1981) *The EDY Course: Trainee Workbook*, Manchester, Manchester University Press.

GALLOWAY, D., and GOODWIN, C. (1987) *The Education of Disturbing Children: Pupils with Learning and Adjustment Difficulties*, London, Longmans.

HARGREAVES, D. (1982) *Challenge for the Comprehensive School: Culture, Curriculum and Community*, London, Routledge and Kegan Paul.

HEGARTY, S., and HODGSON, A. (1988) 'The one term courses', in Hegarty and Moses, *op. cit.*

HEGARTY, S., and MOSES, D. (Eds) (1988) *Developing Expertise: Inset for Special Educational Needs*, Windsor, NFER/Nelson.

HER MAJESTY'S INSPECTORATE (1988) *Education Observed 7: Initial Teacher Training in Universities in England, Northern Ireland and Wales*, London, Department of Education and Science.

HINSON, M. (Ed.) (1987) *Teachers and Special Educational Needs*, London, Longman/NARE.

INNER LONDON EDUCATION AUTHORITY (1984) *Improving Secondary Education*, London, ILEA.

INNER LONDON EDUCATION AUTHORITY (1985) *Equal Opportunities for All?* (The Fish Report), London, ILEA.

JEFFS, A. (1988) 'INSET Contributions to Change in Schools', in Hegarty and Moses, *op. cit.*

JOWETT, S., and HEGARTY, S. (1988) *Joining Forces: A Study of Links Between Special and Ordinary Schools*, Windsor, NFER/Nelson.

MITTLER, P. (1987) 'Towards education for all', *Special Needs in Ordinary Schools* Series Editorial Foreword, London, Cassell.

MOSES, D. (1988) 'Special needs action programmes', in Hegarty and Moses. *op. cit.*

POTTS, P. (1985) 'Training for teamwork', in Sayer and Jones, *op. cit.*

PRINCE OF WALES ADVISORY GROUP ON DISABILITY (1988) *Learning Options: Guidelines on Provision of Further and Continuing Education for People with Disabilities*, London, Prince of Wales Advisory Group on Disability.

ROBSON, C. (1988) 'Evaluating the education of the developmentally young course for training staff in behavioural methods', *European Journal of Special Needs Education*, 3, pp. 13–32.

ROBSON, C., SEBBA, J., MITTLER, P., and DAVIES, G. (1988) *Inservice Training and Special Educational Needs: Running Short, School-Focused Courses*, Manchester, Manchester University Press.

ROBSON, C., and SEBBA, J. (1988) 'Research into inservice training and special needs', in Jones, N. (Ed.) *Special Educational Needs Review*, No. 1, Lewes, Falmer Press.

SAYER, J. (1987) *Secondary Schools for All?*, London, Cassell.

SAYER, J., and JONES, N. (Eds) (1985) *Teacher Training and Special Educational Needs*, Beckenham, Croom Helm.

SEBBA, J., and ROBSON, C. (1987) 'The development of short, school-focused INSET courses in special education', *Research Papers in Education*, **2**, pp. 3–30.

THOMAS, G., and FEILER, A. (Eds) (1988) *Planning for Special Needs: A Whole School Approach*, Oxford, Blackwell.

WHELAN, E. (1986) *The Training Needs of Staff of Colleges of Further Education Working with Students with Special Educational Needs*, Department of Education, University of Manchester (mimeo).

2
Counselling and Special Educational Needs

Jack Gilliland and John McGuiness

Introduction

The recent formation of a Counselling Psychology Section in the British Psychological Society, and the longer existence of the British Association for Counselling,
are two organizational indicators that the helping professions in Britain are
beginning to accept that counselling has a significant contribution to make to professional practice. A wide range of professions, many of them wedded to perfor-
mance-indicator and cost-benefit philosophies, see it as offering potential benefit to
their professional activity. They expect that counselling will work for them. Thus,
general practitioners, nurses, industrial and commercial managers, the armed
services and the police have all in recent years sought training in counselling skills in
the expectation that such training will enhance their professional practice.

Within education, too, there has been a growing interest in the help that
counselling might offer those facing a range of challenging issues. Thus the
Warnock Report (DES, 1978) argued for and formally recommended counselling
for some children with special educational needs. The Manpower Services
Commission advocates counselling for young people on TVEI schemes (MSC, 1985;
White, Pring and Brockington, 1985), and the National Association for Pastoral
Care in Education sees access to counselling services as an important part of pastoral
provision in school (NAPCE, 1984). Several authors (Laslett, 1977; Kolvin *et al.*,
1981; Galloway, 1985; Rose and Marshall, 1974) have discussed the value of
guidance and counselling approaches in responding to disruptive behaviour.

Given the wide range of meanings, contexts and objectives allowed to the
word counselling, it seems important to undertake some definitional groundwork.
The same word can be used to describe the activity of a professional who has a three-
year first degree in psychology, a Ph.D and a one-year supervised course of training
in an educational or a clinical setting and then, at a more basic end of a continuum,
be described as 'nothing more than having big ears and nodding at the right time'
(DES, 1987b). Although that final comment was, one hopes, half-jocular, it was the
only description of counselling in the publication cited and it reflects a deprecatory
view of counselling that prevails still in some educational settings. It parallels

First published in 2009 by Wayland

Wayland
338 Euston Road
London NW1 3BH

Wayland Australia
Level 17/207 Kent Street
Sydney, NSW 2000

Produced for Wayland by Calcium

Editors: Sarah Eason and Robyn Hardyman
Editor for Wayland: Katie Powell
Consultant: Jayne Wright
Designers: Paul Myerscough and Rob Norridge
Picture researcher: Maria Joannou

British Library Cataloguing in Publication Data:
Levete, Sarah.
   Talk about family break-ups.
   1. Broken homes—Juvenile literature. 2. Teenagers—Family
   relationships—Juvenile literature. 3. Divorce—Juvenile
   literature.
   I. Title II. Family break-ups
   306.8'9-dc22

ISBN: 978 0 7502 5737 4

Printed in Malaysia

Wayland is a division of Hachette Children's Books, an Hachette UK Company
www.hachette.co.uk

The author and publisher would like to thank the following for allowing their pictures
to be reproduced in this publication:
Cover photographs: Shutterstock/Suzan (top), Corbis/Rick Gomez (bottom).
Interior photographs: Alamy Images: Catchlight Visual Services 6, Angela Hampton
Picture Library 33; Corbis: Creasource 20, Rahat Dar/EPA 30–31; Fotolia: Duane Ellison 10,
TheFinalMiracle 5; Getty Images: Stone/Kevin Cooley 40; Istockphoto: Bobbieo 11, Robert
Churchill 22, Digitalskillet 9, Fotocromo 32, Sergey Lagutin 24, Andrea Laurita 45, Nikolay
Mamluke 4, Juan Monino 21, Vikram Raghuvanshi 8, Barbara Sauder 37, TommL 27; Rex
Features: Giuliano Bevilacqua 16–17, c.W. Disney/Everett 39, Ken Katz 42, Most Wanted 29;
Shutterstock: Galina Barskaya 15, 43, Andi Berger 28, Bronwyn Photo 41, David Davis 12,
Jaimie Duplass 2–3, Mandy Godbehear 13, Anthony Harris 38, David Hughes 34, Iofoto 18,
Tan Kian Khoon 36, Losevsky Pavel 35, Kristian Sekulic 19, Raluca Teodorescu 1, 14, Paolo
Vairo 25, Tracy Whiteside 44; Wayland Archive: 47.

CONTENTS

Chapter 1

What is family break-up?

Do you live with two parents, one parent, carers or grandparents? Your parents may be living together or living separately. Adult relationships between couples, whether or not they are married, sometimes break down. A break-up is hard for everyone involved, but it is especially difficult when either adult has children – either their own children or children for whom they are responsible. Family break-up affects many children and young people every year.

Breaking up

If a couple decides to separate, their children have to live apart from one parent. Children from a family whose parents have separated or split up are often said to come from a 'broken home'.

There are many terms to describe a family after a break-up. These include a lone parent, single parent and one parent family. These terms can also refer to a family where a parent has died, or where only one parent has ever lived with the children. Are these terms accurate? In many cases both parents remain involved in the care of their children, even if one parent has most of the day to day responsibility.

You may be very upset if your parents split up, but in the long term it might be easier than seeing arguments all the time.

TALK ABOUT

According to the *United Nations Convention on the Rights of Children, 1989*:

"… the child, for the full and harmonious development of his or her personality, should grow up in a family environment, in an atmosphere of happiness, love and understanding."

Consider these questions about the family environment:

✳ What do you think makes a family?

✳ Do you think families are important – why?

✳ Do you think it is better for children to live with two parents or with one and why?

How and when does a break-up happen?

A family can break up at any time, when a baby is young or when the children have grown-up and are living independently. Whenever it happens, and whatever the make-up of the family, a break-up creates many complex feelings and inevitably involves change for all the individuals involved.

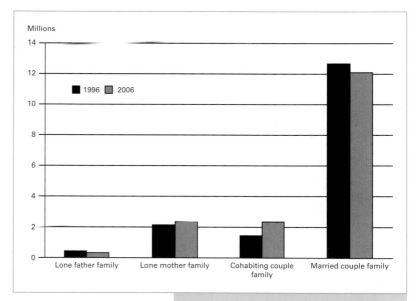

This graph shows the change in family types between 1996 and 2006 in the United Kingdom.
Source: National Statistics website: www.statistics.gov.uk

Some children are aware of difficulties between their parents and may not be surprised when they split up, but for others it can be a total shock. Sometimes, one parent leaves very suddenly; in other families, both parents stay in the house while arrangements are made. However a break-up happens, every family deals with the separation in its own unique way.

Chapter 2

Why do families break up?

Every family has its ups and downs, with arguments, upsets and tensions. But when these become overwhelming, some couples decide there is no future for them together and that they are better off apart. The reasons why a couple separates are unique to them, just as their relationship is unique.

Falling out of love

Sometimes a couple who have been content with each other simply fall out of love. They may begin to treat each other more like housemates or friends rather than loving partners, and find that they don't share any interests, except for their children. Some couples are content to carry on in this way while others are not. There is no right or wrong.

One person may unexpectedly meet someone else, fall in love with them and start an affair. The new relationship may last or it may end – but an affair is often the cause of a family break-up.

Arguments

Everyone argues. Arguments can be about money worries, health problems, work troubles or over simple things, such as who does the washing-up. Arguments and disagreements can be healthy ways of expressing feelings and finding solutions to difficulties in a relationship, but when they become the main way of communicating, a couple may decide it is better to separate.

All relationships have ups and downs, but when a couple is unhappy together most of the time, separation may be the best option.

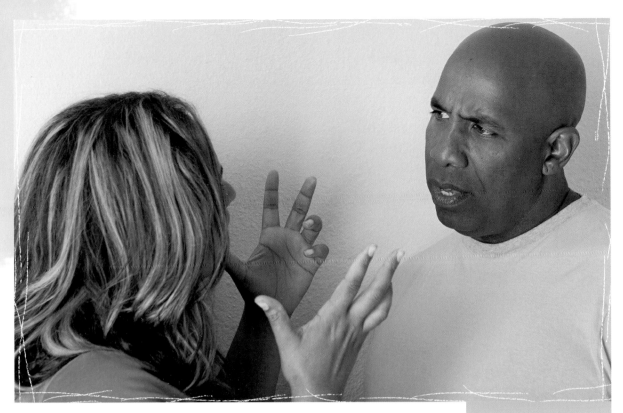

Parents may argue about all sorts of things, from money to who does the household chores.

It's not your fault

Parents often argue about their children – perhaps about how to discipline a young person, or when a child's bedtime should be. You might be concerned that your behaviour has caused rifts between your parents. It may contribute to their arguments, but this doesn't cause a relationship to break down completely. Parents decide to separate because of problems in their relationship as a couple, and not because of any difficulties they might have with their children.

It happened to me

'Me and my sister always argued and fought. We wound each other up about anything. Mum and Dad got really cross with us. Then they'd get cross with each other and argue about how to deal with us. When Dad told us he was moving out, I blamed myself – and my sister. But Mum told me recently it was because she had met someone else and didn't love Dad any more.'

Ali, aged 11.

Harmful relationships

Although a break-up is often caused by the feelings one partner has, or doesn't have, for the other, it can also be caused by one partner's aggressive or unpredictable behaviour. Some adult relationships are abusive – one partner regularly abuses or physically harms the other partner. Such behaviour is unacceptable. A partner in this situation may decide to leave, although this may not always be the easy thing to do.

Domestic abuse is when a parent or partner hits, intimidates or bullies anyone in the home. Abuse isn't always physical; it is also repeatedly saying threatening things or making a person feel very bad about him or herself. A person who suffers domestic abuse may be too frightened to do anything – even to leave. If you are in this situation, talk to an adult you trust or contact one of the organizations that offer confidential support and advice for both adults and children (see page 47).

A problem with alcohol can put great pressure on a family and the relationships within it.

Coping with addiction

Alcohol and drugs can change a person's behaviour. Someone who is often drunk or high on drugs may say or do things that he or she wouldn't usually do. They may become violent and abusive. However guilty the person feels afterwards, or however much he or she may promise that it won't happen again, the behaviour is hurtful, frightening and can even sometimes be very dangerous for the rest of the family.

Coping with a partner's addiction or difficulty with drink or drugs puts a huge strain on the relationship. The partner may not feel able to remain in the relationship. It is unlikely that the addict's behaviour will change until he or she has overcome the addiction.

Why can't they stay together?

Have you ever stayed at a friend's house and seen their parents arguing, and wondered how they can still stay together? If your parents have recently separated you might feel confused about why they couldn't have dealt with their difficulties and stayed together. Different people make different decisions and have their own issues to deal with – comparing your situation with someone else's won't help your family's situation.

No one should feel threatened or unsafe at home. Violence and abuse are unacceptable, either towards a partner or children within the family.

TALK ABOUT

Do you think parents should stay together whatever the situation, to care for their children, or are there situations when it is better for the children if their parents separate?

Chapter 3

How do people feel in a family break-up?

Angry, upset, lonely, scared, glad, relieved, shocked? There are many emotions a young person goes through when his or her family breaks up – sometimes all at once. It can feel like being on an emotional rollercoaster, with no way to get off. Change will happen; things will be different. Overnight, what a person felt secure about may be uprooted. Accepting, understanding and getting used to the changes – which may well be unpredictable – takes time.

But it's their job!

Parents should nurture and love their children from the moment they are born, or as soon as they begin to look after them. That's the job of being a parent. It can seem as if parents give up that job when they separate. Children and young people are usually the main focus of parents' attention. During a break-up, they may suddenly feel they are not important any more – if they were, would their parents have split up?

All young people need a lot of reassurance, support and attention at a time when parents are often preoccupied, worried and unhappy. Family break-up can make young people unsure of where they belong, both in a practical sense of where to live and in an emotional sense.

If you feel angry about your parents' break-up, it is better to talk to them about it rather than hide your feelings.

A young person may feel betrayed by the very people who are supposed to provide security and love. Feelings of anger, hurt and even hatred are often common. But it's important to realize that parents, too, deserve healthy loving relationships; and it usually makes them better and happier parents as well.

Everyone reacts differently to a family break-up. Some people feel glad that the arguments are over, while others may feel very sad that their parents are no longer together.

Relieved or responsible

Some people feel relief when their unhappy parents separate. If life has been a pattern of arguments and unhappiness, it can be better when the rows stop. Feeling glad or relieved is not wrong – it's quite natural.

It's also common to feel responsible for the situation, even guilty. Perhaps you wanted your parents to split up; perhaps you even behaved badly to create more arguments and tension, and they did split, but now you feel guilty. It's important to remember that the breakdown of an adult relationship is just that – a decision taken by the adults alone. A break-up is never the responsibility of a child.

TALK ABOUT

✳ **Is there a right way and wrong way for children to feel when their parents split up?**

✳ **Do you think children should tell their parents how they feel, or is it better not to say anything?**

Lonely

One parent moving out can leave a huge gap in a young person's life and they can feel very lonely. Everyday things, such as not saying goodnight, or not telling a parent about a funny event that happened at school, can highlight these feelings of loneliness. Missing a parent is hard. If you fall out with the parent you live with, you may just want support from your other parent – and feel sad if it is not immediately possible. Sometimes brothers and sisters have to live apart from each other when parents separate, which can add to the feelings of loneliness. Try to talk to friends or other family members about how you feel as it can make you feel less alone.

Young people often feel very confused and alone when parents separate.

Full of hope

Some young people cling on to the hope that their parents will get back together. They may try to behave exceptionally well, and be extra helpful, hoping that will help their parents to mend their relationship. Or they may deliberately express extremes of unhappiness, to put pressure on their parents to 'make everything OK again'. But the parents have made an independent decision – their children's behaviour didn't cause it, and it won't change it. It is better to concentrate on ways to accept the changes and to move on.

Blame

It's easy to blame one parent for a family break-up, particularly if it seems as if one person's behaviour has been the trigger for the separation, or if one parent has left suddenly. However, there are usually lots of things that influence the parents' relationship which children are unaware of. Very few partners in a break-up can be slotted neatly into the roles of the good and the bad.

It happened to me

Perfect parent?

When you stay at home with one parent, he or she still has to ask you to clear up, get ready for school or finish your homework. These everyday things often get on children's nerves and cause arguments. The absent parent isn't there to remind you it's your turn to wash up or to say no to your favourite TV programme, so it's easy to idealize him or her and remember only the good points. It may seem as if he or she is more fun than the parent you live with, but try to be aware of the challenges that each parent faces.

Brothers and sisters

Sometimes, brothers and sisters can support each other when parents split up. After all, they understand the situation better than anyone. At other times, brothers and sisters may take sides with different parents. This can cause more tension and arguments in a period of stress and uncertainty for everyone. Younger children often turn to older ones for comfort; even if you don't feel like supporting anyone else, showing affection to confused brothers or sisters will make a big difference to them.

Brothers and sisters can offer support to each other in times of family break-up.

Unhappy parents

As you are adjusting to the changes in your family, so too are your parents. One or both of them may be really miserable, and it may seem as if they are not there to support you. Indeed, they may even turn to you for advice, reassurance and a shoulder to cry on. If this is the case, it's important that you have an outlet for your own feelings. Talk to other family members, to a trusted teacher or a good friend.

It's common for one parent to be more unhappy than the other, especially if he or she didn't want to split up. Parents may feel very angry with each other. Phone calls and meetings may be tearful, angry, loud and resentful. It's important for children to try to establish their own relationships with both parents in the new situation, regardless of how the adults behave towards each other.

Michael Phelps started swimming as a child to help him deal with his family break-up.

A child may feel great sympathy and concern for one parent, especially if he or she wanted to keep the family together. In this case, the child is dealing not only with the departure of one parent, but also with the unhappiness of the one left behind.

Weapons in a battle

Sometimes parents use children as weapons in their battle with each other. This is unfair on the children. If you think your parents are using you as a go-between to take messages from one to the other, or that one constantly criticizes the other in front of you, try to speak out about it. Ask them not to involve you in that way. Speaking clearly, calmly and directly about this may help them to realize the damaging effect of their behaviour.

It's not getting better

'Everyone will be happier,' or 'We'll all get on better' are the kind of reassuring words parents use when explaining a separation. This can be extremely hard to accept when no one does seem to be happier – in fact everyone appears to be very unhappy. Even though parents have made the decision to part, it can take a while for them to accept that their relationship as a couple is at an end – and there may be great sadness and loneliness for both of them for quite a while. It takes time for everyone to get used to the new situation, even for the people who are responsible for making the decision to break up.

In the media

American swimmer Michael Phelps has won more Olympic Gold Medals than any other individual. He took to swimming when he was seven years old to avoid the arguments between his parents, who were splitting up at the time. Phelps felt that swimming helped him to forget about his family problems for a while and reduced the stress he felt. All family break-ups are stressful. It helps to find a safe and supportive way to express your feelings and let off steam. Not everyone is going to become an Olympic champion, but even just talking to a school counsellor, a relative or a friend can help – as can a good game of football or a swim.

Not the children's responsibility

However upsetting it is to see a parent unhappy or angry about the situation, it's not up to the children to make everything better. Young people can, of course, help more around the house and be sensitive to a parent's feelings and needs, but it's not their responsibility to make their parents happy. If you are concerned about a parent's wellbeing, talk to a trusted relative or school counsellor.

It will help your parent if you help around the house, but you can't solve all your parent's problems.

DOs & DON'Ts

* Do talk about how you feel to friends, family members or trusted teachers at school.

* Don't forget to keep pursuing activities and interests that make you feel good.

* Do write in a journal or draw about how you feel. Expressing your emotions helps to make them seem less overwhelming.

* Do tell your parents how you feel.

* Don't assume that everyone will feel the same about the break-up – not everyone will react in the same way. Some people may be relieved, others may be devastated.

Speak up

Just because your parents are unhappy or preoccupied with sorting out new family arrangements, this doesn't mean that they don't have time to talk to you. You don't need to protect them from your feelings, and it's important to speak up about how you feel.

Talking doesn't mend the situation, but it helps you to deal with your feelings. Friends who have been through a similar situation are great to talk to, because they'll probably be able to identify with lots of your feelings. Talk to grandparents, uncles and aunts, too, but ask them not to take sides. Talking about your feelings is talking about you – it's not about your parents, and it's not the time for other people to criticize either of your parents.

It is good to tell a friend how you feel.

Chapter 4

What happens when a family breaks up?

When a family breaks up, everyone is trying to deal with confused and chaotic feelings. To make matters worse, there are lots of practical things to consider and lots of changes to get used to. For some families, things change overnight and for others, it takes a while before changes are made.

Who lives with who?

The first questions most children ask are: 'Which parent will I live with?' and 'Where will we live?' Parents may choose to agree this between themselves or else a judge in a court makes the decision (see pages 28–29). Most often, children stay with their mother. Some parents choose joint custody where a child lives part of the week with one parent and the rest of the week with the other. Siblings usually stay together, although sometimes one child decides (and is able) to live with one parent, while their brother or sister lives with the other parent.

There are sometimes reasons why a child or young person must stay with one particular parent. It may be to do with their safety, or their parent's ability to care for them. If parents cannot agree between themselves, the arrangements are agreed in a family court. In the case of older children, the court will take their opinions into account when making their decision. The person who looks after the children is said to have custody over them.

Ideally, parents should agree between them who has custody of their children. However, sometimes the only way an agreement can be met is with the help of a family court.

Fostering

If neither parent is able to care for a child for a while, it may be necessary for that child to stay with relatives or to be fostered. Fostering means that another family looks after the child for a while. Being moved away from both parents can make a child feel even more insecure and worried. However, fostering also provides a stable home where a child can feel safe and secure while parents sort out their difficulties. Whatever your feelings, it helps to share them with an adult, such as a teacher or social worker.

Children sometimes stay with a relative such as a grandparent while their parents sort out the new living arrangements.

DOs & DON'Ts

There are some things about your new situation that you can influence, and others that you cannot.

* Do tell a responsible adult clearly what you would prefer.

* Do accept that some decisions have to be made even if you are unhappy about them. Try to understand the reasons why those decisions have been made.

* Don't stay quiet if you feel unsafe staying with one of your parents – tell another trusted adult.

Moving house and school

Sometimes children stay in the same house after a break-up. However, when a parent leaves the home they may need to pay for a new home of their own. They may also pay for the home their children still live in. This can be very costly, so children may need to leave the family home and move to a less expensive home. A family may also move if one parent moves in with another partner.

If you move to a different area, you may well change school, too. This is another big change, but it is also an opportunity to meet new friends. You can still stay in touch with your old friends.

It can sometimes feel as if you have no choice in all this, and there are some things you can't change. But this does not mean you can't make your feelings known and express your views. The living arrangements are usually based on who is in the best position to care for the children and offer them the security they need at this time of great change and upset.

It takes time to settle into a new area and school, but sometimes such moves are unavoidable when parents split up.

Seeing both parents

Just because a parent moves out it doesn't mean an end to the child's relationship with that parent. Arrangements are often made so that children remain in regular contact with the absent parent. This isn't always easy or straightforward – if one parent moves a long way away, it may not always be possible to see him or her every week. If one parent is finding it difficult to adjust to the new set-up, they may need some time before they can see the children on a regular basis. Always ask parents to be very clear about the arrangements for seeing the other parent.

TALK ABOUT

* **Do you think children should be allowed to choose whom they live with after a break-up?**
* **Do you think parents should only make contact arrangements if a child approves of them?**
* **Should parents be legally obliged to remain in contact with their children?**

No contact

In some cases, a child loses all contact with the absent parent. This is in no way the child's fault; it is the adult's responsibility to keep up the contact. Sometimes one parent might feel that the child is better off without contact; perhaps the parent is experiencing difficulties or has problems which make it too hard to remain in contact. If the contact stops, a child can feel rejected and sad. In this situation, try to focus instead on the people who are able to support you.

It happened to me

'My mum moved out and stayed with a friend. Then she got a new flat and Dad couldn't afford the rent on our home. So we had to move. It wasn't far away, but I was fed up with having a smaller room and no garden to play footie. After about a year, things changed again and we moved to a different place. I'm still near my friends and still have a small room, but at least the atmosphere is better now and I see Mum every weekend.'

Ravi, aged 12.

Chapter 5

People's attitudes to family break-up

In recent decades, society's attitudes to families, and family break-up, have changed. Fifty years ago, it was unusual for a couple to live together without being married. Since the 1960s this has become more common, with fewer couples getting married.
It has become easier to get a divorce in many countries, so the number of divorces has increased. Over the last few years however, in the United Kingdom and United States, there has been a drop in the number divorces; fewer people are marrying in the first place.

Many negative stereotypes still exist for children from one parent families. Family break-ups are still often blamed for any bad behaviour by young people.

It happened to me

'When my dad left it was upsetting, but me and my sister were OK and Mum was brilliant. But when I got into a bit of trouble at school, everyone seemed to think it was because my dad wasn't around. It really annoyed me that people seemed to think Mum couldn't manage on her own and it was her fault. It wasn't easy, but we were OK. The trouble at school was down to me – I got mixed up with a bad crowd, but Mum soon sorted me out!'

Leon, aged 14.

TALK ABOUT

Do you agree with the statements below?

✱ Every child benefits from living with two parents.

✱ There are more pressures on a parent who brings up children alone.

✱ Family break-ups are responsible for children doing badly at school, and for negative behaviour in young people.

Stereotypes

It is likely that you either know people whose parents have split up or that your parents have split up. However, just as one parent families have become more common, so prejudices have developed about the effects of this on children. Disruptive and troubled young people can sometimes come from broken homes. Some people think that coming from a one parent family can increase a young person's chances of getting into trouble. Parts of the media even suggest that the majority of teenage troublemakers come from one parent families. However, there are many factors which influence a young person's behaviour and all the difficulties they may experience can not be blamed on the parents alone.

Barack Obama is a positive role model, yet he is from an unconventional family background. He was brought up by his mother and then his grandmother. The media don't talk about unconventional one parent households as much as they dwell on negative role models coming from broken homes.

President Barack Obama is an example of someone who has come from a 'broken home' and gone on to become extremely successful.

Religion and divorce

In many religions, the bond of marriage is sacred and they believe divorce breaks this sacred bond. Different religions have very different attitudes towards divorce.

Within the Christian religion, Roman Catholics believe that marriage is a sacrament, a special bond and blessing witnessed by God. For this reason, there are restrictions on obtaining a divorce and a divorced person is not allowed to take part in some key religious ceremonies. The Protestant Church of England allows divorce, but only permits remarriage in a church in certain circumstances.

The Hindu religion does not allow divorce, but in some countries Hindus still divorce anyway. If a Hindu couple do divorce, there may be a prejudice or stigma against them, particularly the woman.

Muslims accept that divorce may be necessary. Different Muslim cultures and communities have varying ideas about divorce. Some accept that a man can divorce his wife by repeating the phrase 'talaq, talaq, talaq'. Others do not recognize this as the formal ending of the marriage and believe that there should be periods of separation and attempts at reconciliation before a divorce.

Sikhs expect that a couple will stay married, but accept that separation and divorce are sometimes unavoidable. In Judaism, the Jewish religion, divorce is also recognized as an inevitable end to some relationships.

Changing values

Today, many people are not influenced by religious beliefs; they may decide not to marry but to live with a partner. Married or not married, the effect and upset of family break-up is still the same.

In a recent survey of nearly 3,000 adults in the United Kingdom:

* 28% thought that married couples make better parents than unmarried ones.

* 30% thought it should be harder for couples with children under the age of 16 to divorce.

* 40% thought that one parent can bring up a child as well as two.

* 40% thought that two parents are better than one.

* 66% thought that divorce can be a positive step towards a new life.

* 78% thought it is not divorce that harms children, but conflict between their parents.

Most couples, whatever their religious beliefs, enter marriage believing it to be a union for life.

TALK ABOUT

* Do you think that the increasing number of couples choosing not to marry reflects a reduction in the influence of religious values?

* Does religion make any difference to people today when they think about families?

Chapter 6

The law and family break-up

The media often features wealthy celebrities fighting in a divorce court over their money, property and children. Many couples decide on their family arrangements between themselves, but some ask for legal help to reach agreements over the custody of their children and the financial arrangements for supporting them.

Supporting the children

All married couples are bound by a legal agreement. If they separate, they usually end the marriage legally – by getting divorced. A judge decides whether or not to grant the divorce and the couple don't always need to be present when this happens. An unmarried couple do not need to get a divorce, but they must decide who will look after the children and how much money the other parent will pay towards this care, called child support.

Money is often a source of conflict between parents when they break up. In some countries, the parent who does not live with the children is still legally obliged to contribute money for the things they need, such as food and clothes. Sometimes parents argue about the amount this parent pays, and this can lead to tensions.

In most cases the mother has custody of the children from a relationship. This is because in the past it was usually the mother who stayed at home to look after them. In the United Kingdom and the United States some fathers campaign for better rights to see their children, and for different systems to decide how much money they should to pay to support them.

Whomever the children live with, their other parent will usually have rights to see them regularly.

Family break-ups are difficult for all children, but they are especially hard for children who are in the public eye.

In the media

Pop star Britney Spears is the mother of two young children. She and her ex-husband, Kevin Federine, separated, and in full glare of the media they fought over the custody of their children. Spears is said to have begun to take drugs, and as her behaviour became erratic and unpredictable the courts gave custody of the children to her ex-husband. Spears now has visiting rights to see her children. Most family break-ups do not happen in such a public way and with such drama, but any family break-up is very stressful and upsetting, especially for young people.

Mediation

Many couples try to avoid upsetting battles over children and money in court. Instead, they ask for legal support when they are breaking up, to make the separation as easy as possible, especially for the children. This support is called mediation. A trained counsellor, called a mediator, discusses with the parents how to make their separation less traumatic.

Different countries, different laws

Every country has its own laws about when and how people can divorce. For example, in Japan, in some circumstances a couple can divorce by simply signing a formal paper in front of two witnesses. The Philippines, a Catholic country, does not allow divorce. Each country also has its own laws relating to custody. This can cause great confusion, complication and upset if a family breaks up and the each parent wants to live, with their children, in different countries.

With international travel now so easy, many more people have relationships with people from different countries and cultures. If these relationships then break down, there may be disputes about which country the children should live in, particularly if one parent returns to his or her home country after the break-up.

In the
media

Molly Campbell was a 12-year-old girl, also known as Misbah Rana, who used to live with both her parents in Scotland. In 2006, after her parents separated, her father took her to live in Pakistan, against her mother's wishes. There was a great deal of speculation in the media about whether or not Molly/Misbah had been taken against her will. Molly/Misbah currently lives with her father and sisters in Pakistan.

In 2008, a seven-year-old girl called Reigh, who lived with her mother in the United Kingdom, was on a visit to see her father, Clark Rockerfeller, who was living in the United States. A social worker was with Reigh to ensure her safety. Reigh's parents had been separated since Reigh was born. Rockerfeller apparently snatched his daughter and took her away on a variety of means of transport, including yachts. Eventually Rockerfeller was arrested, and Reigh was returned to her mother.

What about the children?

Sometimes a parent may take their child on holiday to their country of origin, but they don't come back. Sometimes children are 'snatched' or abducted and then taken abroad. The other parent may then have to go through lengthy and complicated court proceedings to try and get his or her child returned home.

According to an international agreement called the Hague Convention, children under the age of 16 who are unlawfully taken from the country where they normally live, must be returned to that country. This agreement is signed by over 45 nations, but in practice it is not always easy to enforce. International custody disputes can be both long and bitter; children are caught, literally, between two countries. In some situations, this may be extremely distressing.

A child, such as Molly/Misbah (above), whose parents decide to live in different countries, often has to face the additional pressures of different cultures and values.

TALK ABOUT

* Do you think mothers are better suited than fathers to being the main carers for children when a relationship breaks down?

* Should both parents have equal rights to their children?

Chapter 7

What challenges does the 'new' family face?

Any change within a family, even a happy occasion such as the birth of a new baby, can be unsettling as family members adjust to the changes. When a family first breaks up, young people have to cope with the shock of the situation. Then they have to adjust to everyday life within their new or re-formed family. The impact of the break-up can affect many different aspects of life, from school to other relationships.

Dealing with school

When you're going through a family break-up, school can sometimes seem like a safe place, away from all the upset and arguments at home. At other times, it can seem like another problem – how can you concentrate on schoolwork when your dad or mum has just left home? Exams and choosing subjects can seem like extra problems that you just can't deal with on top of everything else going on in your life.

The feelings children have when their family breaks up don't stay behind at home. Whether the child feels sad or angry, they sometimes let go of their emotions at school by behaving badly. They may mess about in lessons, bully other children or be rude to the teachers. This doesn't help them; instead it often only leads to more problems.

If you are having trouble concentrating at school because of a break-up, try talking to a school counsellor. Most schools have counsellors to help support pupils having a hard time at home.

Schoolwork

If you are moving house or staying with relatives while things are sorted out at home, it's easy to lose track of schoolwork. Perhaps you have to help look after younger children more, or support your parent in other ways, leaving you with less time for homework. Talk about this to a teacher you like and explain the situation. He or she will probably help you find a way to manage your work and keep on top of everything.

Truancy

When parents are preoccupied with the breakdown of a relationship and setting up a new home, perhaps having to work longer hours, some young people think no one at home will notice if they start to miss school. However, the school usually finds out eventually and the child gets into trouble, which only adds to everyone's difficulties.

They just argue

At school events or parents' evenings do you invite both parents, or choose one? If they both come, will they just argue, or will one refuse to come if the other is there? Try suggesting that they take turns attending events that matter to you, and be firm about no arguments if they attend together!

It can be hard to concentrate at school if your family life is unhappy, but missing school will only cause more problems in the long term.

TALK ABOUT

* Do you think a child's bad behaviour at school is excusable if they are experiencing a family break-up?

* Should teachers be more lenient towards children whose parents are splitting up?

Staying in touch

It may not always be easy to see the parent who no longer lives with you. This can be due to bad feelings between the adults, difficulties for the absent parent, or because children feel so hurt by the family break-up that they don't want to see the parent.

Making arrangements to see a parent can be difficult if there is a lot of bad feeling between the two parents. Sometimes the parent with whom children live may feel so angry and bitter that they try to prevent children from continuing their relationship with the other parent. There may sometimes be another reason for this – perhaps the parent is unsure of the children's safety and wellbeing. Ask your parent to explain the situation, so you understand what's going on and why your parent feels this way.

There are many ways to stay in touch with a parent, even if you are unable to see them.

I'm always let down

Imagine you've been looking forward to seeing your mum or dad all week. Just before he or she is due to pick you up, there's a phone call – suddenly the visit is cancelled. This can be very upsetting. It's important to talk about how it makes you feel; although talking won't magically bring your parent to see you, it will help your parents to understand how you feel.

When a parent has left home, it is sometimes hard to pick up the relationship again. At first, things will feel different. It takes time to build a relationship out of a few hours or days a week, when you have been used to spending lots of time together. You may feel angry towards the parent, and let down. The parent may also feel awkward and guilty. Talking and time can help you both to establish a new, happy and positive relationship.

Two of everything

Shared care means living in two homes. Young people often have two toothbrushes, hairbrushes and sets of pyjamas. The benefits of this are that parents jointly share the care and the young person receives love and attention equally from both parents. However, it can take a while to get used to the practical difficulties of moving between two homes.

It takes time and patience to rebuild a relationship with a parent you don't often see.

DOs & DON'Ts

✳ **Do keep in touch with an absent parent by telephone, email, webcam or letters.**

✳ **Don't be surprised if some visits are less successful than others – they can't all be great.**

✳ **Don't assume your parent can guess what you like doing on visits – explain what you like best. He or she will probably be relieved to sit and chat rather than try to organize special treats for every visit.**

✳ **Do talk to your parent if you know a party is coming up that will interfere with your parent's visit, so that no one is disappointed and other arrangements can be made.**

✳ **Do use a calendar to keep track of where you are staying if you have two homes.**

Stressed parents

When both parents live together, they often share the care of their children, such as taking them to friends and activities, preparing food or supervizing bedtimes. When one parent moves out, the sole responsibility falls on the other parent. This can be extremely tiring for that parent and may also be very stressful.

One parent may also have to take on more paid work outside the home, to make up for the reduced income. A parent on his or her own may seem more stressed and tired than usual. This can be hard for a young person to accept just when they themselves need additional support. It helps if they try to understand the demands and pressures on the parent.

It's not just children who have to deal with difficult feelings. There are lots of adjustments for parents following a break-up.

It happened to me

'I dreaded birthdays. Who would I spend the day with? I loved getting two sets of presents, but I always felt bad about leaving Mum or leaving Dad if I stayed with Mum. In the end I said I wanted to go to my granny's. That made my parents realize what a pressure it felt. Since then, it's taken in turns each year – no discussions.'

Sophia, aged 11.

Jealousy

Your parents have split up: you go round to a friend's house and both their parents are together, or you hear a friend telling you about what he or she did with their mum and dad. It can make you feel jealous and resentful. You might feel angry with your parent that he or she couldn't keep your family together, but each family's situation is different. You cannot know what really goes on in other families. Indeed, your own parents may not have told you everything that led to their own relationship breakdown – remember, parents will often try to protect their children from difficult or upsetting information.

If a parent remarries, it may be difficult to accept that they have formed a new relationship. Try to remember that just because they have a new partner, it does not mean they love you any less.

No boundaries

Some young people feel that after a parent has left, all boundaries are broken. They feel angry. Why should they obey either parent? They go out, come back late and behave rudely. Acting in this way won't help anyone. It's more useful to talk openly and calmly to your parents about how you feel, or to other relatives or friends if you don't feel your parents are listening to you or understand how you feel.

Dating game

Parents may also start new relationships, and in time they may want to live with their new partner. This can be hard to accept. It can feel embarrassing to see your parent going out on dates and behaving more like a love-struck teenager than a responsible parent. You may not like your parent's new boy or girl friend. Perhaps you want to spoil any chances he or she has with new relationships. Try to see that this is unfair – everyone has a right to healthy, happy relationships.

Step families

When a parent meets and sets up home with a new partner, the new partner becomes a step parent. New partners may often come with children, too! A single parent family might suddenly grow into a family with a new parent and new brothers and sisters. There is a lot to adjust to, and everyone has to find a way of fitting in. It doesn't happen overnight, and it's not always simple.

New family, new house – it can seem like too much change. But remember, everyone is getting used to the new situation.

DOs & DON'Ts

* **Do try to work out why you don't like the new partner. Perhaps you're angry that he or she has replaced your other parent, or put out that he or she has caused yet more change just when you were getting used to being with only one parent.**

* **Do tell another adult if you feel unsafe with the step parent, or any new partner.**

* **Do talk to your parent and step parent about any difficulties with step brothers and sisters. It's normal for brothers and sisters to argue, but it can feel more complex when you're forced into sharing a home with other young people you would not choose to know!**

* **Don't expect that bad behaviour or rudeness will make your step parent disappear – it won't.**

New relationships

What happens if a child doesn't get on with the parent's new partner? These feelings are probably manageable if the couple doesn't live together, but there may be problems if they move in with each other. Much younger step brothers and sisters often come with a step parent – much older ones may have left home. It can be hard to suddenly have a toddler around, or an older sister who is allowed to do things that you aren't yet allowed to do. It's a time of adjustment for everyone. You may not ever become best friends with step siblings, but life will be a lot easier if you can find a way to get along.

It may be that everyone in the new family seems to be happy with the new set-up and to find it exciting – except you. No one seems to care what you think. You may feel invisible and left out. It's up to you to explain to the others how you feel, so that they can then help you.

Not all stepmothers are as wicked as the character in the Snow White story! Try to forget the stereotype and see that a stepmother is an ordinary person, just like you.

In the media

From Snow White's wicked stepmother (below) to the negative stereotypes of modern step parents, step parents have a rough press. They are often presented as trying to replace the child's biological parent, or as treating their step children less kindly than their own. It's a difficult job for everyone involved. Whereas children and their biological parents have had years to build their relationships with each other, step parents and step children are expected to establish close living relationships in a short time.

The absent parent

A step parent does not replace your absent biological parent. A step parent has few legal rights over the children of another relationship, unless he or she adopts the children or arranges to take on parental responsibility in law. The rights of the other parent are not affected.

When one parent falls in love with someone new and sets up home with him or her, the other parent may feel very upset. Although it is distressing to see either parent unhappy, it is important not to get caught up in their feelings. One parent's new relationship should not affect the arrangements made for children to see their other biological parent. If you are worried that a new relationship will make it harder for you to see your other parent, tell your parents about your anxieties and ask them to explain how existing arrangements will continue.

Try to see things from your step parent's viewpoint – they too may be finding living in a new family difficult.

It happened to me

'My dad remarried and I went to live with him, his new wife and her two children. For a while, it felt like I was just living in a stranger's house. There were different rules about going out, computer time, bedtime, homework. I was so fed up with it because the way I'd been allowed to do things changed – the others carried on as normal. There was a big argument between me and my dad and stepmum. I think they must have realized it was unfair – now there are new rules for all of us.'

Tom, aged 12.

TALK ABOUT

* **Do you think a parent should ask their children's opinion before moving in with another partner?**

* **Do you think parents have the right to start a new relationship?**

New people

A change of home, sharing a room with a step brother or sister who you really wouldn't choose to be friends with and seeing your parent meet a new partner is a lot to take in. But it's not just you who has to deal with the change – so too do your step siblings. They might not want to share a room with you either, and they might not want your parent as their step parent.

Rather than arguing, try to calmly explain how you feel if you are finding life in a new family hard.

It's common to feel jealous of a parent's new partner or other children in the family. You might think that your parent only cares about the new partner, or seems to favour the step children. But new relationships take time for adults, too. At first they might not get the balance right in making everyone feel included and special. Talk to your parent, and your step parent, about your feelings. Ask your parent to spend some time with you, separately from the new partner or siblings.

Chapter 8

Moving on

Change can be positive! You didn't want things to change, and things won't go back to the way they were, but people can move on. A family that changes is nothing to be ashamed of and it happens to thousands of people. Any change takes time to get used to. Things will be different, but they can also be good.

Children from famous families face the same difficulties after a relationship break-up.

In the media

Madonna and Guy Ritchie divorced in 2008. This extremely wealthy couple have three children: one biological child, one child from a previous relationship and one young adopted child. After all the attention has died down and the family members get used to their new living arrangements, the family will be re-formed. Famous or not, every family break-up creates new family formations and new relationships within it.

Time for change

Unhappy parents who live together argue, ignore each other, say mean things, look sad and are bad-tempered. Once they have separated, they both usually find that things work much better. After a break-up, there is time for everyone to adjust to the new situation. During this time, don't be afraid to ask friends and family for help and support. If things are difficult at home, or you need a break, spend some time with friends or other family members – but make sure your parent always knows where you are.

A family break-up often brings other family members closer, such as grandparents and grandchildren.

DOs & DON'Ts

It's important to look after yourself:

✳ **Don't feel guilty about going out with friends and having a good time. Your parents' relationship has changed, but that doesn't mean you have to feel sad all the time. It's OK to have fun and look after yourself.**

✳ **Do talk to a parent, doctor or school counsellor if you find that your mood remains very low for a long time.**

✳ **Do speak up for yourself. When a family is changing, there are a lot of pressures on everyone. It's easy for children to sink into the background as the adults try to sort everything out. But it's important that those adults know how you feel.**

✳ **Do ask your parents about their relationship if you are worried about them arguing a lot. You can't change their relationship, but it does no harm for them to know about your anxieties.**

43

A deeper relationship

Many young people find that they develop better and deeper relationships with their parents after a break-up. They become closer to each parent in different ways. Brother and sister relationships can also become stronger, as there are fewer tensions in the new family set-up, and the siblings have supported each other through a difficult period.

Your own relationships

The fact that one couple's relationship didn't last does not mean that your own relationships won't work out. The parent left because the adult relationship broke down – not because of the relationship between parent and child. There is no reason why your own relationships, with friends and boy or girl friends, will not last.

Don't be afraid of healthy arguments! Just because you argue with a parent or friend, it doesn't follow that the relationship is about to collapse. You may associate arguments with your parents' break-up, but in lots of other relationships arguments are one method people use to sort out their problems and issues. They can be helpful and positive as well as negative.

The breakdown of a parents' relationship has an effect on everyone in the family, but young people in the family can continue to develop their own strong and independent relationships.

Support

Grandparents, friends, teachers and schools counsellors – all of these people can be great sources of support for young people experiencing the difficulties of a family break-up. Chatting about your feelings or letting off steam about how unfair it all feels doesn't change the situation, but it does make it feel easier to deal with.

There are also lots of organizations that offer free and confidential advice and support. Check out the list of websites on page 47.

Families are about strong, loving and caring relationships. A family can take on a new shape, wherever you live and whomever you live with.

TALK ABOUT

✳ **What positive things happen when a family breaks up?**

✳ **Do you think it is possible to enjoy a newly shaped family without betraying the memory of the old family?**

✳ **How can a newly shaped family look towards the future?**

Glossary

abduct To take a person without permission.

abuse To cause physical or emotional harm to another person.

addiction When someone cannot stop doing something that is bad for them, such as drinking alcohol or taking drugs.

adopt To have permanent legal responsibility for a child or young person.

biological parent Parent who created a child.

child support Money one parent gives to another to help pay for things a child needs.

counsellor Someone who you can talk to about your feelings and who is qualified to help you work out your problems.

couple Two people in a relationship.

court A place where a judge hears about issues and conflicts and makes decisions about them.

custody To have responsibility for looking after a child the majority of the time. A child lives with the parent who has custody.

disagreement When people can not agree on a particular subject.

divorce The legal ending to a marriage.

foster When a couple temporarily looks after and takes on responsibility for someone else's child.

homosexual relationship Sexual relationship between two women or two men.

issues Emotional problems or difficulties.

legal agreement A document that is accepted by a court of law.

nurture To care for someone or something.

mediation Professional support for couples who are splitting up, to help them do so with as little conflict as possible.

prejudice To have negative thoughts about someone based on their background.

preoccupied When someone is absorbed in their own thoughts and can seem distant as a result.

reassurance Telling someone everything will be okay.

separation When a couple splits up.

sibling A brother or sister.

social worker A person who is trained to help support individuals and families.

stereotype Labelling someone as a particular type of person because of their background, class, social situation or other type of category.

Further information

Notes for Teachers:

The Talk About panels are to be used to encourage debate and avoid the polarization of views. One way of doing this is to use 'continuum lines'. Think of a range of statements or opinions about the topics that can then be considered by the pupils. An imaginary line is constructed that pupils can stand along to show what they feel in response to each statement (please see above). If they strongly agree or disagree with the viewpoint they can stand by the signs, if the response is somewhere in between they stand along the line in the relevant place. If the response is 'neither agree, nor disagree' or they 'don't know' then they stand at an equal distance from each sign, in the middle. Alternatively, continuum lines can be drawn out on paper and pupils can mark a cross on the line to reflect their views.

Books to read

When Parents Separate (Choices and Decisions) by Pete Saunders and Steve Myers (Franklin Watts, 2007)

Family Crises (Emotional Health Issues) by Jillian Powell (Wayland, 2008)

Relationships (Know the Facts) by Sarah Medina (Wayland, 2008)

Websites and helplines

Kids' Health

A site for young people with advice on how to deal with divorce of parents and adjust to new step families.

Website: www.kidshealth.org/teen/your_mind/Parents/divorce.html

Youth Information

A site with advice about the legal issues around divorce.

Website: www.youthinformation.com

Families Change

A site for young children and teenagers giving information about the process of divorce and separation, and discussing the issues that are involved for young people.

Website: www.familieschange.ca

Divorce Aid

Advice, support and information for parents and young people experiencing the break-up of a family.

Website: www.divorceaid.co.uk

NSPCC

A site run by the NSPCC for young people aged 12 to 16. There are confidential online advisers and a message board to help sort out a range of issues, including family problems.

Website: www.there4me.com

It's Not Your Fault

Practical information for children, young people and parents going through a family break-up.

Website: www.itsnotyourfault.org

ChildLine

A website and a free telephone helpline for children and young people in the United Kingdom. Trained counsellors offer comfort, support, advice and protection on a range of issues, including family break-up.

Website: www.childline.org.uk

Phone: 00 44 (0) 0800 1111 (Free 24-hour helpline)

RISKY TRADE

This book is dedicated to my family, especially Alice and Fred Kimball, and Keith, Lindsey, Kimberly, John and Alison.

Risky Trade
Infectious Disease in the Era of Global Trade

ANN MARIE KIMBALL
University of Washington, USA

ASHGATE

Published by
Ashgate Publishing Limited
Gower House
Croft Road
Aldershot
Hants GU11 3HR
England

Ashgate Publishing Company
Suite 420
101 Cherry Street
Burlington, VT 05401-4405
USA

Ashgate website: http://www.ashgate.com

British Library Cataloguing in Publication Data
Kimball, Ann Marie
   Risky trade : infectious disease in the era of global trade
   1. Communicable diseases – Transmission 2. International
   trade – Health aspects
   I. Title
   616.9'0471

Library of Congress Control Number: 2005933814

ISBN 13: 978 0 7546 4296 1

Reprinted 2006, 2008

Typeset by Bournemouth Colour Press, Parkstone, Poole.
Printed and bound in Great Britain by MPG Books Ltd, Bodmin, Cornwall.

Contents

List of Figures

List of Tables

List of Abbreviations

AIDS	acquired immunodeficiency syndrome
APEC	Asia Pacific Economic Cooperation
ASEAN	Association of Southeast Asian Nations
BSE	Bovine Spongiform Encephalopathy
BWC	Biological Weapons Convention
CAR	Central African Republic
CDC	Centers for Disease Control and Prevention
CISET	The White House Committee on International Science, Engineering, and Technology
ELISA	enzyme-linked immunosorbent assay
FSIS	Food Safety and Inspection Service (USDA)
EIS	Epidemic Intelligence Service
EU	European Union
FAO	Food and Agriculture Organization of the United Nations
FDA	Food and Drug Administration
FERN	Food Emergency Response Network
GAO	General Accounting Office/Government Accountability Office (post 2004)
GATT	General Agreement on Tariffs and Trade
GATS	General Agreement on Trade in Services
GOARN	Global Outbreak Alert and Response Network
GSS	Global Salmonella Survey
HEPA	high efficiency particulate air
HIPPA	Health Insurance Portability and Accountability Act
HIV	human immunodeficiency virus
HPAI	highly pathogenic avian influenza
IHR	International Health Regulations
IOM	Institute of Medicine
IPPC	International Plant Protection Commission
ISO	International Organization for Standardization
MBM	meat and bone meal
MMWR	Morbidity and Mortality Weekly Report
nvCJD	new variant Creutzfeldt-Jakob disease
NARMS	National Antimicrobial Resistance Monitoring System
NAFTA	North American Free Trade Agreement
NIH	National Institutes of Health
OECD	Organization for Economic Co-operation and Development
OIE	Office International des Épizooties

PAHO	Pan American Health Organization
RNA	ribonucleic acid
SARS	Severe Acute Respiratory Syndrome
SPS	Sanitary and Phytosanitary Agreement
TBCA	Thai Business Coalition on AIDS
TEPHINET	Training Programs in Epidemiology and Public Health Interventions Network
TBT	Technical Barriers to Trade Agreement
TRIPS	Trade-Related Aspects of Intellectual Property Rights Agreement
UK	United Kingdom
US	United States
USDA	United States Department of Agriculture
WHO	World Health Organization
WPRO	Western Pacific Regional Office
WTO	World Trade Organization

Foreword

Dr. David Heymann

During the past thirty years I have had the opportunity to work in countries where infectious diseases regularly emerge, re-emerge and resurge; and globally, at the World Health Organization, during a time when the world has begun to come to grips with the public health risks that occur when these diseases spread internationally in a globalized and interlinked world. As Professor Ann Marie Kimball clearly demonstrates in her book *Risky Trade: Infectious Disease in the Era of Global Trade*, microbes are resilient, and able to survive and multiply through adaptation and natural selection. They also relentlessly find entry points to human populations through weaknesses in public health or risky human behaviour; and freely travel the world in humans, insects, food, animals and biological products.

At the same time, when microbes cross, or threaten to cross international borders, they enter a world where information about infectious disease outbreaks travels at high speed on the electronic highway; and where countries, their scientists and their public health experts are increasingly working together to detect, prepare for and respond to public health events that threaten international public health and economic security. The recent outbreak of Severe Acute Respiratory Syndrome (SARS), fully described by Professor Kimball in her book, clearly demonstrated that it is no longer the exclusive privilege of countries to report and respond to infectious diseases occurring in their own territories, but that the global community has also assumed this role, aided by the ease and power of electronic communication through the world wide web. Demands on countries during the SARS outbreak were unprecedented, and they were accepted. Countries were first asked to report probable cases of SARS in real time using electronic reporting formats. They were then asked to screen airline passengers and prevent those with SARS, or a history of contact with SARS, from travelling internationally. And finally, international travellers themselves were asked to postpone travel to certain areas were SARS was occurring.

Infectious disease outbreaks not only cause human suffering and death. They severely impact national economies, either directly due to the need for measures to contain disease and manage those who become infected, or indirectly because of decreases in travel and trade limitations. This was once a strong disincentive for reporting of infectious diseases, but new norms and standards that have been reinforced during the SARS outbreak have mandated a change. In Asia, governments have been remarkably frank about reporting when poultry flocks become infected with the H5N1 influenze virus, and have rapidly reported any human infections that occur, keeping both their own citizens and the international community informed. These governments have reported despite financial consequences to the agricultural sector – with culling of entire flocks of poultry. National and international public health interests are no longer being suppressed in the context of national sovereignty.

Other countries have also demonstrated their willingness to forego previous concepts of national sovereignty with the recent international spread of wild poliovirus. Since the latter part of 2003, wild poliovirus has spread internationally to 18 previously polio-free countries across Africa, into the Middle East and then onwards to Asia. These countries continue to freely exchange genetic information about the viruses through the global polio surveillance networks, linking each imported virus to its country of origin. Solidarity in surveillance and response, with synchronized immunization campaigns in countries with common borders, again confirms that international collaboration prevails over issues that were previously considered the domain of a sovereign nation alone.

Some scholars have cited international reporting of infectious diseases, and internationally-driven collaborative response as a potential infringement on national sovereignty, compromising the concept that states reign supreme over their territories and peoples. As we enter the 21st century there are many positive signs of a new world order, crowned in May 2005 by intergovernmental agreement to the revised International Health Regulations that will serve as a formal framework for pro-active international surveillance and response to infectious diseases. Captains of industry have reason for optimism that infectious diseases will not disrupt the waters as they continue to navigate the seas of our globalized world.

David L. Heymann, M.D.
Special Representatative for Polio Eradication, formerly
Executive Director of Communicable Diseases
World Health Organization

Introduction: Reversing the Microscope

As the World Health Assembly wound up its agenda in Geneva in May of 2005, a new regime of International Health Regulations was approved. This is a landmark event both in terms of the potential importance of the regulations themselves and the amount of effort that went into their formulation, vetting, negotiation and final passage. But the regulations are modest in what they bring to the efforts to bridge the yawning void between the worlds of commerce and health into which the health of the populations of the world may be teetering. It is a gap built on mutual misunderstanding, lack of cooperation and clashing cultural values. I write here as a member of the world of health who has dared to wander into the other camp and try and learn what the conflict is all about. So my opinions are not those of an expert on both camps, but those of a member of one and an interested observer of the second.

The modern day commercial enterprise activity is unprecedented in its reach, wealth and ingenuity. The way that economic statistics and other national measures are reckoned encumber the appreciation of the change in ownership of resources that has occurred. According to press reports in financial periodicals, the ten richest men in the world hold between $18.6 billion and $46.5 billion in personal wealth, for a total of $316.6 billion.[1] If these ten individuals were a country, and their GDP were $316.6 billion, they would nestle comfortably between Belgium and Switzerland. Of course the measurement of total assets and gross domestic product are not comparable, but they give a rough idea of the unprecedented concentration of wealth in the private sector that has occurred since World War II. There are not good figures available on total public sector assets versus total private sector assets, nor are there reliable measures of annual product within these two sectors on a global basis. Nationalizing such figures would be even more problematic since the creation of wealth has become a transnational activity. This presents an extraordinary new reality in the search for solutions to global ill health.

The wheels of enterprise, predominantly driven by the private sector, is what I regard as the global express. It is the physical transfer of millions of human beings and tons of goods across thousands of miles every single day. It is also a brand new mobility for microbes that is haphazardly tracked through outbreaks. And the outbreaks are the business of public health to fix. Public health, which has suffered from profound neglect for two decades, is woefully behind in catching up with the challenges presented in this scenario. We need help from the "other side."

Against this background, the aim of this book is to explore a very concrete and important challenge to population health: the emergence of new human pathogens.

---

1 All currency references are to US dollars.

The book traces the rise in commerce and travel as part of the globalization we are living. Chapters 2 through 4 describe the behavior of three kinds of pathogens within this system of the global express: foodborne diseases, which are usually of short incubation period and relatively non lethal; "stealth" infections, which are of very long incubation period and more often lethal; and new, highly contagious diseases that have short incubation periods and are more often lethal. Intentional threats are covered in Chapter 5, and vary widely in the biology of the agents and their incubation period and lethality.

Based on the evidence presented in the first five chapters, I begin to focus on constructing a conceptual framework to consider prevention of the emergence and transmission of new pathogens within the global system. This discussion is oriented around a "pyramid of prevention" and seeks to examine the potential for prevention at every level of intervention: initial emergence, and local, national, and international spread. In the final chapter, some promising areas of work are set forward that I hope will invite others to begin to join the thinking.

In a sense the book turns the microscope upside down. Working from the microbial level of emergence, infection and disease, it works up to the macro level and tries to unmask the "why" of pandemic threats. The text works up from the meeting of microbes with hosts and attempts to understand how the overall system that allows or encourages that may operate.

I write with the hope that the general reader will find it understandable and useful in his or her thinking about the connections between the fast-paced world of commerce and travel and the unseen changes at the microbial level. Behind the book is my firm conviction that the challenges facing the modern world require the genius of the entire human family to find solutions. Confining such discussion to "experts," top level bureaucrats, or politicians is too frail a strategy to assure success. In my experience, the best answers often come from the most unlikely places. Genius is not confined to those with a high profile. The book puts forward more questions than it answers, in the hope that the reader will review the evidence presented, and come to his or her own conclusions. Even better, I hope the reader starts to jump into the discussion of emergence.

Preventive medicine is a discipline that works its way up the chain of causality of human illness. The goal is to find the cause and prevent the problem. It is in that effort that this book hopes to serve. The catastrophes of epidemics such as SARS, HIV/AIDS and enteric diseases are often preventable. But to prevent them, the root cause and factors contributing must be discovered and addressed. Often there is not a single cause, but many. Those causes that are known are presented here. Those that are hypothesized and yet to be proven are also presented here.

My own journey in this area of inquiry was sparked by a visit to the Central African Republic (CAR) in 1982. Outside of the capital, Bangui was a marketplace with stalls made of bamboo. The CAR was in a time of hardship and on market day, few items made it to the market for trading: some beans, some palm wine. And yet, the marketplace was full of people who came to buy and to trade. While some were brought by their search for food, most were brought by their desire to socialize, exchange news and dicker. The urge to bargain, barter, trade, buy and sell is central to the way humans are built. In the modern age it has created an unparalleled global system of trade and travel. This I dub the "global express." The system connects us across oceans, continents, national boundaries, cultural differences, language groups and ethnicity. It is bringing us closer and closer together all the time, and it is inexorable.

But what of the unseen world? What is going on with the microbial world as all of this "macro" stirring is occurring? I believe that the emergence of new human pathogens is tied, in part, to the changes that we cannot see at the microbial level. It only makes sense. Our understanding of those changes is in its infancy whereas the global system of trade and travel is decades old. We need to catch up with our own activities and understand the risks we are creating.

This book owes a great deal to many people who have kindly provided information, interviews, and insights and shared their work. These include but are not limited to Dr. Kelley Lee, University of London; Professor David Fidler of the University of Indiana; Mr. Bruce Plotkin of Seattle; Dr. David Heymann; Dr. Gunael Rodier; Mr. Mike Ryan; Mr. Nick Drager; Ms. Benedickte Dal; Dr. Max Hardimann and Margery Dam of WHO; Ms. Gretchen Stanton, Ms. Marie Isabelle Pellan, Ms. Mirielle Crossy, and Ms. Carmen Pont-Vieira of WTO; and Professor Alan Swinbank, University of Reading, UK.

My colleagues at the University of Washington have contributed their support and forbearance during this process of writing. I would acknowledge in particular the kind financial support of Dr. Craig Hogan, Vice Provost of Research; Dean Patricia Wahl, School of Public Health; and Professor Scott Davis, Chair of the Department of Epidemiology. This work was also supported by the generosity of the Guggenheim Foundation, without which it would not have been possible. My work in this area advanced greatly with the support of the New Century Scholars Program of the Fulbright Foundation, which enabled me to generate the first proposal for this book.

Ms. Jill Read Hodges assisted in the research, writing, editing and organization of the text as my research associate. Ms. Gail Boyer and Drs. Heymann and Fidler provided early reads of the manuscript to assist in the finalization of the book. Mr. Yuzo Arima, PhD candidate, contributed to the discussion of influenza. Illustrations were organized by Ms. Judith Yarrow and Ms. Alicia Silva assisted with the text.

Finally, I would presume to dedicate this work to those who find themselves in the path of public health emergencies such as pandemics. There is no greater injustice than that of the indiscriminate, often preventable loss of health and welfare wrought by epidemics and pandemics. It is in the earnest hope of prevention of such calamities to the human family that this work is offered. The modern world can afford to assure the safety of all of its citizens; the primary question is whether our global community will choose to do so.

Chapter 1

The Global Express

In the quiet of the World Trade Organization auditorium in Geneva, delegates from dozens of economies leaned forward, listening intently to the translated testimony streaming through their earphones. The delegate from the People's Republic of China, an economy highly affected by the SARS epidemic, was attempting to head off further damage in the form of trade restrictions on Chinese agricultural products. The country's products are safe, he argued; the new disease is transmitted person-to-person – there's no evidence it can be passed on through food (World Trade Organization Committee on Sanitary and Phytosanitary Measures 2003).

The delegate's task was a difficult one. The recent Severe Acute Respiratory Syndrome (SARS) outbreak had caused considerable alarm around the globe, and even today many questions remain unanswered. By late June 2003, more than 8,000 cases of the new, highly fatal, highly infectious pneumonia had surfaced, and more than 700 people had died. In China alone, there had been more than 3,000 SARS cases and nearly 350 deaths. SARS epitomized a threat that had been anticipated in public health circles for more than a decade: the emergence of a new human pathogen that would spread across wide expanses of the Asian Pacific. The SARS microbe "hitchhiked" on travelers from community to community, flying on commercial aircraft. Compounding concerns was the belief that before the virus had begun zipping across continents in humans, it had jumped across species – from animals to humans. While the crossover has not been completely defined, it appears that SARS, a corona virus that had its entire genome mapped by a network of international laboratories in just one month, came from animals. The specific route is in any case unknown, but one possibility is that the virus was transmitted via food handlers who raise civet cats, slaughter the cats for sale as food, and provide the goods in the marketplace in Guangdong, China. (Trade in civet cats was halted in Guangdong in the summer of 2003 because of the outbreak, but resumed in August of that year.) Microbes moving from animals to humans is not new. In fact more than two thirds of new infections in humans arise from other vertebrate animals. However, with the potential amplification resulting from modern global trade and travel, it is becoming more important to understand.

The SARS outbreak brings into sharp relief the challenges of globalization and the accompanying emergence of human infections. Global trade continues to increase in volume, diversity of product, and speed. Likewise, the volume and speed of travel for both business and pleasure continue to grow. Microbes, invisible to the human eye and undetectable by normal human senses, have been, are, and will continue to be potential travelers on the burgeoning global express. Meanwhile, the safety nets protecting humans against this proliferation of disease are growing threadbare in spots. Science is struggling to keep pace with the ever-evolving microbes. Access to public health and personal health services across the globe are vastly uneven. Moreover, access to basics, such as clean water and sanitation, are not assured for all of the world's inhabitants. These realities are increasingly creating risk. The evidence of this risk is the surge of emerging infections. Some of these diseases, such as salmonellosis from food products, are foes we have long known that are changing their behavior in modern times; others, such as SARS, are brand new threats.

So the delegate from the People's Republic of China was trying to palliate concerns about his country's products in the face of an unknown threat. Concerns about contagion are the most powerful motivator for trade restrictions. When embargoes are put into place they cost millions, even billions, of dollars in lost trade. But the global express of trade and travel among nations has increasingly shown its power in amplifying and spreading new and frightening human infections. Thus the challenge faced by the delegate in the cool, dark auditorium of the WTO on that hot Geneva day was considerable.

Factors of Emergence – "Trade-related Infections"

In 1991, the prestigious Institute of Medicine Working Group on Emerging Infections identified trade and travel as a "factor of emergence." The landmark study group, chaired by Nobel Laureate Joshua Lederberg, produced a chilling view of the changing world of microbes and humans in the report *Emerging Infections* (Lederberg, Shope et al. 1992). The Clinton White House was so alarmed that an interagency group was convened shortly thereafter to more fully describe the security and safety issues the report raised and to outline policy options for response. The White House Committee on International Science, Engineering, and Technology (CISET) emphasized the intersectoral nature of the threat and, in turn, the response. Epidemics of disease are not solely the concern of the health care or public health system; they are products of human activities in numerous areas of endeavor, including global commerce and travel. Just so, an effective response cannot be limited to the health sector. In line with the policy direction suggested, the US Office of Science and Technology Policy began to promote discussion of emerging infections in virtually every forum in which the US participated. This included political, economic, and international arenas as well as health related groups. While a brilliant beginning, the agenda for response over the intervening years has taken a detour, and the multidisciplinary approach has been slighted.

I began working with the Asia Pacific Economic Cooperation (APEC) on the issue of emerging infections in 1994, following their high profile Leaders' Summit in Seattle. APEC, which counts 21 member economies, is one of the largest trading cooperations with 2.6 billion people and more than 60 percent of global trade within its community. Also in 1994, at an Industrial Science and Technology meeting in Vancouver, I encountered a delegate from the White House Office of Science and Technology Policy. We found we were on the same quest for intersectoral cooperation on fighting the emergence of new human pathogens. We teamed up, and founded the first electronic network for emerging infectious disease alerts in the region. The APEC Emerging Infections Network has been tracking the drumbeat of new emergence for a decade.

A "trade-related infection" is one that:

1. is facilitated by the ramping up of production to meet global demand (a massive slaughterhouse or overcrowded pens, or pooling of large lots of biological product in preparation for a specific end product, for instance);
2. is disseminated or amplified through global distribution of goods (for example, *Escherichia coli* traveling from the US to Japan on radishes); or
3. has a major economic impact, through its occurrence and reporting, on the flow of trade (SARS' toll on China, or "mad cow" disease's toll on the United Kingdom's beef industry).

A similar working definition has not been developed for travel-related infections per se. However, the following excellent description of the role of the traveler provides a thought-provoking context:

> Travellers are interactive biological units that pick up, process and drop off microbial genetic materials at different times and in different places. Travellers alter places and populations during and after travel. Changes in the biota may be sustained if a traveller carries a pathogen into a new environment where it is transmitted and then survives, replicates and persists in a new geographic area.
>
> (Wilson 2003 p. 1S)

The Unseen Travelers: Microbes

In both trade and travel, microscopic travelers emerge and then are borne to far distant locations in products and humans, transported by trains, boats and planes. Our understanding of the ways the bugs travel – on melons, almonds and snow peas; in burgers, humans and shipping containers – and their ability to survive in a variety of circumstances is continually evolving. Infectious agents are not "thinking" entities as far we know. Nonetheless, they are intrepid survivors, thanks to short life spans and prolific reproduction. We count their generations in hours or days, and their numbers in logarithms of 10. In this way, evolutionary biology tells us, they are able to flourish because there is a natural selection of individual agents that are best adapted for survival. And with hundreds if not thousands of generations occurring over a single human lifespan, the opportunity for continuous adaptation is extraordinary.

Just as "know thine enemy" is key to successful military strategy, so it is to a successful safe trade strategy. The microbial world is diverse. In the world of trade-related infections, we describe four basic types of "bugs": bacteria, spores, viruses, and prions. The differences among these are important. Bacteria can often live independently of a human host; spores are protected forms of bacteria that are dormant but blossom in certain environments; viruses need humans or other animals to reproduce themselves; and prions are not actually bugs but proteins. In fact, prions remain hypothetical in that the research thus far suggests, but has not proven, that they cause mad cow disease in cattle and new variant Creutzfeldt-Jakob disease in humans. This is called the "Prion Hypothesis" because it has yet to be proven in the way that other agents have been proven to be the cause of the diseases with which they are associated.

Koch's Postulates

Causality is always tricky in science. In the early 20th century, German scientist Robert Koch advanced his famous postulates that had to be fulfilled to prove that any given microbe was responsible for a particular agent:

- The microorganism must always be observed in association with the disease.
- It must be possible to isolate the agent from the host and grow it in a pure laboratory culture.
- The microbe must produce the disease when it is introduced into a susceptible host.
- It must be possible to recover the microbe from that host and once again grow it in a laboratory culture.

The fact that prion research remains a working hypothesis should not be alarming or even surprising. In fact most areas of microbiology and virology are relatively new and many are still being understood by science. The prion disease hypothesis is a radical change from our traditional understanding of disease. There is no genetic material involved. Replication appears to be related to spatial factors and folding of proteins; it stands James Watson and Francis Crick's DNA helix on its head, or at least puts it into a more modest context. The take-away message is that science is not as solid as most casual readers believe in the area of infectious diseases. As we will see, our recent decades of complacency regarding infectious disease was foolhardy to the extreme; with most new infections, the knowledge base is still under construction.

While there are many known microbes, there are even more that are unknown. Some of these are pathogenic in humans, some are not. Microbiology focuses on those that cause disease in humans. Isolating and describing these bugs requires the ability to see or detect the agent. The agent is then isolated and grown in culture to be further studied. Our tools for this work have evolved over the later 19th century and throughout the 20th century and, with this evolution, our vista on the microbial world has widened. This progressive discovery and description of microbial agents over time has proven to be critical in the comprehending of the health repercussions of global trade and travel. As diagnostic technologies become increasingly sophisticated, it becomes possible to detect and follow the movement of particular bugs across continents.

Science has only recently begun to outline the vast body of undescribed agents through the new technologies that display microbes' genetic make-ups and enable comparison between known and unknown agents. GenBank, a global bank of genetic mapping information maintained by the US National Library of Medicine, contains some 30,000 species of bacteria (Figure 1.1).

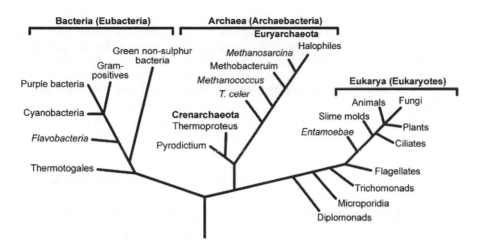

Figure 1.1   The eubacteria tree

However, recent studies in the Sargasso Sea estimate that seawater might support two million different bacteria and a ton of soil might contain four million species. In fact, only about half of the bacteria whose genes have been stored in GenBank have been formally described. This means that we know the characteristics of less than half of the organisms for which scientists have obtained genetic information. It is becoming clear that even our understanding of agents that we discovered long ago can be imperfect or outdated. Many of the "facts" attributed to these agents are based on observations from 50 to 100 years ago that have not been rigorously tested with modern methods. Science is always based closely on observations. This means that the better we can see, the more accurately we can test and describe. When we had only simple microscopes to look through, testing was largely a matter of description. How big is it? What color is it? What does it look like if I stain it this way? How about when I put it into this liquid? Occasionally "facts" related to older microbial agents stay with us long after new ways of testing them have been discovered. For instance, many textbooks state that tuberculosis increases in people exposed over previous decades to asbestos – this "fact" dates from the 1930s and has not been well tested since. So while we readily recognize shortcomings in our knowledge of new agents, we sometimes fail to remember that our understanding of older agents can be tenuous as well. The unexpected behaviors of trade-related infections serve as a reminder of this fact. Almost monthly, we see old agents behaving in new and unexpected ways. Who knew that *Salmonella enterica* would penetrate mango skins? (For details, see Chapter 2.)

Classic microbiology classifies bugs into groups and then generalizes how these groups act. However the newer infections we tend to see related to global trade have been redefining these rules, and so understanding how particular agents work offers a more useful framework here than placing them in categories. Usually the bug is detected because of how it acts in the human. How does it cause infection? What are the clinical signs and symptoms of the infection? How long does it take for the infected human to become ill? How serious is that illness? Can it be fatal? Is it treatable? The Institute of Medicine's Emerging Infections Report prompted scientists to consider anew the impact of changes in the larger global environment on the infinitesimal world of microbes. While this makes sense, it articulated a shift in the way many scientists of microbiology, virology and other "micro" studies viewed the subjects of their work. Looking through a microscope and cataloguing, describing and testing new agents in the test tube or on culture had been standard practice since the early 1900s. Now scientists also are examining the constant evolution of the microbial world as it responds to environmental changes due to the ever expanding human community. And they are recognizing that these microbial mutations are every bit as rapid and powerful as major events in the "macro" scale of existence.

Historically the science of ecology has defined the relationships that occur in nature between an organism, such as a turtle, and its environment – i.e., how that organism interacts with its immediate natural environment. This science has been key in describing global trends in species endangerment or loss, as well as human interactions with the environment. Ecology in the 1960s focused on the natural environment: the lifecycle of forest communities, the ecological niches of the rainforest. Increasingly, scientists are focusing on the "built environment" that mankind is creating. Roads, buildings, and coastline bulkheads all change the way humans and other organisms interact with their living environment. In some sense, trade and travel provide a new conceptual framework for examining the ecology of microorganisms. Trade and travel constitute a built environment that is mobile and constantly changing, presenting challenges as well as opportunities for survival and successful reproduction for microorganisms. In these tumultuous conditions, microbes often find humans convenient hosts. It is this continuously changing, manmade environment that sets the stage for the drama of the emergence of new human infections through trade and travel.

In his crosscutting work, *Evolution of Infectious Disease*, Paul Ewald and his colleagues have begun to try to marry ecology, evolution and infectious disease (Ewald 1996). They have begun the work of bringing the science of ecology and its pressures into an understanding of the rapidly evolving world of microbes. Some human activities, such as the provision of pure water, appear to have a definite impact on the evolutionary strategies of microbes. The areas of trade and travel that have created unprecedented mobility for the microbial world remain to be systematically explored in this way. Increasingly they are playing a part in human epidemics, so the time has come to pay serious attention.

By Air, by Sea, by Land

In 2004, the World Tourism Organization counted a record 760 million international arrivals (World Tourism Organization 2005). An estimated 1.4 million people cross international borders every day (Wilson 2003). Human travel was the key to the rapid global spread of SARS and has been key to "stirring" a number of other emergent infections as well, among them dengue, influenza, measles, and polio. The link between travel and the spread of disease is not new. History is replete with examples of indigenous populations being decimated when conquerors or settlers arrived, bringing with them infections previously outside the population's experience. However the modern era of global travel is unprecedented in (1) the volume of individuals traveling, (2) the speed of travel over long distances, (3) the range of travel and the increasing interconnectedness it brings to populations. Air transportation moves 40 percent of global trade by value, in addition to its human cargo. The time in transit from point A to point B, even when thousands of miles distant, is less than the time it takes for most diseases to become evident in an infected person. Thus an infected individual may board a flight in Canada, pass his or her journey feeling well, and become clinically ill some days after arriving in India.

When public health laws were first passed to limit travel-related contagion in Italy in the 14th century they focused on quarantine. Quarantine, from the Italian word *quaranta* for forty, described the amount of time ships were required to stay out of port prior to allowing passengers to disembark. After 40 days the threat of plague or yellow fever from those on board was thought to have passed, in that any infected individuals would be clearly ill by that time. In today's world of travel, airlines radio ahead one hour prior to landing if the crew suspects a passenger is ill. Even then, it is rare that an aircraft is placed in quarantine on arrival – and certainly not for forty days. The specialty of travel medicine has historically focused on maintaining wellness for travelers during their journeys. However, the last decade has seen the specialty begin to expand to embrace the increasingly urgent agenda of emerging infections and the role of travelers in their biology and dissemination.

Global Trade: A Recent History

Products, like people, are traveling further and faster. Since the 1970s, world trade has expanded at a steady clip, averaging about 6 percent a year with occasional dips, such as the worldwide recession in 1992–3 and the more pronounced decline following the 9/11 attacks on the US in 2001. Although most international trade dollars are linked to manufactured goods, agricultural products consistently have accounted for a sizable chunk, from nearly 30 percent in 1963, to about 9 percent – some $583 billion worth – in 2002, as shown in Figure 1.2 (World Trade Organization 2004).

Developed countries dominate agricultural exports and imports; Brazil is the only developing country among the top 10 exporters of agricultural goods (Arcal and Maetz 2000). A growing portion of agricultural exports are processed products, from cheese to sausages. In 2002, processed goods made up nearly half of all agricultural exports. As later chapters will illustrate, the additional steps entailed in processing often present more opportunities for pathogens to be introduced into products.

Myriad technical, cultural and economic dynamics drive the global exchange. Advances in communications and transportation have telescoped time and distance.

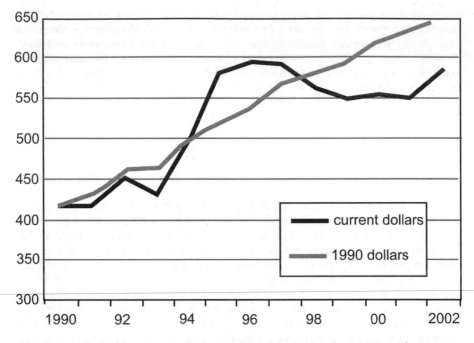

Figure 1.2   World exports of agricultural products, 1990–2002 (US$ billions)
Note: Refers to WTO, ITS definition of agricultural products.
Source: WTO, International Trade Statistics, 2003.

Innovations in packing and refrigeration have transformed even the most delicate items into portable goods. The steady flow of people across borders to visit or live has globalized palates. Affluent, health-conscious consumers have come to expect fresh fruits and vegetables year round. The value of the global fruit and vegetable market expanded from $3.4 billion in 1961 to almost $70 billion in 2001 (Huang 2004). Increasingly, concepts like in season, exotic, and local cuisine are becoming quaint notions.

This globalized food trade has spawned integrated supply chains constructed by transnational enterprises that stretch literally thousands of miles, spanning continents and oceans. Your melons at the grocer's today may have traveled from the southern cone of the Americas to reach your table. This fundamentally changes the way product safety operates. Product safety, particularly food safety and safety of biologically derived medicines, is one of the domains of public health. To pick up contamination of product, and its human consequence of disease, the public health safety net needs to stretch across thousands of miles.

Paving the way for crossborder commerce are bilateral and regional trading blocs such as the North American Free Trade Agreement (NAFTA) and the European Union, which enable exchanges with fewer hurdles. Member countries might agree, for instance, that their food safety practices are roughly equivalent and that therefore goods will not require an extra inspection at the border. Regional and bilateral agreements have flourished since the 1950s; more than 100 are currently in force. Beyond the regional agreements are the overarching agreements under the World Trade Organization (WTO), founded in 1995 to assure "free trade" as a means of improving the economic lot of the peoples of the world.

"Free" Trade

Central to the creation of the WTO was the institutionalization of a number of agreements governing the various aspects of international trade, from tariffs to safety requirements. Among them are the Sanitary and Phytosanitary Regulations (SPS), which guide negotiations between countries about the flow of a broad variety of agricultural goods of plant and animal origin. Simply put, the SPS determine how that trade takes place and defines fair and unfair practices in shipping produce, live animals, seeds, and other commodities. Countries use these guidelines in their bilateral talks about their commerce. If they fail to reach agreement, formal mechanisms are in place to alert the rest of the trading community to issues that need to be resolved between exporting and importing economies.

Policies on the importation of goods are complex, and are the product of national decision making in most economies. In addition to considering their domestic market for the potential imports, each economy regulates the quality and to some extent the quantity of goods brought in. Depending on the nature of the product, there are regulations that stipulate the production quality, the purity of ingredients, and allowable levels of contaminants and microbial content. With the international trade agreement, these standards increasingly are becoming globalized as trading economies are being urged to adopt the same or similar measures.

While the area of agricultural trade is seen as an opportunity for economic development for poor countries, these countries are often absent from WTO negotiations. The WTO recognized this during their annual meeting in 2001 in Doha, Qatar, and called for more participation, representation and consideration of the needs of poor and middle income economies. The "Doha Declaration" formalized this effort and has been a basis of subsequent discussions to attempt to even out the playing field in agriculture and other primary product trade for developing countries. Periodically, in an effort to jumpstart or redirect an economy, international aid organizations attempt to help a poor country develop crops for the export market. Unfortunately, these attempts to draw developing countries into the global marketplace can have negative health repercussions. Resources that might otherwise go toward health and social services may be redirected toward economic development and trade (McMichael 1993). Or an export market may collapse after an outbreak tied to a particular product, with devastating consequences for small farmers.

Even as developing countries are woven into the international trade network, gaping inequities remain – creating, among other problems, ripe conditions for the spread of disease. Of the world's 6.4 billion people, more than a billion lack access to clean water and nearly 2.6 billion live without adequate sanitation (UNICEF and

World Health Organization 2002). Developing countries' capacity to detect and treat disease may consist of only a nominal health officer facing countless pressing matters, or a loosely contrived reporting system, making it difficult, if not impossible, to comply with international trade safety standards.

Chapters 2 through 5 will explore the various dynamics of travel, trade, and health, from the implications of long-incubation or "stealth" diseases, such as Bovine Spongiform Encephalopathy (BSE) and new variant Creutzfeldt-Jakob disease (nvCJD), to fast-moving diseases such as avian flu, to the prospect of bioterrorism.

Trade Negotiations and Sanctions: David, meet Goliath

Many developing countries still rely heavily on agricultural exports such as cocoa, meat products and bananas as an integral part of their economies, leaving these countries particularly vulnerable to the vagaries of international markets, disease and trade agreement sanctions. Take, for instance, the emergency notifications system that allows countries to embargo goods from other countries to avoid potential contagion. While this is used primarily by nations that are heavily involved in the business of trade, the system occasionally snares those economies that are limited traders in its web of negotiations and embargoes, with disastrous results. Thus in 1998 when the European Union (EU) filed a notification it was restricting the importation of fresh fish from the four Lake Victoria African states of Uganda, Tanzania, Mozambique, and Kenya, the David and Goliath nature of trade disputes became apparent. In 1997 European Union economies became concerned about the microbial safety of fish products from Lake Victoria after a cholera outbreak had been reported in the region. A mission from the EU was dispatched to discuss the need for reinforcing sanitation around the lake with the "competent authorities," i.e., the governments of each of the four states. After a follow-up visit, it was deemed by the European Union that adequate steps had not been taken to assure safety and import restrictions were in order.

It is notable that no cases of cholera had actually occurred at this point among European consumers. In placing import restrictions on fresh fish from the region, the European Union followed the "precautionary principle" of taking protections against a potential health risk even in the absence of scientific proof that a true danger existed. The restrictions involved a five day mandatory inspection period that essentially ended the trade in fresh products. A formal notification of the restriction was filed with the WTO in 1998. At this point, the four African states sent representatives to Geneva to protest the restrictions. These are not countries that have regularly participated in the WTO working group process. Meanwhile, the World Health Organization issued an unprecedented statement that sanctions were not advised in this setting.

While the sanctions were technically lifted within six months, the economic impact on the small economies was profound. My colleagues and I have done careful analyses of the trade volumes in affected products from the four exporting African countries that flowed to the EU states. Information was only available for about half of the trading partners through the UN statistical system, which makes the numbers shown in Table 1.1 an underestimate.

Table 1.1 **Ratios of loss in trade (LIT) to total GDP or exports of four African countries to the EU**

Year	Total GDP (billion US$)	LIT/GDP	Total export*	LIT/Total export*
1997	24.7	0.26%	$2,959,996,288	2.13%
1998	25.7	0.47%	$3,056,564,000	3.47%
1999	26.8	0.72%	$2,798,671,552	6.10%
2000	27.6	0.74%	$2,628,410,784	6.97%
2001	28.9	0.87%	$1,213,393,824	18.33%
2002	30.3	0.96%	$2,769,109,024	9.02%

Note: *Export data from Mozambique is not available and the values and percentages are computed without Mozambique.
Source: Kimball, Taneda et al. 2005.

As shown, because the economies were small in scale, the impact of the restriction really hurt. The hurt continued for years after the formal sanctions were lifted. This demonstrates the risk to poor economies that have not been part of making the rules of global trade when those rules are invoked. Economics are particularly fragile if, like these four African states, they have modest trade in few commodities and rely on a single large export market. Fishermen in the Lake Victoria region reported losing up to 80 percent of their livelihood, and the ripples of these losses were felt throughout the exporting economies.

The United Nations Development Programme (UNDP) has studied the participation of African states in the negotiations of the WTO. It found that, in 2000, 15 African countries had no representative in WTO headquarters in Geneva and that "few developing country members are able to participate effectively in negotiations and decision-making" (United Nations Development Programme 2002 p. 135). The devastating impacts of the embargo enacted as a precaution due to the cholera outbreak demonstrate the risks to very poor economies of non-participation in WTO proceedings. Countries are particularly vulnerable if they produce for export "value added" products for which there is no domestic market or new customer waiting in the wings.

On the other hand, countries in Asia have consistently seen trade as central to economic development and have participated regularly in the WTO process. For these countries, the promise of economic development facilitated by global trade is coming true. Asian economies have organized themselves into two major trading blocs with many countries members of both: they are the Association of Southeast Asian Nations (ASEAN) and Asia Pacific Economic Cooperation (APEC) (see Table 1.2). APEC spans the Pacific, including members from North and South America as well as Asia. ASEAN membership is made up of countries on the Asian side of the Pacific.

Increasingly both ASEAN and APEC have included infectious diseases in their policy agendas. SARS galvanized this response in 2003 and regional trade groups

Table 1.2   APEC and ASEAN membership

APEC members	ASEAN members
Australia	Brunei Darussalam
Brunei Darussalam	Cambodia
Canada	Indonesia
Chile	Laos
People's Republic of China	Malaysia
Hong Kong, China	Myanmar
Indonesia	Philippines
Japan	Singapore
Republic of Korea	Thailand
Malaysia	Vietnam
Mexico	
New Zealand	
Papua New Guinea	
Peru	
Philippines	
Russia	
Singapore	
Chinese Taipei	
Thailand	
United States of America	
Vietnam	

have moved from reluctant partners to enthusiastic proponents of public health safety. How these trade and economic regional groups can best interact with the global and regional public health authorities to meet the common challenge is under development, with a number of hopeful initiatives underway. Our work with APEC, which has articulated emerging infections as a priority in Leaders' Declarations (declarations by heads of member states) consistently since 2000, is one such example.

International Health Regulations

In addition to the WTO agreements guiding world trade, another important body of regulations spanning trade, travel and health are the World Health Organization's recently revised International Health Regulations. These regulations, among other things, provide a framework for determining what health threats should be reported to WHO and when they should be reported. Reporting incidents to WHO helps alert the international community to potential disease outbreaks and also can warrant assistance in the forms of sophisticated diagnostic, surveillance and communications equipment and international experts. Reporting also can result in travel advisories. These advisories issued by WHO, which typically warn travelers to put off non-essential travel to affected regions, can have enormous economic repercussions both in tourism and in trade, as we saw with the SARS outbreaks. Consequently, there may be a reluctance on the part of a country to come forward with information of a potential epidemic, particularly when that country may lack the resources to address the problem. Theoretically, though, both the WTO agreements and the International Health Regulations play key roles in preventing local outbreaks from becoming international pandemics.

Disease Prevention Pyramid

In the science of prevention, there are three levels: primary, secondary and tertiary prevention (Figure 1.3). For instance, in the context of HIV/AIDS:

● Primary prevention is the prevention of HIV infection in the first place.

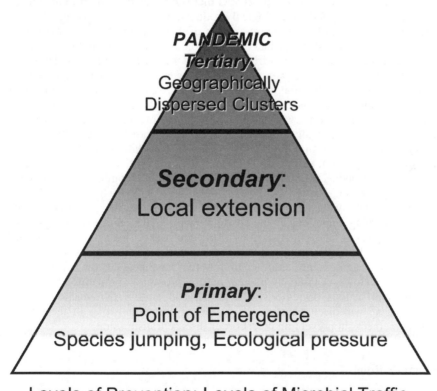

Figure 1.3 The prevention pyramid

- Secondary prevention is the prevention of clinical illness from infection or AIDS.
- Tertiary prevention is the prevention of complications from infection, such as tuberculosis, or death.

The analogy for protecting the world's peoples from new infectious diseases is imperfect. But it can provide a useful framework to begin to talk about how to go about preventing the emergence of new infections as well as their amplification and transmission on the global express of trade and travel.

As illustrated in Figure 1.3, in this model, primary prevention would entail preventing the initial emergence of new infections. We know some things about how emergence happens: the agents usually cross over from other vertebrate animals to humans; viruses, especially RNA viruses like influenza, SARS and HIV, seem to be more adept at jumping the species barrier. The exact method remains a mystery to science. And as we will see in coming chapters, some factors appear to facilitate this process: the absence of clean water and sanitation for human populations and sanitary animal husbandry, the pressure of human populations on spaces that are home to other animals, and new processes that short-cut tried and true disinfection processes for animal feeds or biological products. As we will discuss in Chapter 6, there are steps we can take to address some of these factors to limit emergence – these steps can be considered primary prevention. Secondary prevention in this case would be preventing an infection from spreading locally to cause an epidemic. Key to curbing this spread are, again, clean water and basic sanitation facilities, sufficient health and regulatory resources, and reasonably good diagnostic, surveillance and epidemiological capabilities. We will examine these elements in Chapter 7. Finally, tertiary prevention involves preventing an international pandemic, or geographically dispersed clusters of disease conveyed by trade and travel. This is where the International Health Regulations and World Trade Organization agreement guidelines come in. Here, it is critical for the international trade and health bodies to collaborate. The World Health Organization's mandate is, of course, promoting health worldwide, but until recently its International Health Regulations (IHR) were woefully out of date and consequently, not much help in curbing emerging infections. That changed with SARS, and the newly-revised Regulations, set to take effect in 2007, will continue to take on an increasingly important role. But ultimately, when it comes to trade, the regulations with the most clout are the agreements crafted under the auspices of the World Trade Organization. However trade, by its very nature, promotes competition and a focus on individual nations or regions, not global cooperation (Koivusalo 2003). In Chapter 8, we will discuss further the current and potential roles of the IHR and WTO agreements in preventing crossborder disease transmission.

Industry's Role

At this point, private industry is not pictured in the pyramid. But it should be. Private enterprise is at work in each of the examples we will review. Generally, private enterprise and transnational corporations prefer to self-regulate and eschew regulatory interference. However it is an open question whether and how the proprietary isolationism of the business world could effectively be marshaled to address what are global threats of this magnitude. This is a question which is important to consider carefully. There are industry groups that bridge corporations and corporations that cross national boundaries. Again, the fine filaments of the web of contacts between trade and public health appear to be too fragile to hold in the face of increasing pandemic pressures.

Global Problem, Global Solutions

The reality is that microbes do not recognize national and regional boundaries or preferred trading partners. Piecemeal approaches to tackling emerging infectious disease are bound to fail, particularly when some regions of the world – and participants in the global marketplace – lack the basic necessities to prevent, detect and treat disease. The following chapters will examine in greater depth the global dynamics at play in the emergence of trade and travel-related diseases in hopes of illustrating why health considerations must be a core component of trade discussions. Nature is increasingly sending us warnings in the form of outbreaks and epidemics. Examining these events provides clues and suggests strategies for prevention and control. The challenge is enormous, and time is probably short given the increasing pace of emergence in the past decade.

Study Questions

1. Define a trade-related infection.
2. Microbes have a different reproductive strategy than human beings. What is that strategy and what key advantage over human beings does it afford them in survival?
3. The "incubation period" for an infectious disease is the time from infection to the time of clinical illness in the individual. Given the speed of modern travel, what practical problem does this raise for infectious disease control in populations?

Chapter 2

Elusive Enterics

For decades, health care providers have cautioned international adventurers to steer clear of untreated water, undercooked food and fresh fish to avoid unwanted gastrointestinal souvenirs. But thanks to today's global marketplace, you can contract "travelers' diarrhea" from food products sold right down the street at your local grocer's (Osterholm 1997). As food production and distribution practices evolve both domestically and internationally to keep pace with consumer demand and international competition, new pathogens are emerging and long-known microbes are expanding their reach.

Among the culprits are bacteria such as *Salmonella*, *Escherichia coli*, *Listeria monocytogenes* and *Cyclospora cayetanensis* – resilient bugs that insinuate themselves into fruit, vegetables, poultry, beef and dairy products as they circulate around the globe (see Table 2.1). They hang on for the ride, often multiplying and spreading to humans along the way. And just as scientists begin to close in on the problematic pathways, the microbes mutate, or appear somewhere they have never been detected before. *Salmonella* makes its way from eggs to fruit to nuts. *E. coli*, originally linked to ground beef, turns up on radish sprouts.

Table 2.1   Foodborne pathogens in the US

Pathogen	Infections (Cases per 1,000,000 population[a])
Cyclospora	0.7
Vibrio	2.1
Listeria	3.4
Yersinia	4.4
E. coli 0157:H7	21
Shigella	79
Salmonella	144
Campylobacter	157
Total Pathogens	411.6

Note: [a] Incidence baesd on data from selected FoodNet sites which include CT, MN, GA, OR, and selected countries in CA, MD, NY, TN; total population 30.5 million. FoodNet is the Foodbourne Diseases Active Surveillance Network (CDC, 2000a).
Source: US FDA (2003).

While imported foods are not necessarily more likely to be contaminated, practices designed to meet the demands of global trade – to produce more goods more quickly and more cheaply – can intensify food safety problems. Antimicrobials designed to bring about bigger sides of beef prompt new drug-resistant bugs. Massive processing facilities provide prime opportunities for broad contamination. Farmers from developing countries without adequate sanitation or regulation infrastructures struggle to produce products that meet importing customers' health safety standards. Intercontinental delicacies such as soft cheese and foie gras run afoul of health authorities. In this chapter, we explore some of the key characteristics of international trade that are fueling the spread of infectious disease through food and compounding the challenge of detecting and curbing that spread. Table 2.2 provides a starting point for this exploration.

Table 2.2   The nexus of global trade and foodborne pathogens

Pathogen	Origin	Trade-related interaction
Salmonella	Described in the late 1880s in swine. Subsequently recognized in humans, poultry, cattle, rodents and exotic pets.	Use of antimicrobials in livestock in response to heightened global competition has contributed to emergence of antimicrobial-resistant strains such as *S. typhimurium* DT104 and *S. Newport*-MDR Amp C.
Escherichia coli O157:H7	Identified as a pathogenic agent in humans in 1982. Hosts include cows, deer, sheep, horses, pigs and dogs.	Intensified production and far-reaching distribution channels in the meat industry enable widespread dissemination in vehicles such as ground beef.
Cyclospora cayetanensis	First documented cases observed in humans 1978. Only known host is humans.	Hardy oocysts are transported on produce exported to geographic regions where the parasite previously had been largely unknown.
Listeria monocytogenes	Detected in 1926 in rabbits and guinea pigs, identified as a source of human infection in 1929 and perinatal contamination in 1936.	Increased popularity on the global market of raw milk cheeses and ready-to-eat products contributed to surge in listeriosis.

Mutating Microbes and Other Surprises: *Salmonella*

While *Salmonella* is among the longest-known and most common foodborne pathogens, the Salmonellosis outbreaks stemming from the growing global exchange have revealed areas in which our current knowledge is limited or outdated. *Salmonella*, traditionally linked primarily with poultry, eggs, raw meat, and dairy products, has been associated with a growing number of nuts, vegetables and fruits. Meanwhile, multi-drug-resistant strains such as *Salmonella enterica* serotype *typhimurium* DT104 have emerged, defying traditional expectations about how the bug will behave and can be subdued.

Salmonella

Salmonella was first described in the late 1880s by US Bureau of Agriculture director Dr Daniel E. Salmon and fellow researcher Theobald Smith. The bacterium, part of the Enterobacteriacae family, initially was isolated as a veterinary pathogen affecting swine. It has since been recognized in humans, along with a variety of domestic and wild animals (including poultry, cattle, rodents) and exotic pets, such as iguanas and turtles. The bug lives in the intestinal tracts of these birds, reptiles and animals and is transmitted to humans through contaminated foods.

Historically, *Salmonella* was widely diagnosed in part because it was easy to identify with early technology. The bacterium, which prefers environments of low oxygen, is relatively simple to grow in the laboratory using blood agar and warm temperatures. But even with current, more sensitive, surveillance and detection techniques, *Salmonella* remains one of the most commonly identified sources of foodborne illness, accounting for some 1.4 million cases worldwide every year. More than 2,000 strains of *Salmonella* have been classified based on their serotypes (particular combinations of antigens).

Salmonella has a short incubation period, from six to 72 hours; the illness typically surfaces an average of 12 to 36 hours after exposure. The infection can be communicable for days, weeks, and in rare cases, months. The bacteria penetrate cells in the intestine, multiply and spread. Common symptoms of Salmonellosis include diarrhea, fever, nausea and sometimes vomiting. The disease is rarely fatal; the most vulnerable individuals are infants, elderly people and those with compromised immune systems. While most *Salmonella* cases resolve without treatment, severe cases customarily have been treated with antimicrobial drugs such as fluoroquinolones.

The microbe is found worldwide, with different serotypes prevalent in different regions – making it possible to track the incursion of new strains that may be linked to international commerce. *Salmonella* reproduces quite nicely in a variety of foods, especially milk, quickly reaching a high infectious dose if the food is not refrigerated. In the right conditions, the bug can persist in the environment for weeks, even months. Infection commonly results from inadequately processed or undercooked eggs, poultry, dairy or meat. But humans also can transmit the bacterium through fecal-oral contact, and fruits and vegetables can be infected by contaminated water, work surfaces and utensils.

The bug has caused massive outbreaks of illness. In 1994, an estimated 224,000 people across the US developed *Salmonella enteritidis* infections from ice cream produced by The Schwan Food Company, a frozen food distributor based in Minnesota. The outbreak was detected after health officials in Minnesota noted an increase in reports of *S. enteritidis* infections in September 1994 and, upon further inquiry, learned that a disproportionate amount of infected people had consumed Schwan's ice cream. Shortly thereafter, the manufacturer recalled all of the ice cream that had been produced at its plant in Marshall, Minnesota, and temporarily halted production. Investigators estimated the scope of the infections based on the number of affected consumers in Minnesota and the product's distribution nationally (Hennessy, Hedberg et al. 1996). After inspecting the ice cream plant, the facilities that produced premix for the ice cream and the tankers that transported the mix, investigators concluded that several batches of mix probably were contaminated when they were transported in tankers that previously had carried nonpasteurized eggs (Hennessy, Hedberg et al. 1996). The food company took a series of corrective measures, including establishing containers dedicated exclusively to products that would not be repasteurized after transport, such as ice cream, and resumed operations. The cross contamination from the tankers, some of which may even have been washed between runs, highlights the tenacity of *Salmonella* and the low doses required for infection.

New Pathways

Salmonella-related outbreaks increasingly are associated with a diverse range of sources, including internationally traded food products, from parsley to coconut milk (Jones and Schaffner 2003). The mechanisms of contamination of these newly identified sources of infection are in some cases surprising and, in others, poorly understood. For instance, while raw almonds grown in California have been the suspected source of *Salmonella* outbreaks in the US and Canada on at least two occasions, in each instance investigators were not able to determine how the nuts were contaminated (Centers for Disease Control and Prevention 2004). The harvesting, drying and shelling processes are all possibilities. The bacteria could be transmitted through fecal-oral contact via infected workers who handle the almonds when they are harvested, processed or packaged. Alternatively, the source of contamination could be work surfaces or equipment harboring the bug. Even when equipment is washed, bacteria can survive in inaccessible crevices, where they can multiply and ultimately cause additional contamination.

Similarly, sprouts are a relatively recent and especially problematic player in pathogenic circles (Taormina, Beuchat et al. 1999). Sprouts, which began appearing in sandwiches and salads in the US during the 1970s emergence of so-called health foods, are part of the burgeoning world seed trade. International seed exchanges have more than tripled over the last three decades, shooting from nearly $1 billion in the 1970s to more than $4 billion in 2004 (Figure 2.1). Along with potato, beet,

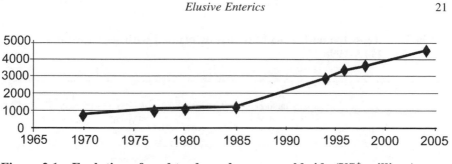

Figure 2.1 Evolution of seed trade exchanges worldwide (US$ millions) 1970–2004

Source: International Seed Federation, http://www.worldseed.org/statistics.htm.

radish, and wheat seeds, the global exchange includes alfalfa and mung bean seeds destined to become sprouts. Once the well-traveled seeds reach their destination, they are hydroponically nurtured into sprouts. During one of the many steps in their production, from growth to harvest to shipment, the seeds can be contaminated, primarily by contact with animal feces. Sometimes the sprouts are fertilized with soil containing feces harboring *Salmonella*; in other cases, they are grown near pastures with feces that spread to the seed-growing area in run-off. During harvest and shipment, the seeds can be exposed to infected workers and equipment or storage vessels containing the bug. The dry conditions under which the seeds are stored enable *Salmonella* and other pathogens to survive for months. All the while, the seeds sheltering the bacteria appear unharmed. During sprouts' warm, moist germination process, the microbes thrive. Sprouts have been linked to a series of outbreaks across North America, Western Europe and Japan (Taormina, Beuchat et al. 1999). These are summarized in Table 2.3. In 1999 and again in 2002, after spates of *Salmonella* and *E. coli* infections, the US Food and Drug Administration issued warnings to consumers about the health risks of eating raw and lightly cooked sprouts.

One of the first outbreaks linked with sprouts involved seeds produced in a home sprouting kit in the US in 1973. Since then, many larger outbreaks have involved imported seeds. A 1995 outbreak of *Salmonella Stanley*, for instance, spanned 17 US states and Finland. The infection ultimately was traced to a distributor in the Netherlands who had obtained seeds from Italy, Hungary and Pakistan; investigators were never able to determine which source was implicated in these outbreaks (for details on the international investigation, see Chapter 7).

The contamination pathway in the first known case of an outbreak associated with imported mangoes is particularly paradoxical. In 1999, 78 people in 13 US states became ill from a common strain of *Salmonella enterica*; 15 patients were hospitalized and two died (Sivapalasingam, Barrett et al. 2003). Investigators traced the mangoes back to a farm in Brazil. They discovered that, surprisingly, no Europeans who had consumed mangoes from the same farm were affected. Investigators deduced that the mangoes destined for the US had probably absorbed the microbe as a result of a hot water treatment used to fend off fruit flies. The treatment was required to meet US standards barring produce carrying the

Table 2.3   Reported outbreaks of illness associated with seed sprouts, 1973–1998

Year	Pathogen	No. of culture-confirmed cases[a]	Location	Type of sprout	Likely source of contami-nation	Ref.
1973	*Bacillus cereus*	4	1 US state	Soy, cress, mustard	Seed	3
1988	*Salmonella* Saint-Paul	143	UK	Mung	Seed	5
1989	*S.* Gold-Coast	31	UK	Cress	Seed and/or sprouter	7
1994	*S.* Bovismorbificans	595	Sweden, Finland	Alfalfa	Seed	8,9
1995	*S.* Stanley	242	17 US states, Finland	Alfalfa	Seed	10
1995-96	*S.* Newport	133[b]	>7 US states, Canada, Denmark	Alfalfa	Seed	11
1996	*S.* Montevideo and *S.* Meleagridis	~500	2 US states	Alfalfa	Seed and/or sprouter	13
1996	*Escherichia coli* O157:H7	~6,000	Japan	Radish	Seed	16
1997	*E. coli* O157:H7	126	Japan	Radish	Seed	17
1997	*S.* Meleagridis	78	Canada	Alfalfa	Seed	15
1997	*S.* Infantis and *S.* Anatum	109	2 US states	Alfalfa, mung, other	Seed	14
1997	*E. coli* O157:H7	85	4 US states	Alfalfa	Seed	18
1997-98	*S.* Senftenberg	52	2 US states	Clover, alfalfa	Seed and/or sprouter	*
1998	*E. coli* O157:NM	8	2 US states	Clover, alfalfa	Seed and/or sprouter	*
1998	*S.* Havana, *S.* Cubana, and *S.* Tennessee	34	5 US states	Alfalfa	Seed and/or sprouter	*

Notes: [a]The number of culture-confirmed cases represents only a small proportion of the total illness in these outbreaks, as many ill persons either do not seek care or do not have a stool culture performed if they do seek care.
[b]Includes only culture confirmed cases in Oregon and British Columbia
*Mohle-Boetani J., pers. comm.
Source: Taormina, Beuchat et al. 1999.

Mediterranean fruit fly – standards the Europeans did not impose. The farmer had adopted the hot water treatment to avoid employing cancer-causing pesticides to repel the fruit flies. But investigators discovered that dipping the mangoes in hot water, then submerging them in cool water before packing initiated a process in which gases inside the fruit contracted, drawing in contaminated water. So steps that the farmer had taken to clear the mangoes of insects without using carcinogens had ultimately provided an entree for the pathogen.

Antimicrobial Resistance

Even as scientists track the expanding web of *Salmonella* transmission pathways, the bug mutates and takes a new tack. While overall rates of *Salmonella* have been dropping in the US since 1996, the rates of drug-resistant strains have been on the rise. More than a quarter of *Salmonella* isolates are resistant to at least one antimicrobial; a significant portion has multiple resistances (Smolinski, Hamburg et al. 2003). Infections resulting from these strains are not only difficult to treat because of their resistance to drugs, they also can cause more serious illnesses and hospitalizations (Martin, Fyfe et al. 2004). The Institute of Medicine estimates that the national tab for treating antibiotic resistant illnesses approaches $3 billion annually.

Among the most prominent drug-resistant strains is *Salmonella typhimurium* definitive phage type 104 (*S. typhimurium* DT104), which began appearing with increasing frequency in the 1990s after fluoroquinolones were approved for use in food-producing animals. The bug is unresponsive to a handful of common antimicrobials, including ampicillin, chloramphenicol, streptomycin, sulfonamides and tetracyclines (Centers for Disease Control and Prevention 1997; Threlfall 2002). *S. typhimurium* DT104 was first detected in the UK in 1984 and quickly became one of the most commonly reported strains of *Salmonella* in England and Wales, linked with consumption of chicken, pork sausage, meat cakes, and eventually, beef (Centers for Disease Control and Prevention 1997). In 2000, a DT104 outbreak affecting 361 people in England and Wales was associated with lettuce served at several take-out food establishments; the source of the lettuce and of the contamination never were definitively identified (Horby, O'Brien et al. 2003). While isolated cases of DT104 appeared in the US in the early 1980s, by the mid-1990s, the pathogen had become widespread (Glynn, Bopp et al. 1998). The first reported outbreak in the US affected 18 school children in Nebraska in October 1996. Investigators identified as potential sources consumption of outdated milk or contact with a potentially infected turtle or kitten (Centers for Disease Control and Prevention 1997). In 1997, three outbreaks of the resistant strain in Washington State, California, and Vermont were linked to consumption of raw milk (Villar, Macek et al. 1999).

More recently, a drug-resistant strain of *Salmonella Newport*, *Newport*-MDR Amp C, has emerged in the US. *Newport*-MDR Amp C is resistant or less susceptible to at least nine antimicrobials, including those on DT104's list, and to cephalosporins, which often are used to treat children with serious cases of salmonellosis (Gupta, Fontana et al. 2003). The proportion of resistant *S. Newport* isolates identified by the National Antimicrobial Resistance Monitoring System (NARMS) rose from 1 percent in 1998 to 26 percent (33 of 128 isolates) in 2001 (Centers for Disease Control and Prevention 2002). At the same time, the incidence of *Newport*-MDR Amp C has increased among cattle. Infections in humans have been associated with handling of cattle or consumption of related meat. Investigators linked a 2002 outbreak affecting 47 people in five states to exposure to raw or undercooked ground beef (Centers for Disease Control and Prevention 2002).

One of the factors in the emergence of these resistant strains is the controversial use of antimicrobials in animals. Although most drug-resistant infections in people have resulted from the use of antibiotics in human medicine, another contributing factor is antimicrobial applications in food-producing animals. Of all the antimicrobials used in the US each year, the proportion administered to food animals is estimated to be anywhere between 40 percent and 80 percent (Shea 2004). Since the 1950s, farmers have employed antimicrobials to fight disease and promote growth in their poultry, swine and cattle. Concerns over disease transmission have heightened as more livestock are confined in closer quarters. The drugs are thought to promote growth by fending off small infections, enabling animals to process feed more efficiently – one strategy for getting an edge in the face of heightened global competition. The use of antibiotics as growth enhancers is particularly problematic because it entails applying low doses over long periods to large numbers of animals, potentially transforming the livestock into reservoirs for antibiotic resistant bugs (US General Accounting Office 2004). Once the bacteria in the animals develop resistance to the drugs, those new strains of resistant bacteria can in turn be transmitted to humans through contaminated meat, soil, and water. (See Chapter 6 for further discussion of resistance.) While few dispute the importance of antimicrobials in fighting disease in food-producing animals, the line between therapeutic and nontherapeutic uses remains ill-defined. At the same time, global competitive pressures continue to grow, prompting producers to consider all means available to develop plumper chickens and cheaper cheese.

Mass Production and Transnational Corporations: *E. coli* O157:H7

In addition to spurring the use of antimicrobials in food producing animals, competitive pressures of the global market also have incited the consolidation of food production. Increasingly, mammoth transnational corporations, leveraging economies of scale, are elbowing smaller farms out of the market (Lang 1999). The number of farms in the US shrank from 6.3 million in 1929 to 2.2 million in 1998 (Chalk 2004). Cattle cohabit in feedlots that hold more than 30,000 head. Along with the efficiencies of intensified production come increased opportunities for cross contamination – and significant challenges in tracing the original source of infections. Ground beef from a single cow may be mixed with that of thousands of other cows at several different stops along the production process, from slaughter to processing to retail packaging. The emergence and spread of *Escherichia coli* O157:H7 illustrates the headaches that can accompany mass production.

In the winter of 1982, health officials in Oregon noticed a spate of illnesses with uncommon symptoms. Patients complained of severe abdominal pains, bloody diarrhea and, distinctively, little or no fever (Riley, Remis et al. 1983; Wells, Davis et al. 1983). A similar outbreak in Michigan followed a few months later. All told, at least four dozen developed the mysterious infection. Tests at local hospital labs for the usual suspects (*Salmonella*, *Shigella*, *Camploybacter*) came up negative. Eventually tests revealed the presence of *Escherichia coli* O157:H7, a serotype discovered in 1975 that had been identified in a human only once before. Through interviews with patients, epidemiologists tracked the source of the infection to undercooked beef patties served at local McDonald's outlets and, ultimately, a lot in Michigan that had supplied the outlets with ground beef.

Escherichia coli O157:H7

While *E. coli* is a regular resident in human intestines, where it fights bad bacteria, several pathogenic strains have developed, including the particularly toxic *E. coli* O157:H7, which was first identified as a pathogenic agent in humans in 1982. It is named for its components: the 157th somatic (O) and 7th flagellar (H) antigens. The pathogen, which has been reported in at least 30 countries since its discovery, is linked to an estimated 73,000 cases and 60 deaths annually in the US alone, mostly in the northern and western states. Outbreaks tend to occur in warmer, summer months.

For a minority of people, infection does not result in any symptoms; an estimated 70 to 90 percent of patients experience painful abdominal cramps and bloody diarrhea (hemorrhagic colitis). In about 5 percent of those cases, the infection develops into hemolytic uremic syndrome (HUS), a serious condition that leads to kidney failure. Much of the damage results from Shiga toxins produced by *E. coli* O157:H7 that cause fluid accumulation and histological damage. At greatest risk are the elderly and children under five; HUS is most common cause of renal failure in children. The incubation period for *E. coli* O157:H7 is two to 10 days. It is infectious one week in adults and three weeks in children. In most cases, treatment entails avoiding dehydration and letting the illness resolve, which usually happens in five to 10 days. But serious cases of HUS can require a kidney transplant. The use of antimicrobials in more severe cases is a subject of debate; while some studies indicate they can be protective, others have found they exacerbate the illness. There is no vaccine.

Most infections result from eating bovine products, especially ground beef or raw milk. Beef was associated with nearly half of the foodborne outbreaks in the US between 1993–99 in which the source was identified (Codex Alimentarius Commission 2002). The bacterium, which lives in cows' intestines, typically is introduced into the meat during the grinding process. Pathogens present on cows' udders can be transmitted directly or via contaminated equipment when cows are milked. More recently, O157:H7 also has been linked to produce. And in 2003, investigators traced an outbreak in Ohio to inhalation of manure-contaminated sawdust (Varma, Greene et al. 2003). Along with cows, the virus has been identified in other domestic and wild animals, among them deer, sheep, horses, pigs and dogs. Infected humans spread the virus as well through various avenues, from food preparation to crowded swimming areas, day care centers and nursing homes. The bug also has stowed away on more than a few cruise ships. *E. coli* O157:H7 can survive moderate heat and freezing, and exposure to as little as 50 to 200 organisms can cause infection in humans.

Over the next decade, a handful of *E. coli* 0157:H7 outbreaks, mostly tied to ground beef, cropped up across the western and midwestern US. But it was not until the infamous Jack In the Box outbreak that the microbe registered on the general public's radar. In December 1992, more than 500 people in Washington, Idaho, California and Nevada developed the trademark symptoms, and four people died. The *E. coli* 0157:H7 outbreak was associated once again with undercooked, contaminated beef patties served at a fast food restaurant.

The outbreak was first detected in January 1993 when a pediatric gastroenterologist in Washington state noted a surge in HUS cases and emergency room visits for bloody diarrhea (Bell, Goldoft et al. 1994). Subsequent contacts with hospitals, laboratories, and physicians, along with public announcements, ultimately revealed hundreds more cases. Interviews with patients led investigators to conclude that the outbreak might be linked to hamburgers served at Jack in the Box restaurants. Health officials tested lots of meat patties produced at the time of the infections and found several of the lots contained the bacteria. As a result, Jack in the Box recalled more than a million patties. About 20 percent of those patties ultimately were recovered, preventing an estimated 800 additional cases (Bell, Goldoft et al. 1994). Upon inspection of the restaurant's food preparation practices, investigators found that most of the regular hamburger patties tested had not been cooked sufficiently to reach the internal temperature of 68.3°C required by state health laws. A team from the Centers for Disease Control identified one Canadian and five US slaughter plants as potential sources of the contaminated lots, but they were not able to definitively pinpoint a single source.

Today *E. coli* 0157:H7 is a significant health concern in a growing number of regions around the world, particularly areas of Europe and North and South America; and South Africa and Japan (see Figure 2.2). *E-coli* O157:H7 infections are linked with a range of meat and produce products, from salami to melons to lettuce. In most cases, produce is contaminated by water or soil containing feces, commonly from agricultural run-off. The bacteria can survive several months in standing water or frozen products. In February 2004, three cases of *E. coli* 0157:H7 infection in Okinawa, Japan, were linked to hamburgers made from frozen ground beef purchased at a local US military base. A subsequent investigation revealed the meat had been produced some six months earlier in the US and also might have been responsible for several cases of infection that had been reported in Orange County, California, the previous August and September (Centers for Disease Control and Prevention 2005). A 1991 outbreak in Massachusetts traced to apple cider highlighted the microbe's ability to endure acidic conditions. Unwashed apples had been pressed in a mill, which then passed on the infection to subsequent batches. Investigators discovered the *E-coli* O157:H7 survived nearly three weeks in refrigerated, unpasteurized cider (Besser, Griffin et al. 1999). Similarly, the microbe has survived in mayonnaise and other fruit juices with relatively high acid levels.

Conspiring to make *E. coli* O157:H7 an emerging threat in the international marketplace are the bug's virulence and resilience, along with the relatively low doses required for infection, enabling ready transmission and enhancing opportunities for large outbreaks. With the intensified meat production processes designed to meet global demand and competition, the scope of potential

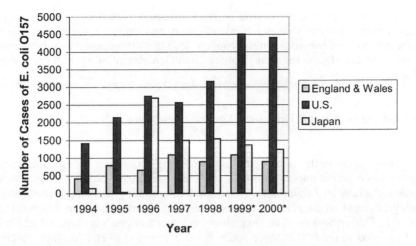

Figure 2.2   Comparison of reported cases of *E. coli* O157:H7 infection in three countries

Notes:
1. US figures are for 1994–2000; England and Wales for 1994–2000; Japan for 1996–2000. *Provisional figures for the US for 1999 and 2000.
2. CDC, NNDSS; Cases include suspect and confirmed human isolations.
3. PHLS Laboratory of Enteric Pathogens; Cases include only isolates (obtained from stool samples) that are submitted to PHLS from laboratories in England and Wales. They are confirmed, serotyped, phage typed and VT typed at PHLS.
4. Ministry of Health and Welfare, National Epidemiological Surveillance of Infectious Diseases; Cases are restricted to those with stool samples that have been culture confirmed and include all O157 serotypes.

Source: Risk Profile for Enterohaemorrhagic *E. coli* including the Identification of the Commodities of Concern, including Sprouts, Ground Beef and Pork. Codex Committee on Food Hygiene, 35th Session, Orlando, USA, 27 Jan–1 Feb 2003.

contamination is vast. Colorado-based ConAgra Beef Company, for instance, recalled nearly 19 million pounds of suspect beef trim and ground beef in 2002 after an outbreak was linked to their meat.

Further contributing to the risk of spread is the growing list of contaminated produce. US-grown radish sprout seeds, for example, were implicated in a massive outbreak in Japan. In the spring and summer of 1996, more than a dozen clusters of *E. coli* 0157:H7 infection swept through central Japan, resulting in 10,000 cases – 6,000 among school children and the rest among factory workers. Laboratory tests revealed that the isolates from the various clusters had identical patterns, suggesting the outbreaks were connected. Investigators then determined that white radish sprouts were the only common uncooked ingredient served at both the school and factory cafeterias on the days leading up to the outbreaks. The radish sprouts were traced to a particular farm in Japan that had supplied both cafeterias. That farm had purchased its seed from a grower in the US. Interestingly, the US beef trade also took a hit as a result of the outbreak. Beef imported from the US was among the suspect ingredients early on in the investigation, and although it was later ruled out as the cause of the outbreak, public concern lead to a 40 percent dip in beef imports to Japan over the following year (State of Utah Department of Agriculture and Food 1998).

Uneven Resources and Unknown Agents: *Cyclospora*

One of the appeals of global commerce is the prospect of bringing formerly excluded players to the table – stoking struggling economies by enabling them to supply more prosperous markets. In an ideal world, developing countries with tropical climates and abundant acreage stock their trading partners' grocery shelves with year-round produce, and everybody benefits. Of course, it is more complicated than that. One critical issue is determining whether a nation's resources and land are best invested in crops that serve and rely on external markets. Another concern is whether small growers in developing countries have the basic infrastructure necessary to develop products that can compete internationally. While farmers in many developed countries have enjoyed decades of government subsidies and publicly constructed water and sewage systems, their counterparts in developing countries historically have had fewer similar benefits. As a result, growers in poor countries are at once more prone to and more vulnerable to the consequences of foodborne pathogens. The situation becomes even more complex when it involves little-known, and consequently unpredictable, microbes such as *Cyclospora cayetanensis*.

When *C. cayetanensis* was first detected in humans in the late 1970s, it appeared to be confined mostly to tropical and subtropical areas of the developing world, affecting primarily children and people with compromised immune systems. On the occasions that cases of cyclosporiasis appeared in developed countries, it struck travelers who had visited areas where the disease was known to exist – and who presumably had been exposed to contaminated water. For two decades, the microbe remained relatively obscure and vaguely understood. In the 1990s, a series of outbreaks reported in North America prompted new discoveries about the disease and its transmission. Almost all of the outbreaks had potential links to imported food; several of the largest implicated berries from Guatemala (see Table 2.4).

The first reported US outbreak, in 1990, spread through a dormitory at a teaching hospital in Chicago, Illinois, where at least 21 participants in a training program developed the gastrointestinal symptoms. An investigation revealed a strong association with drinking dormitory tap water (Huang, Weber et al. 1995). A number of infected people also had attended a party in the dormitory at which food was served. However, the dorm had a broken water pump and food had not yet been confirmed as a vehicle for transmitting *C. cayetanensis*, leading investigators to conclude that a tainted water supply was the likely source of the outbreak. More recent discoveries about the nature of *C. cayetanensis* suggest that, alternatively, contaminated food from the party possibly could have been the culprit (Herwaldt 2000).

Cyclospora cayetanensis

The first documented cases of infection of the protozoan parasite *Cyclospora* in humans were observed by British parasitologist R. W. Ashford in Papua New Guinea in 1977–78. He determined that the oocysts excreted in feces of the infected humans did not sporulate for several days – suggesting that the pathogen not only endures, but requires, time outside the host to become infective, typically several days or weeks. It would become evident two decades later that this feature enables *Cyclospora* to survive on produce and, in the process, mature into an infectious agent.

In 1993, scientists in Peru classified the coccidian parasite as a member of the *Cyclospora* genus, with two sporocysts, each containing two sporozoites (Ortega, Sterling et al. 1993). The following year they dubbed it *Cyclospora cayetanensis*, named for the primary site of their research, Universidad Peruana Cayetano Heredia.

The resulting disease, cyclosproriasis, is characterized by bouts of watery diarrhea, fatigue and weight loss that may last up to several weeks. While the disease generally is not serious, the symptoms will reoccur if it is not treated (typically with trimethoprim-sulfemethoxazole). Cyclosporiasis also has been associated with complications including Guillain-Barré and reactive arthritis syndromes (Shields and Olson 2003). The infection also can be asymptomatic. People with no previous exposures and young children appear more susceptible to symptomatic infection. The incubation period is about one week.

Much remains unknown about *C. cayetanensis*. The only known host for the parasite is humans; to date, it has not been detected in animals. Humans contract the infection by ingesting sporulated oocysts. The time required after excretion before infective spores are produced suggests that human-to-human transmission is unlikely (Herwaldt 2000). The only established means of transmission are through contaminated water or produce, including berries, lettuce and basil.

C. cayetanensis appears to be more prevalent in tropical and subtropical regions, such as Guatemala, Nepal, Peru and Haiti. But it also has been documented in North America and Eastern Europe. It appears to be seasonal, emerging in during wet or warm months. It has not been determined whether the pathogen can survive high heat or refrigeration.

In May of 1996, health departments in New York, Florida, Texas and Canada reported clusters of cyclosporiasis to the US Centers for Disease Control. By the end of the following month, the CDC had received reports of some 55 clusters encompassing 725 cases from 14 states, the District of Columbia and two Canadian provinces (Ostroff 1998; Herwaldt 2000). Eventually nearly 1,500 cases spanning 20 states, Canada and DC were reported to the CDC. Because *C. cayetanensis* is relatively recently identified and therefore under-recognized, health officials estimate the scope of the outbreaks likely was even larger than the numbers suggest (Ostroff 1998). Investigators examined patterns among the outbreaks and

Table 2.4 Documented outbreaks of cyclosporiasis in the US and Canada in the 1990s[a]

Month and year of outbreak[b]	Location	No. of clusters[c]	No. of cases[d]	Vehicle[e]	Source of vehicle	Comment
June or July 1990	Illinois	1	21	Water or food (if food, unidentified vehicle)		If waterborne, related to repair of water pump on 5 July; if foodborne, related to party on 29 June
May–June 1995	New York	1[f]	32	Possibly food		Fresh raspberries of unknown source were among the fruits served
May 1995	Florida	2	38	Raspberries?	See comment	Guatemala was a possible source
May–June 1996	US, Canada	55	1465	Raspberries[g,h]	Guatemala	
March–April 1997	Florida	—[i]	—[i]	Mesclun	Peru (or US)	If evidence from December 1997 outbreak also is considered, most likely source of mesclun was Peru
April–May 1997	US, Canada	41	1012	Raspberries[h]	Guatemala	
June–July 1997	Washington, D.C. area[j]	57	341	Basil	Multiple possible sources	See text about possibility that basil was contaminated locally
Sept 1997	Virginia	1	21	Fruit plate	See comment	Fruit plate might have included raspberries (non-Guatemalan) but not blackberries
Dec 1997	Florida	1	12	Salad (mesclun)	Peru (mesclun)	If evidence from March 1997 outbreak also is considered, most likely vehicle was mesclun
May 1998	Ontario	13	315	Raspberries[h]	Guatemala	
May 1998	Georgia	1	17	Fruit salad?	Undetermined	Multiple combinations of many fruits were served
May 1999	Ontario	1	104	Dessert (berry)[h]	See comment	Implicated dessert included fresh Guatemalan blackberries, frozen Chilean raspberries, and fresh US strawberries
May 1999	Florida	1	94	Probably fruit, most likely a berry[h]	See text	Multiple combinations of many fruits were served
July 1999	Missouri	At least 2	64	Basil	Mexico or US	

Notes:

[a] See text for further description of the outbreaks. Some of the outbreaks that are listed separately might have been related (that is, the outbreaks in New York and Florida in 1995 and those in Florida and Ontario in 1999). Some potential outbreaks were not included in the list.

[b] If the outbreak included both cluster-related and sporadic cases, the months listed are those in which the events (for example, parties) associated with the clusters of cases occurred. Implicated produce might have been harvested in the previous month.

[c] A cluster of cases of cyclosporiasis was defined as ≥ 2 cases among persons with similar exposures (for example, attended same party). At least 1 case per cluster had to be laboratory confirmed.

[d] The case counts are inexact because of under recognition and underreporting of cases and partial investigations of some outbreaks (for example, not all event attendees were interviewed). Both laboratory-confirmed and clinically defined cases are included. If the outbreak included sporadic cases that were not related to events, those are included in the case counts.

[e] The produce was served fresh

[f] The cases were related to exposures, on various days, at a country club.

[g] Raspberries were not served at one event at which blackberries that reportedly were from Guatemala were served (whether the blackberries were fresh is unknown) [22].

[h] See text for discussion of the possible role of blackberries.

[i] The investigation that implicated mesclun focused on persons who ate at a restaurant in Tallahassee in mid-March (case count, 29; 14 other cases, including two cases involving persons who had eaten salads containing mesclun at another local restaurant, were not included in the main investigation). Other identified cases that might have been linked to mesclun and might have been related to this initial cluster of cases were associated with eating at a restaurant elsewhere in Florida in early April (case count five) and with being on a cruise ship that departed from Florida on 29 March (257 of 783 persons who completed a questionnaire had been "ill", 77 of 249 respondents in a case-control study had had diarrhea, and 45 of the 77 met the case definition).

[j] The outbreak occurred in the Northern Virginia–Washington, D.C.–Baltimore metropolitan area [24, 25].

Source: Herwaldt 2000.

determined that virtually all were linked to events at which fresh raspberries had been served. (Earlier outbreaks involving fruit had been reported the previous year, but they were small and the investigations were inconclusive.) The raspberries, in turn, were traced to Guatemala.

In the 1980s, in an effort to jumpstart its battered economy, Guatemala cultivated a handful of crops for export, among them berries destined for markets in North America. At its peak in the mid-1990s, the $5 million-a-year industry, in which berries were harvested by hand from October to May, employed as many as 30,000 workers (Hart and Sutton 1997). But a series of outbreaks in North America linked to Guatemalan raspberries would ultimately take a serious toll.

By the time the initial outbreaks had been recognized, it was too late to establish the precise source of the contaminated berries. Generally, the symptoms of cyclosporiasis do not surface for at least a week. After the berries had been imported and consumed and the infections had become evident, the berry season was over. Consequently, it was impossible to inspect the growing, harvesting, packing and transport procedures, or to conduct tests along the way. Moreover, any raspberries from the contaminated batches had long ago been consumed or disposed of. Further complicating the investigation was the limited knowledge about *C. cayetanensis*, particularly in relation to foodborne transmission. The far-reaching nature of the outbreak suggested that a common practice among several suppliers, rather than a single farm, was responsible for the contamination (Herwaldt 2000). Investigators concluded the most likely source of the infection was contaminated water used in some step of the berry-growing process.

In response to the findings, the Guatemalan Berry Commission implemented precautionary measures targeting water and sanitation practices on the farms, and classified individual growers according to risk. But the efforts failed; the berry season in 1997 was a repeat of the year before – the CDC received reports of 41 clusters involving a total of 762 cases from 13 states, the District of Columbia and one Canadian province. The investigation once again led to Guatemala, which then suspended raspberry exports, incurring millions in lost income (Powell 2000). For the 1998 spring season, based on the previous outbreaks and its knowledge of current farming practices, the US FDA banned imports of fresh raspberries from Guatemala. At the time, barring imports without lack of physical evidence of contamination was highly unusual, although the practice is more common today (Calvin 2003). That year, Canada once again experienced a series of outbreaks that affected more than 300 people in Ontario, but the US did not, eliminating any lingering doubts about the source of the infections.

Berry growers managed to restore access to US markets the following year by taking corrective measures, establishing the so-called Model Plan of Excellence, which included implementing food safety practices with which exporting farmers were required to comply and applying codes linking berries with the farms where they were grown (Calvin 2003). The FDA again halted exports in 2001. By 2002, only three farms were approved to export raspberries to the US (Ho, Lopez et al. 2002). Subsequent outbreaks have been far smaller than those in 1996–98, and investigations have been more successful at linking those outbreaks to particular farms. But the export market also has diminished considerably. The smaller farms had largely been eliminated from the export market. At the height of the exchange in 1996, the US imported more than 300 metric tons of raspberries from Guatemala. Even after a modest recovery, in 2001 the number of exports was 16 percent less than it had been at the peak levels five years earlier (see Figure 2.3). In some respects, the costs of implementing the safety measures required to continue exports exceeded the benefits (Calvin 2003).

Along with raspberries, *C. cayetanensis* infections have been associated with other produce, including basil, mesclun lettuce and snow peas. In only a couple of cases – one involving basil, the other frozen raspberries – has the microbe been identified on the produce suspected of causing the outbreak. Similarly, the modes of contamination have been even more elusive. Cyclosporiasis' week-long incubation period, coupled with the fact that *C. cayetanensis* often travels on fresh produce that is long gone by the time the infection is discovered, can make it difficult to identify the source of the infections. Adding to the challenge is the fact that very low doses of exposure apparently are required for infection – consumption of a single, unmemorable raspberry can be sufficient (Herwaldt 2000). These propensities, along with *C. cayetanensis'* apparently hardy constitution and mysterious nature due to its recent discovery, make this bug a significant obstacle to growers in countries without reliable access to clean water and sanitary facilities, not to mention extensive networks of surveillance and laboratories.

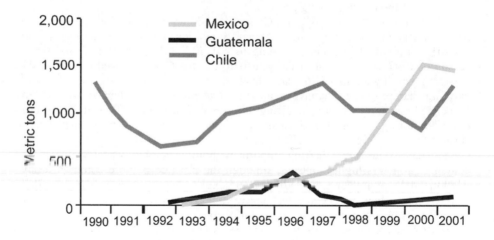

Figure 2.3   US fresh raspberry imports, 1990–2001
Source: US Department of Commerce (from Calvin, L. Food Safety in Food Security and Food Trade, Case Study: Guatemalan Raspberries and Cyclospora. International Food Policy Research Institute, FOCUS 10 • Brief 7 of 17, September 2003).

Listeria monocytogenes

L. monocytogenes, one of six species of *Listeria*, a gram positive, rod-shaped nonspore-forming bacterium, is the primary cause of listeriosis in animals and humans. First detected in 1926 in rabbits and guinea pigs, it was identified as a source of human infection in 1929 and as a source of perinatal contamination in 1936.

The microbe lives chiefly in soil, water, mud and animal feed, but wild and domestic mammals, fowl and people also serve as hosts. It can be transmitted directly from animals to humans as well as among humans, but most cases are foodborne.

L. monocytogenes is associated with two conditions – listerial gastroenteritis, which generally occurs in healthy adults and involves mild flu-like symptoms; and the more severe and invasive listeriosis, which can cause sepsis, meningitis and, in roughly a quarter of cases, death. About a third of listeriosis cases occur in pregnant women; while some women experience fever and abortion (approximately 25 percent), others have few symptoms and unsuspectingly pass the bug on to the fetus, which can be born with septicemia or appear healthy but then quickly develop meningitis. Infections are fatal for up to 30 percent of infants; the rate is even higher (about 50 percent) for babies who become ill in the days after birth.

The incubation period for *L. monocytogenes* ranges from days (three) to months (two plus), but signs of infection generally surface about three weeks after exposure. It can be treated by penicillin or ampicillin but has some resistance to tetracycline. The threat of listeriosis is greatest for fetuses, newborns, people over 60, and adults with other illnesses such as diabetes or cirrhosis.

Because symptoms are often severe enough to require medical attention, *Listeria* infections are reported more frequently than those by less potent pathogens, such as *Salmonella*. The majority of reported cases have been in industrialized nations in North America, Europe and Oceania. The Centers for Disease control estimates about 2,500 cases and 500 related deaths occur in the US annually. Most cases occur sporadically, rather than as parts of clusters or outbreaks.

The bacteria can survive in a variety of food preparation and distribution settings; thrives in many refrigerated foods; and can endure acidity, salt and relatively low moisture. It is most commonly found in dairy and meat products. Along with frankfurters and brie, outbreaks have been linked to chocolate, imitation crab, and pig's tongue. Contaminated raw fruits and vegetables account for a small portion of infections.

Product Innovations and the Global Palate: *Listeria*

Increasingly, appetites are bridging borders. Grocery stores feature "ethnic food" aisles and delis are stocked with luxury imports from around the world, from foie gras to smoked duck. At the same time, food producers are hard at work developing "ready-to-eat" foods that require no more than a quick stint in the microwave. In 2002, processed goods made up nearly half of all agricultural exports (World Trade Organization 2004). Left behind in the whirl of innovation are food safety regulations drafted before many of these delicacies made it to the table, providing an opening for bacteria that were not part of the plan, such as *Listeria monocytogenes*.

The *L. monocytogenes* bacterium, rare but also relatively dangerous, became a public heath concern in the 1980s, when the illness was linked definitively with the ready-to-eat foods that dominate many a grocery list. A veritable Happy Hour spread comprises many of the bug's vehicles of choice – deli meats, smoked fish, fresh soft cheeses and pâté. Refrigeration provides little deterrent; the bug can thrive under cool conditions. *L. monocytogenes* was first identified as a foodborne pathogen in 1953, when a pregnant woman who had consumed milk from an infected cow developed the infection herself and had stillborn twins. For the next few decades, however, it went largely unnoticed until several major outbreaks in the 1980s caught health officials' attention. In 2000, it was the pathogen most commonly associated with hospitalization in the US, and accounted for a third of reported pathogen-related deaths (US Food & Drug Administration Center for Food Safety & Applied Nutrition 2003).

A study examining the 54 *L. monocytogenes* outbreaks reported around the world from 1970 to 2002 found that roughly one third occurred in the US (Table 2.5). In more than 90 percent of the cases, contaminated meat or dairy products were identified as the source of the infections (US Food & Drug Administration Center for Food Safety & Applied Nutrition 2003). In 2002, for instance, an outbreak tied to contaminated turkey spread through nine states, resulting in 54 illnesses and eight deaths, including three unborn babies. The contaminated poultry was traced to Pennsylvania-based Pilgrim's Pride Foods, which consequently recalled 27 million pounds weight of turkey and chicken products.

Recent sanitation and pasteurization efforts have helped reduce infection rates in the US – the rate declined 44 percent from 1989 to 1993 and another 38 percent from 1996 to 2002. But ever-changing food preparation and distribution practices, along with breakdowns in existing systems, hamper progress. In some cases, for example, food that is properly pasteurized (heat treated) or cooked is then recontaminated before it is packaged. Consequently, *L. monocytogenes* remains on the top of health officials' priority lists. In November 2002, the USDA's Food Safety and Inspection Service (FSIS) stepped up inspections of production facilities perceived as high and medium risk. And in October 2003, the agency issued a "Listeria rule" designed to encourage manufacturers of ready-to-eat foods to take more aggressive measures to fight *L. monocytogenes* contamination, such as adding an additional step to kill pathogens after the food has been cooked and cooled. In December 2004, the FSIS reported that recalls related to *L. monocytogenes* dropped from 40 in 2002 to 14 in 2003, suggesting that the efforts may be paying off. However, the listeriosis rate in the US rose slightly from 2.7 cases per million in 2002 to 3.3 cases per million in 2003 (see Table 2.6).

Table 2.5   Outbreaks of listeriosis in the US (1970–2002) with known food vehicle(s)

Year	Food Vehicle	State	Cases	Perinatal cases (% of total)	Deaths (% of total)	Serotype	Reference
1979	Raw vegetables or cheese	MA	20	0 (0)	3 (15.0)	4b	Ho, 1986
1983	Pasteurized fluid milk	MA	32	7 (21.9)	14 (43.8)	4b	Fleming, 1985
1985	Mexican-style cheese (raw milk)	CA	142	93 (65.5)	48 (33.8)	4b	Linnan, 1988
1986-1987	Ice cream, salami, brie cheese	PA	36	4 (11.1)	16 (44.4)	4b,1/2b, 1/2a	Schwartz, et al., 1989
1986-1987	Raw eggs	CA	2	Unknown	Unknown	4b	Schwartz, et al., 1988
1987	Butter	CA	11	Unknown	Unknown	Unknown	Ryser, 1999
Not specified	Frozen vegetables	TX	7	3 (42.9)	Unknown	4b	Simpson, 1996
1998-1999	Hot dogs, deli meats	22 states	101	Unknown	21 (20.8)	4b	Mead, 1999
1999	Pâté	CT, MD, NY	11	2 (18.2)	unknown	1/2a	Carter, 2000
2000	Deli turkey meat	10 states	29	8 (27.6)	7 (24.1)	unknown	CDC, 2000
2000-2001	Homemade Mexican-style cheese (raw milk)	NC	12	10 (83.3)	5 (41.7)	unknown	CDC, 2001
2002	Deli turkey meat, sliceable	8 North Eastern states	63	3 (4.8)	7 (11.1)	unknown	CDC, 2002b
Total			466				

Source: US FDA (2003), http://www.cfsan.fda.gov/~acrobat/lmr2-2.pdf. http://www.cfsan.fda.gov/list.html.

The challenges *L. monocytogenes* entails are particularly evident in the burgeoning world cheese market. In recent decades, the cheese varieties on offer have proliferated from several dozen to several hundred, among them myriad soft cheeses and boutique or artisan cheeses – many of them potential *L. monocytogenes* vehicles. The pathogen can invade early on in the process and endure in raw cheeses, or reinfect a cheese after pasteurization. In Switzerland, between 1983 and 1987, 122 infections and 34 deaths were linked to Vacherin Mont D'Or cheese before it was determined that the contaminants were lingering in the aging caves, contaminating one batch after another (BC Centre for Disease Control 2002). Homemade raw milk cheeses have been the source of periodic outbreaks in the US. In the Los Angeles area in 1985, the cheese was linked with 86 cases of *L. monocytogenes* infection that resulted in 29 deaths, including 13 stillbirths and eight newborns (Centers for Disease Control and Prevention 1985). In that instance, the infections were associated with a commercially produced cheese and the potentially

Table 2.6 Outbreaks of human foodborne listeriosis

Country	Year	Food vehicle[a]	Numbers of cases					Serovar
			Total	Pregnant	Non pregnant	With underlying disease	Deaths	
US	1976	?Raw salad	20	0	20	10	5	4b
New Zealand	1980	?Shell or raw fish	22	22	0	0	7	1/2a
Canada	1981	Coleslaw	41	34	7	0	18	4b
US	1983	?Pasteurised whole milk and 2% milk	49	7	42	42	14	4b
US	1985	Mexican-style soft cheese made from unpasteurised milk	142	93	49	48	30	4b
Switzerland	1983–1987	Soft cheese	122	65	57	24	34	4b
UK	1987–1989	Pate	355[b]	185	129	NK	94	4b and 4 not 4b
US	1989	?Shrimps	2	NK	NK	NK	NK	4b
Australia	1990	Pate	9	NK	NK	NK	NK	1/2a
Australia	1991	Smoked mussels	4	0	4	0	0	1/2a
New Zealand	1992	Smoked mussels	4	2	2	2	1	1/2a
France	1993	Pork tongue in aspic	279	NK	NK	NK	NK	4b
France	1993	Pork rillettes	38	31	7	NK	10	4b
US	1994	Commercially pasteurised chocolate milk	45	1	44	1	0	1/2b
Sweden	1994–1995	Cold-smoked rainbow trout	9	3	6		2	4b
France	1995	Soft cheese	17	11	9	5	4	4b
Italy	1997	Sweetcorn salad	1566	0	1566		0	4b
Canada	1996	Crab meat	2	0	2	0	0	1/2a
US	1998–1999	Hot dogs and delicatessen meats	50	NK	NK	NK	>8	4b
Finland	1998–1999	Butter	25	0	25	24	6	3a
Finland	1999	Cold-smoked trout	5	0	5	NK	NK	1/2a
England	1999	Cheese and cheese and salad sandwich	2	0	2	2	1	4b
France	1999–2000	Pork rillettes	10	3	7	6	2	4b
US	2000	Turkey meat	29	8	21	NK	7	NK
France	1999–2000	Pork tongue in jelly	32	9	23	11	10	4b
US	2000–2001	Mexican-style soft cheese made from unpasteurised milk	12	10	2	1	5	NK

Notes: a ? = Food implicated through epidemiological study only.
b Information was not available to classify 41 patients.
Source: McLoughlin 2004.

contaminated cheese products were recalled. But often queso fresco – a fresh, soft cheese made from unpasteurized, or "raw," milk – is produced in private homes, making it difficult for health officials to enforce sanitary regulations. Consequently, roughly half the states in the US have banned the sale of raw milk to individuals.

Presently, commercially manufactured cheeses must either be made from pasteurized milk or, if they are made from raw milk, be cured for a minimum of 60 days to outlast any remaining pathogens. However, the so-called "60-day" rule, developed in the 1950s before many of the cheeses it regulates existed, has come under scrutiny in recent years as it has become evident that a number of pathogens, including *Salmonella* and *E. coli* O157:H7, can withstand the 60-day aging period. Investigators demonstrated that *L. monocytogenes* can endure for up to 434 days (Ryser and Marth 1988; Food and Nutrition Board, Institute of Medicine et al. 2003). Further complicating the issue is the fact that the pathogens can survive outside the food product on equipment or storage facilities and contaminate cheeses via that route, rendering the aging process moot. Discussions about modifying the 60-day rule are under way. Meanwhile, regulations require that raw milk cheeses, among them some of the finest French imports to the US, must be labeled as such.

Among many gourmets, however, labeling with a warning of raw milk tends to serve, if anything, more of an incentive than a deterrent.

Conclusion

In response to the growing market pressures of global commerce, producers are scrambling to meet the challenge by making more diverse and better products. The accompanying innovations have in turn created new challenges for health authorities. New, more efficient mass production operations that entail pooling mass amounts of meat or produce, sometimes from numerous sources, are proving to be fertile ground for the broad spread of infections. Increasingly popular fresh produce can carry difficult-to-detect microbes capable of causing infections at very low levels of exposure. Moreover, the short shelf life of fruits and vegetables make sources of infection especially difficult to identify and address. Particular strains of disease that were once mostly contained by geographical boundaries now are spreading with food products that are making their way around the globe to meet year-round demands. Not only are new strains appearing in new areas, they are being transmitted via vehicles that had not previously been suspected, and mutating into forms that have not previously been seen and often resist microbial treatments. These constantly evolving dynamics of the global market are rendering existing safety systems outdated and in some cases simply impractical even as they are being adapted.

Study Questions

1. How much does the global marketplace present itself in your neighborhood store? What items can you get year-round that are imported?
2. The marketing of food is extremely important. What campaigns for certain food stuffs, by food councils or industry groups, have you seen on television in the past two weeks?
3. Have you ever heard of a recall of beef or cheese by lot?

Chapter 3

New Agents with Speed

The most immediate and widely feared infectious disease threat is the global spread of a highly contagious, unknown and dangerous agent. The prospect has become increasingly realistic in this era characterized by high-speed international travel – in a matter of hours, we can move from one continent to another over thousands of miles away. Even the most rapid infectious diseases require six hours from the time of infection to the manifestation of illness. Most agents require a longer period of days, months or even years. This means that we can be infectious before we really know we are ill. We can bring new infections into communities that are naïve to those infections. This is not new; travelers introduced and spread syphilis through Europe in the 18th and 19th centuries, and adventurers and explorers caused great epidemics in the Americas when they introduced measles and smallpox. The great plague of the 14th century is thought to have arrived in Europe via traders traveling from Asia. But now things are faster. Time increasingly is not on the side of public health and safety. In this chapter, we discuss the relationship between travel and emerging disease and examine two new challenges: SARS and avian influenza. The lessons they bring about the new era of the global express are sobering.

Transmission On Board

Modern conveyances carry passengers in close proximity in enclosed spaces for increasingly long periods of time. SARS demonstrated the hazard that this can create for the onboard traveler, but this is only the latest dramatic example. The problem has been "on board" the global express for decades. Person-to-person transmission can occur anywhere people are crowded together. On short journeys, the travelers disperse from the conveyance before they become ill, and their contact on board may not be identified as their source of infection. When small groups travel together, the rate of infection may be such that only a few individuals become ill from the exposure. However, when lots of people travel together and the disease is highly contagious or unusual, investigations are more likely to turn up the common exposure of sharing, for instance, a cruise ship or airplane space.

In recent years, cruise ships have become notorious for outbreaks of respiratory and gastrointestinal diseases among passengers and crew. The number of outbreaks of gastrointestinal illness on cruise ships reported to the US Centers for Disease Control's Vessel Sanitation Program jumped from seven in 2001 to 24 in 2002 and has continued to rise. While some of the increase may be due to better reporting and the growing popularity of cruises, also contributing is the nature of cruises, upon which hundreds of passengers, many of them elderly and more vulnerable to disease, share common water and food sources and regularly engage in social activities. Onboard outbreaks typically affect relatively large numbers of passengers, are transmitted by several routes and may persist from one cruise to the next despite decontamination efforts, perhaps in part because the crew continues to remain infectious (Widdowson, Cramer et al. 2004).

Some 10 million people a year embark on cruises (Schlagenhauf, Funk et al. 2004). While the majority of passengers are North Americans, the ships have people of various nationalities boarding at different ports, presenting the opportunity for the spread of disease from diverse regions. Additionally, when passengers from the southern and northern hemispheres mix, there is potential for off-season exposure to diseases that normally emerge at particular times of the year. So people who normally receive vaccines in anticipation of the winter flu season may be unexpectedly exposed in the summer when they encounter people from countries where the seasons are reversed. For instance in August 1997, a group of passengers from Australia, which typically has a flu season that runs from May to September, boarded a cruise ship in New York, where the flu is more common in the opposite months. The Australian passengers were disproportionately represented in an initial attack of acute respiratory illness that subsequently spread through the ship, suggesting that they may have been infected before boarding (Miller, Tam et al. 2000). Moreover, the outbreak marked the first of that particular strain of virus in North America. Similarly, a summertime influenza outbreak in Alaska's Yukon Territory between May and September of 1998 was linked to an infusion of cruise ship passengers and crew into the area (Uyeki, Zane et al. 2003). This cruise, up the inside passage along the coast of Canada, seeded influenza into communities along the route during the summer, which is off-season for flu in the northern hemisphere.

Aircraft travel, which typically entails briefer but often more proximate exposure, presents different and in some respects greater risks for disease transmission. An estimated 1.5 billion people travel by plane every year, many of them on flights of 10 hours or longer and 50 million of them to the developing world (Leder and Newman 2005; Mangili and Gendreau 2005). Travel related infectious disease "events" have been a consistent feature of the jet age. Malarious mosquitoes hop a ride in Africa, and infect unsuspecting humans as they arrive at airports in Europe or the US. This "airport malaria" has been described for at least a decade. Mosquitoes can survive in the wheel wells of modern aircraft for hours of journey at tens of thousands of feet quite handily. They then disembark and bite passengers and others within their flying radius at the destination point. However, because they cannot sustain their reproduction in such places, only a handful of human cases of disease occur through this route.

Much discussion has focused on the potential for respiratory disease transmission when hundreds of people are confined for hours in an aircraft with a recirculating air supply. The risk of pathogens circulating through aircraft ventilation systems is minimal; only the most robust microbes survive the high efficiency particulate air (HEPA) filters, dry air and frequent circulation (Leder and Newman 2005; Mangili and Gendreau 2005). Aircraft circulation systems generally divide the jet into sections in which the air circulates from one side of the jet to the other; the air typically does not move along the length of the plane. Of course, the systems only work when they are used. In a 1977 case, for instance, 72 percent of the 54 passengers on board a commercial plane developed influenza within three days after being exposed to a single ill passenger – the plane had been grounded with mechanical problems for three hours before take-off, during which time the ventilation system was not operating, potentially contributing to the contamination (Moser, Bender et al. 1979). While HEPA filters are extremely effective, only one in seven flights is equipped with the newer filtration systems. Regardless of the circulation system, passengers risk direct exposure to infected people who are coughing and sneezing on board. There are documented cases of onboard transmission of multi-drug-resistant tuberculosis, influenza, and now SARS in this manner (Centers for Disease Control and Prevention 1995; Olsen, Chang et al. 2003; Leder and Newman 2005). Figure 3.1 illustrates the spread of SARS on a commercial aircraft flight.

Measles clusters related to the arrival of children incubating measles has plagued local health departments across the US. In typical conditions, the possibility of in-flight transmission varies depending on the stage of the illness in the index case (the person with the original infection), as well as the length and proximity of exposure. Increased risk of infection is associated with flights of eight hours or greater for those sitting within two rows of a contagious passenger (Mangili and Gendreau 2005).

But onboard transmission is in many respects less of a concern than the "vector" function of modern air travel and trade. Whether a passenger is exposed onboard or at home before taking a flight, that contagious person may travel thousands of miles, expose countless people in their paths, and carry the disease to a new region before the infection becomes evident. The infected traveler may be at home, in his or her community, carrying on the activities of life and exposing his or her neighbors for days or weeks before becoming ill. This reality challenges traditional means of disease containment, such as quarantine.

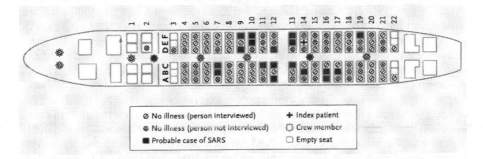

Figure 3.1   SARS transmission aboard a commercial aircraft
Note: Schematic diagram of the Boeing 737-300 Aircraft on Flight 2 from Hong Kong to Beijing.
Source: Olsen, Chang et al. 2003, Figure 2.

Quarantine and Containment Strategies

The quarantine system in the US has languished over the past 30 years, coincident with the complacency about infectious diseases and, ironically, with the burgeoning of international travel. Illness on board is reportable to port authorities under US quarantine law. For aircraft, notice is required one hour prior to landing. For ships, 24-hour notice is required. Similar procedures are in place for most nations that receive traffic by sea or air from the global express. By early 2004, between six and eight active quarantine stations were operating in US airports. These stations were staffed by quarantine officers who were not, by and large, trained in infectious diseases, and much of the expertise needed to handle infectious disease threats was contracted to local physicians. I served as a consulting quarantine physician for Seattle-Tacoma International Airport between 1992 and 2000, and was called just once to see an incoming European child with a rash. Having determined the rash could not be measles, I reviewed several other past cases with the quarantine officer and found that referral was haphazard and payment depended on agreements with affected airlines. Clearly if the airline had to pay for the consultation, there was probably less motivation for calling in the quarantine officer for assistance.

The inadequacy of this system was starkly outlined during the 1994 plague outbreak in India. For the first month of the epidemic, intensive surveillance was put in place to prevent the introduction of plague into the US via air travel. The system (see Figure 3.2) relied on both active and passive surveillance – which is to say persons potentially ill with plague were actively sought during airline travel from India to the US by airline personnel, and local health authorities were alerted to watch for signs of patients with plague (Fritz, Dennis et al. 1996). Information sheets about the symptoms of plague were distributed to passengers. However, the airline personnel are not medically trained and their ability to detect illness among passengers was not known.

Ultimately, over the 30-day alert period, just 13 people were identified in the US who might have had plague. Only six of these were evaluated before they left the airport. Happily none had plague. But clearly airport-based quarantine would not have been effective if all 13 had actually had the highly infectious pneumonic plague, since half of the possible cases were not detected before they had left the airport and interacted with family, friends and business associates, potentially further spreading the disease.

For quarantine strategies to be effective, access to medical care – the ability to go to a trained health care provider with little wait and little cost – is important. Without being seen by a medically trained provider, a patient cannot be isolated, diagnosed or treated. Assuring that this process works easily is clearly important for protecting communities from emergent infectious diseases. Given the current crisis in health insurance coverage in the US, we figure among the more vulnerable populations for broad transmission from disease introduction, and we are unique among developed countries in this vulnerability. According to the Kaiser Foundation Commission on Medicaid and the Uninsured, 44 million Americans have no health insurance (Kaiser Commission on Medicaid and the Uninsured 2004). The uninsured are less likely to seek medical care, and more likely to defer

Plane with ill passenger
arrives at US airport

Ill passenger examined by Quarantine
Officer and airport contract physician,
in consultation with CDC medical officer

Suspect plague patient?

 Yes

No

Suspect plague patient
1) transported to hospital under respiratory isolation
2) diagnostic specimens obtained
3) antibiotic therapy initiated

Non-suspect plague patient
1) obtain locating information
2) monitor temperature for 7 days
3) Quarantine Officer notifies state epidemiologist

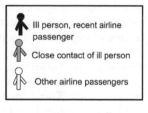

Other passengers
1) complete surveillance form
2) provided with Plague Alert Notice
3) monitor temperature for 7 days

4) antibiotic prophylaxis initiated for close contacts

Other passengers
Provided with Plague Alert Notice

> Ill person, recent airline passenger
>
> Close contact of ill person
>
> Other airline passengers

Figure 3.2 Plague surveillance system in action
Source: Fritz, Dennis et al. 1996 p. 31.

preventive care and delay in seeking care when ill. Thus when and if a new emergent infection, natural or deliberately launched, hits a community the uninsured will be the last to be diagnosed and treated. They are likely to remain in their communities enhancing transmission until they are ill enough to drag themselves before a health provider for evaluation, treatment and care. So, returning to the plague example, if a person with pneumonic plague had entered the country, and returned to his or her community, and if that community were low income with poor medical insurance coverage, the lack of access caused by this unacceptable fact could have caused epidemic plague. Moreover, most US medical practitioners have never seen plague, so even if an uninsured person became so ill that he decided to make that budget-busting trip to the emergency room, the illness still may not be recognized.

The bioterrorism threats and SARS epidemic early in this decade have stirred the US government into reconstituting the quarantine system. The budget and staffing have improved. However the role of the quarantine system still is under discussion.

The Institute of Medicine's Forum on Microbial Threats convened an expert group to assist in defining just what the role of quarantine should be and how the system should work. The report and recommendations of that group are still in process. But as the SARS outbreak highlighted, there are acknowledged limitations to border control in the modern age. It is not a stand-alone strategy.

SARS – A Cousin of the Common Cold Goes Bad

On a recent visit to Shanghai, my hosts from Fudan University took me to visit the new Shanghai Municipal Hospital for Infectious Diseases, which is located 65km away from the city center. Shanghai is a city of 16 million people that was miraculously spared during the 2003 SARS epidemic. Nonetheless, the decision to invest $150 million in building this facility was a direct result of SARS. The new facility will have a capacity of 550 beds, expandable to 1,500 if necessary. The walls of the buildings are color-coded for the level of potential contagion and precaution necessary for health workers, and the whole campus, which encompasses several acres, can be completely sealed or locked down in case of quarantine.

The SARS crisis developed quickly, and it reached two continents with direct contagion and illness in a matter of weeks. Worldwide attention and concern was focused on the situation as the World Health Organization (WHO) issued unprecedented alerts and travel advisories. It was highly fatal; an estimated 10 percent of clinically ill people succumbed to their disease. This contrasts with the 1918 influenza pandemic's mortality rate of 2.5 percent. That pandemic killed 40 million people worldwide, and remains etched in history as the most fatal epidemic in the human community in modern times. As the mortality of SARS became apparent, the risk and need for extraordinary controls was sobering.

SARS is primarily related to human travel, not to trade in commodities. The unknown SARS agent traveled intercontinentally by aircraft to more than a dozen countries prior to its formal identification by science. However it seems the SARS agent jumped the species barrier from animals traded in the marketplaces of Guangzhou in the first instance. Fully a third of the early cases in China have been linked to animal handling. The dramatic story of SARS should be seen not as a battle victory that ended a war, but as battle won at great cost that was likely just a first skirmish in an ongoing war. SARS brought into high relief the inadequacy of public health systems, the gaps in science, and the urgency of repair.

Despite the exotic and mysterious media stories of Ebola and HIV coming from the jungles of Africa, the Asia Pacific region has in fact been the area of origin of most of the major newly reported human infections. SARS followed a decade that included the steady drumbeat of emergence in the region: Nipah Virus in Malaysia, Enterovirus 71 in Taipei, Dengue hyperendemicity throughout the region, *Escherichia coli* 0157:H7 in Japan (through trade with the US), avian influenza in China, increasing drug resistance in tuberculosis in Vietnam and the Philippines, just to mention a few. So SARS originated in a region already sensitized to the risk of emergence. The APEC and the ASEAN trading blocs had both incorporated the emergence of infections (including HIV) as a priority in their policy portfolios and

---

SARS

Severe Acute Respiratory Syndrome is a severe respiratory infection with associated gastrointestinal symptoms in an as-yet unknown percentage of those infected. Thought to have originated in Guangdong Province, China, the disease presents with malaise, myalgia and fever, quickly followed by respiratory symptoms including cough and shortness of breath. Diarrhea may occur. Symptoms worsen for several days, with maximum viremia at 10 days after onset. The incubation period is from three to 10 days. The agent persists in the environment for at least one to two days, and in the stools of persons with diarrhea up to four days. The SARS agent is a coronavirus, similar to animal coronaviruses. Transmission is person-to-person by direct contact with respiratory secretions or body fluids of infected persons. Possible fomite or aerosolized sewerage transmission has been described.

---

working groups prior to SARS. The potential threat was known; the real threat was galvanizing.

When SARS first emerged in the People's Republic of China, the government kept the appearance of the mysterious disease secret – a move that potentially contributed to the international spread. In November of 2002 an unknown but serious and often fatal pneumonia afflicted the population of Guangzhou province in Southern China. The Chinese health authorities investigated and, on the basis of laboratory work done in Beijing by the China Centers for Disease Control, announced that the outbreak was probably due to Chlamydia, a known, treatable, bacterial pathogen. However, treatment did not work, and the number of cases and deaths began to mount. The population of Guangzhou began to panic. Pharmacies were mobbed. Finally on February 20, doctors in Guangzhou broke ranks with their colleagues and alerted the world that in their opinion the specimens were not Chlamydia, but a virus they could not identify. By then more than 300 cases had occurred in the province, and five people had died. One 62-year-old physician traveled from Guangzhou to Hong Kong and stayed in the Metropole Hotel. His stay was unremarkable, but he was very ill. He succumbed shortly afterwards to SARS.

Ominously, cases of serious atypical, untreatable pneumonia began to occur in Vietnam, Hong Kong (March 11 notification, Program for Monitoring Emerging Diseases (Pro-Med), International Society for Infectious Diseases) and Toronto, Canada (March 14 notification, Pro-Med). Hospital staff – doctors and nurses – were succumbing to this very serious illness, with a high rate of contagion and mounting mortality. The French Hospital in Hanoi was sealed after 16 cases occurred in its staff and patients. The World Health Organization (WHO) issued a global alert as it became clear that the "index" or first case linked to those seen around the world was that of the physician who had traveled from Guangzhou to Hong Kong before becoming ill. The new, unknown virus was going global, traveling by airliner. It defied medicine and killed a high percentage of its victims. The global public health and scientific communities did not even know what it was.

In Vietnam, Dr. Carlos Urbani was dispatched by WHO to investigate. It was he who ordered the sealing of the French Hospital – a step that is credited for preventing significant spread to the rest of the city of Hanoi. It was also he who was infected with and died of SARS shortly thereafter. Numerous staff members in the French Hospital also died, and tended to their dying colleagues. However, because no one was allowed in or out of the hospital after lock down, the community at large was protected from contagion. Dr. Urbani and the Vietnamese staff at the French Hospital are justly recognized for their tremendous heroism, literally laying down their own lives for their fellows.

Because SARS was infecting so many health workers, the ability of governments and their health systems to respond was under fire. In Taipei, Taiwan, hospital workers began to balk at going to work; in Singapore, janitorial staff required additional bonuses to show up. The hospitals were rapidly putting in place barrier protection and isolation precautions, but it was a scramble. At Singapore General and in Toronto, duct tape and visquene plastic sheeting were stretched across hallways to create additional isolation wards. The toll continued to mount.

Meanwhile researchers raced to identify the new pathogen. WHO coordinated an unprecedented laboratory collaboration. Instead of an individual research group racing for scientific acclaim or the Nobel Prize, researchers across 12 laboratories became a relay team, working together to reach the finish line and identify a common threat. In record time of one month, the entire genome of the new pathogen, a coronavirus, was identified. A new way of working together resulted in an unparalleled success in scientific discovery. However, describing the genome and knowing the agent is only the first step. There was no arsenal of medical treatments for this new coronavirus. A vaccine was years away. Known antiviral medications were only modestly effective in practice, although clinicians tried whatever seemed to make sense. Antivirals were used empirically to treat patients but results were mixed. Treatment schemes were shared on an ad hoc basis among doctors and hospitals as the cases occurred, but looking back at the evidence it is not possible to say that this treatment was effective.

Coronaviruses are not unknown in medicine; in fact they are thought to be responsible for 10 to 15 percent of occurrences of the common cold. But that is about as much as most physicians and human infection scientists knew of these viral agents when the outbreak hit. And SARS is not due to the common cold virus, but to an entirely new virus of the same family. The human health medical community was only familiar with the family of the common cold virus, because that was the only disease the coronavirus was known to cause in humans. Veterinarians were much more well-acquainted with coronaviruses, and the prestigious journal *Nature* issued a general call for collaboration with veterinarians. It was time to bring the animal and human scientists together to compare what was known, and not known, about the new agent. Most new human pathogens have come from animals, and the communications between the worlds of medicine – human and animal – needed a major boost. The Centers for Disease Control had a number of veterinarians in their Epidemic Intelligence Service, but most of these scientists worked as epidemiologists of human infections rather than in their primary area of veterinary medicine. Since SARS, this has shifted and the agency has deliberately brought veterinary science into their work.

Identifying the virus was one hurdle; the next was figuring out how to contain it. SARS had a mixed picture of contagion: it was highly contagious in some settings such as the Metropole Hotel in Hong Kong and in hospitals. However at the community level, it appeared to be less contagious. In other words, it was not as consistently contagious as influenza would be. Control of viral infections, especially those that are highly contagious, focuses on three lines of attack: isolating infectious people to prevent spread to others, administering antiviral medications to the infected to shorten the course of illness and, ultimately, developing vaccines to prevent or to shorten illness. With the urgency of SARS, isolation was the only immediately available option. Two levels of isolation were put into place: within hospitals and, when community clusters occurred, in those settings. Hospital control was essential. At Singapore General, people arriving at the hospital were evaluated in the parking lot, where their temperatures were taken. Those with fever were sent to one room, those without fever to another. The workers receiving the febrile patients were gowned, gloved and given personal protective equipment such as masks. Patients also wore masks until they reached their hospital isolation room, where there was "negative pressure" air flow. In other words, the rooms were ventilated in such a way that the air was vented outside rather than recirculated to other areas of the hospital. All personnel working with the patients in the rooms did so in full personal safety protection. Similar precautions were adopted in Toronto, Hong Kong, and other locales where the illness struck. In fact, in hospitals all across Asia and North America, SARS protections were put into place. Experience as the epidemic progressed suggested that a single patient could infect many others in the absence of such safety measures. Indeed, in Toronto, the early "stand down" from strict hospital infection control measures is faulted for the resurgence of the SARS epidemic in that city.

Remarkably, investigation revealed that the early international "index" cases in the numerous outbreak sites could be traced to the doctor from Guangzhou, and his stay for a single night on a single floor at a single hotel in Hong Kong. As Figure 3.3 illustrates, this individual was the source of illness across two continents and in at least five locations. Investigators were not able to determine exactly what had happened to cause such a high level of contagion. However, six weeks after the events, SARS coronavirus genetic material was still detectable in the carpet at the doorway of the room occupied by this "super spreader" case.

The bug's tenacity also was evident in the Amoy Gardens residential compound in Hong Kong. People living in the multi-towered complex, which housed 1,500, began to develop the mystery illness. The apartments were arranged in blocks of 33 floors with eight apartments on each floor. There was an apparent concentration of cases in block E. Authorities quarantined the entire complex. All of the residents were evacuated, and relocated to temporary shelter – still in isolation – as the compound was completely disinfected and environmental investigation was carried out. A total of 321 cases of SARS occurred in the complex, 41 percent of which were in block E. The index case was a 33-year-old man who visited his brother in the complex on March 14 and March 19. He had chronic renal disease and was under care at the Prince of Wales Hospital. During his visit he was suffering diarrhea and subsequently shown to have SARS. A careful environmental assessment of

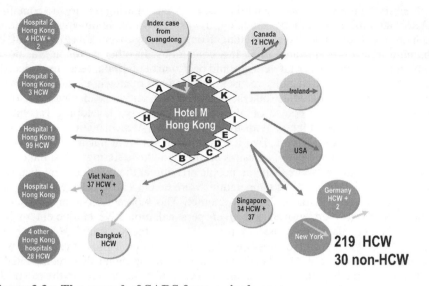

Figure 3.3   The spread of SARS from a single case
Notes:
1. This diagram shows the spread of SARS from a single case via other guests at Hotel M, Hong Kong, 21 February to 26 March.
2. HCW denotes health care worker.
Source: David Heymann, WHO; University of Washington lecture 2004.

block E revealed a cracked sewage pipe and poorly functioning "U traps" in the sanitary fixtures. The investigation suggested that taking a shower was a risk factor associated with disease. Most of the Amoy Gardens cases also reported having diarrhea; the SARS coronavirus has been shown to be excreted, and capable of prolonged survival in the environment after excretion. It appears that cross connections within the building between plumbing for sewage and plumbing for shower drains had probably allowed aerosolization of the virus within the showers to infect the residents. In other words, the agent was in the fine sprays in the showers. Thus SARS had at least one non-hospital route for contagion.

In China, Hong Kong, Singapore, Toronto and Taipei, unprecedented quarantine was put into place. Despite the 21st-century bench science at hand, public health relied on the containment strategies of the 19th and 20th centuries. Developing information about cases and quarantine was greatly facilitated in Hong Kong, where academia and public health worked together to fashion an innovative database for keeping cases and contacts. Later, again in Hong Kong, collaboration with police facilitated the implementation of the "no fly" lists that succeeded in stemming more international spread. During the outbreaks, some 40 flights carrying suspected SARS passengers were investigated for possible disease transmission. Onboard transmission was associated with five of those flights, resulting in 37 additional SARS cases (Mangili and Gendreau 2005).

Hong Kong's collaborative approach was not the rule during the crisis. While virtual networks facilitated communications among epidemiologists and microbiologists responding to outbreaks, WHO and their Western Pacific Regional Office (WPRO) in Manila adopted a "need to know" basis for sharing information. While the WPRO office was the front line for country coordination, much of the decision making waited on Geneva. Restriction of information in a crisis setting is unavoidable, but disquieting for the rest of the world, connected by airlines to epidemic areas. Indeed our own network, the APEC Emerging Infections Network, was besieged with inquiries from unaffected countries about what was going on in epidemic areas. We also received numerous "unofficial" reports elaborating on the terse information shared internationally by the World Health Organization. All in all, SARS demonstrated the need for fast, accurate communications across borders.

Avian Influenza: "It's only the Flu..."

Yet another threat of a fast-moving virus hovers over Asia, the world's most populous continent. This one, influenza, is well-known for its ability to wreak devastation across continents. But it is behaving in new and surprising ways, due in part to intense ecological pressure that mounts as the population and the poultry industry that feeds it continue to grow, particularly in Southeast Asia. Poultry are central to the diet of Asia, and the local palate dictates that birds should be served as fresh as possible. Consequently, large live bird markets are the norm in most major cities in China, as well as in Taipei and Hong Kong. Meanwhile, rice, another staple, is cultivated in a symbiotic process between farmers and ducks. Waterfowl are raised near the rice paddies and, during the growing season, the ducks eat the weeds but leave the young rice shoots untouched, greatly facilitating the work of the farmer. But when the ducks migrate, they also can transport disease among poultry pens. As we will see, these dynamics have helped set the stage for the current flu crisis.

Influenza

Influenza is an acute viral disease of the respiratory tract characterized by fever, headache, myalgia, prostration, coryza, sore throat and a cough that is often severe and protracted. Airborne spread predominates among crowded populations in enclosed spaces and may also occur through direct contact. The influenza virus may persist for hours, particularly in the cold and in low humidity. Incubation period is short, from one to three days, and individuals are infectious for three to five days following the onset of illness. There are three types of influenza viruses – A, B and C – and the emergence of new strains occurs only with type A viruses.

In 1997, a new kind of influenza – a "bird flu" or avian influenza – was isolated from the throat swab specimen of a three-year-old boy who had died in Hong Kong. Because of the lag time in testing (results take several weeks in the laboratory), the kind of flu the boy had could not be determined until some weeks after he died. The finding of an avian kind of influenza (H5N1) was unexpected, and an investigation by public health authorities was launched. Meanwhile, additional cases were occurring, and the virulence of the new virus was alarming. A total of 18 people became ill and six died – a mortality rate of 30 percent. The virus, which had first been noted by Chinese scientists in geese in Guangzhou in 1996, did not seem to travel from person to person; cases appeared to be linked to direct contact with poultry. The three-year-old boy had been in a preschool that kept ducks as pets. Hong Kong officials suspected that the source of the problems might be the live bird markets; bird flu had killed many of the birds there. Over the next weeks, all markets were closed and disinfected, 1.5 million fowl were slaughtered, and new regulations were put into place: the markets were to segregate birds by species, and close one day a week for cleaning. Behind the scenes, an ambitious program of testing and tracking for flu was put into place, focusing on people, poultry and pigs.

The alarm regarding the 1997 outbreak stemmed from the unprecedented "jump" of avian influenza from birds directly into humans. Influenza viruses historically have been thought to circulate from birds to pigs to humans. Pigs are believed to serve as "mixing vessels" because they possess receptors for both avian and human influenza viruses and thus can act as intermediate hosts (Smolinski, Hamburg et al. 2003). In this theoretical construct, avian influenza or "bird flu" would need to be contracted by a pig in order to be transmitted to humans, and then on from human to human. But in retrospect, the whole area of influenza research is relatively new. Influenza viruses were only identified in the 1930s in pigs and ducks. The hypothesis that an avian influenza virus had to go through a pig to reach a human was just that, a hypothesis. In 1918, when the most severe global epidemic of influenza swept around the globe, science had no ability to characterize the virus, much less track its presence in other species.

Epidemic Flu

In the intervening years, our experience with and knowledge of influenza has increased, although much remains to be discovered. The influenza virus causes regional epidemics in temperate regions every two to three years, marked by excess mortality and hospitalizations due primarily to respiratory infections (Mandell, Bennett et al. 2000). In the US alone, influenza causes an average of 20,000 to 36,000 excess deaths annually in non-pandemic years (Smolinski, Hamburg et al. 2003). Attack rates can range from 10 to 40 percent during seasonal outbreaks and are highest among school-age children; mortality rates peak among people over age 65 and younger than five years. Societal and economic costs from influenza outbreaks extend well beyond these high-risk groups to young, healthy people; each case of illness is associated with an average of three missed days of school or work (Mandell, Bennett et al. 2000).

As a communicable disease with a large, worldwide reservoir in migratory waterfowl populations, influenza is an essentially uncontrolled and non-eradicable zoonotic disease (Lederberg, Shope et al. 1992; Shortridge, Peiris et al. 2003). Influenza poses a severe threat not only in developing countries but also in developed countries; studies in Canada, the US, and Holland have shown that annual non-pandemic (interpandemic) influenza epidemics already have a major impact on hospital costs and reduced productivity (Smolinski, Hamburg et al. 2003). Influenza viruses come in three types: A, B and C. The type of virus is determined by the proteins it carries on its coat. Influenza A viruses, the pandemic variety, are named for two sites on the viral particle: the hemagglutinin or "H" site and the neuraminidase or the "N" site. These are sites that can be described in a standard way in the laboratory through serological testing. Viruses are also commonly named for the city or country where they are first identified. Thus in 1957 the "Asian flu" swept through the US, causing 70,000 deaths and extensive illness (Centers for Disease Control and Prevention 2005). While the scientific name for this strain was the H2N2 virus, most people who got sick would tell you they had the Asian flu.

Hong Kong has always been a bell-wether for influenza and a critical part of WHO's Global Influenza Surveillance Network. However, after 1997 the intensity of surveillance efforts increased and new technical tools were brought to bear. It became evident that the close quarters of human and avian populations in this region, along with the presence of other animals, seems to be tipping the balance of nature towards the emergence of pandemic flu. At the time of this writing, two ominous events are unfolding in parallel: unprecedented geographically dispersed outbreaks of avian influenza of the H5N1 type among birds in Southeast Asia and an increasing human toll, with 53 deaths to date (World Health Organization 2005).

Influenza pandemics in the 20th century

Influenza pandemics, defined as global outbreaks of influenza due to viruses with new antigenic subtypes, result from the emergence of an influenza A virus that is novel for the human population (Glezen 1996; Horimoto and Kawaoka 2001). It must have the ability to replicate in human beings and the potential to rapidly spread from person to person (Claas, Osterhaus et al. 1998). Such pandemics have occurred throughout recent history. The first pandemic is believed to have taken place in 1580, and 31 such events have described since then (Mandell, Bennett et al. 2000). There have been three major influenza pandemics during the 20th century. The most severe – the largest recorded outbreak of any infectious disease (Gamblin, Haire et al. 2004) – occurred in 1918–19 and resulted in up to 40 million deaths worldwide (Stephenson, Nicholson et al. 2004), including 549,000 in the US alone (Mandell, Bennett et al. 2000). This "Spanish flu" pandemic, caused by the H1N1 strain, may have entered the human population directly from a zoonotic reservoir without a reassortment event involving exchange of different viral genes in a third species such as a pig (Claas, Osterhaus et al. 1998). This direct transmission probably contributed significantly to the extreme virulence and high mortality of this pandemic influenza, especially in healthy young adults.

The subsequent 1957 "Asian flu" (H2N2) and the 1968 "Hong Kong flu" (H3N2) pandemics were similar in that they both emerged first in Southeastern Asia, and they were antigenically distinct from influenza viruses then circulating in humans (Horimoto and Kawaoka 2001). Both pandemics are thought to have been caused by a reassortment event between avian and human influenza viruses, where pigs may have acted as the mixing vessel (Claas, Osterhaus et al. 1998; Horimoto and Kawaoka 2001). Scientists now believe there are at least two possible mechanisms by which influenza pandemics can be generated; via direct transmission from avian sources or via an intermediate "mixing vessel" host, such as the pig (Horimoto and Kawaoka 2001). It is imperative to consider both transmission modes, and attempt to minimize opportunities of either from realizing. There is evidence that pigs in China have been sporadically infected with avian H4 and H5 viruses in addition to swine and human H1 and H3 viruses (Ninomiya, Takada et al. 2002). Recently, both H9N2 and H5N1 subtype avian influenza viruses – both of which are known to threaten humans – have been isolated from pigs in China (Hai-yan, Kang-zhen et al. 2004). These findings from former pandemic strains and recent zoonotic hosts depict the complex ecologic and epidemiologic role that animals play in human influenza pandemics through their ability to facilitate creation of new influenza subtypes to which the human population has little or no existing immunity.

The last major influenza pandemic occurred more than 35 years ago. Many believe that the next influenza pandemic is not only inevitable, but long overdue (Smolinski, Hamburg et al. 2003). Evidence from the current bird flu outbreak in Southeast Asia suggests that, like the devastating "Spanish flu," the influenza H5N1 strain responsible for this outbreak may also be capable of direct transmission from poultry to humans. The recent reporting from China regarding the finding of avian influenza viruses from pigs add further concern – co-circulation of avian, human, and pig viruses in pigs is of significant concern because of the potential for reassortment (World Health Organization August 25, 2004). It has also recently been reported that 70 percent of waterfowl (ducks) are infected with H5N1 in affected areas in which ducks and chickens are raised together (Schuettler April 19, 2005).

Source: Yuzo Arima.

Table 3.1 Influenza pandemics during the 20th century

Pandemic	Subtype	Species of origin	Region of origin	Human impact	Notes
1918–1919 Spanish Flu	H1N1	Contains mammalian and avian genes – possibly jumped from birds to humans, with very little mutation	Debatable	20-40 million human deaths; unusual W-shaped curve	Extremely pathogenic and virulent with high mortality in healthy young Isolated from pigs and humans at approximately the same time
1957 Asian Flu	H2N2	Avian (reassortment–combination of avian and human viruses)	Southeast Asia/ southern China	>1 million deaths worldwide	Antigenically distinct from influenza viruses then circulating in humans
1968 Hong Kong Flu	H3N2	Avian (reassortment–combination of avian and human viruses)	Southeast Asia/ southern China	>1 million deaths worldwide	Antigenically distinct from influenza viruses then circulating in humans Isolated from pigs and humans at approximately the same time
1977 Russian Flu (may not be considered a pandemic)	H1N1	Debatable – frozen source, accidental release from laboratory?	Russia/ China	Low mortality; older population immune	Reappearance of H1N1 virus essentially identical to those circulating among humans in 1950s
					Low death rate attributed to immunity of persons over age 20 years who had been infected previously

Source: Yuzo Arima, with reference to Horimoto and Kawaoka 2001; Smolinski, Hamburg et al. 2003.

Avian Influenza in Asia – The Beat Goes On

Late in 2003, Korea notified international authorities of an outbreak of highly
pathogenic bird flu in its territory. Early in 2004, Cambodia, Hong Kong, Laos,
Thailand, Japan and Vietnam filed similar emergency reports with the World Animal
Health Organization (OIE). With the exception of Laos, where the final
identification beyond the H5 designation was not made, all of the outbreaks were of
the H5N1 virus, the same virus that caused the cluster in Hong Kong in 1997.
Indonesia and China reported outbreaks in February of 2004, and Malaysia also
recently reported outbreaks. The geographic breadth of this continuing pandemic is
unprecedented. Control has been elusive.

The chief means of control has been the slaughter or "culling" of hundreds of
millions of chickens. The actual count of how many chickens have been killed is
difficult to know because the highly pathogenic avian influenza also kills chickens
rapidly. In total, the losses have been staggering. Trade impacts have also been
severe, since trafficking in chickens is virtually halted when influenza affects an
area. In Vietnam, for example, "the virus wiped out 17 percent of the fowl
population totaling 43.2 million poultry across 57 of 64 localities," causing losses
of VNF 1.3 trillion ($83.3 million) (Vietnam News Brief Service September 10,
2004). While Hong Kong requires vaccination documentation on any imported
chickens, vaccination generally has not been seen as an option in most countries for
a variety of reasons. In Thailand, for instance, after a small trial of vaccination, the
Thai Agricultural Ministry banned the practice because it confounded their control
efforts. The concern was that farmers, strapped by the ongoing crisis, would be
tempted to claim their fowl were vaccinated to avoid their slaughter.

While the economic losses have been devastating, the most disquieting
development has been the clusters of human cases of influenza in Vietnam, Thailand
and Cambodia with high mortality. As of May 2005, in Vietnam, 76 cases of
laboratory-confirmed human bird flu had been reported, and 37 of those cases were
fatal; in Thailand, 17 cases had been reported, 12 of which were fatal; and in
Cambodia, four cases had been reported, all of which were fatal (World Health
Organization 2005).

Asia is not the only geographic area where influenza has flexed its muscles (see
Figure 3.4). In Europe in 2003, the Dutch, German, and Belgian poultry industry
suffered heavy losses from an outbreak of another strain of the virus (H7N7). By
that May, Germany had destroyed 4,000 birds, Belgium had destroyed 2.77 million
birds and Netherlands had culled 26 million birds in efforts to curb the avian
epidemic. Evidence of infection in pigs also was detected and the Dutch Ministry of
Agriculture halted transport of pigs and pig manure. The measures taken to control
the outbreak were vigorous.

Protective measures taken in North-Rhine Westphalia, 30 May 2003

This followed the European Commission decision of May 16, 2003.

- A total standstill imposed on all transport of live poultry, hatching and poultry slurry.
- The entire poultry flock affected by the disease as well as the adjacent flocks were destroyed immediately and safely disposed of after the official determination of disease suspicion (approximately 80,000 birds).
- Within a radius of 3km around the outbreak, all poultry flocks were destroyed and safely disposed of within 48 hours after the suspected presence of avian influenza had been established.
- Within a radius of 10km, a protection zone was established followed by a surveillance zone with a further radius of 10km, with a total standstill on movements of live poultry.
- Neither live poultry, hatching poultry eggs, nor untreated slurry or bedding material from flocks in North Rhine-Westphalia Land may be dispatched to other regions of Germany, European Union Member States, nor third member countries.
- Fresh poultry meat from the protection zone established in North Rhine-Westphalia may be sold only within Germany (with specific labeling and must be cut, transported and stored separately).
- All events involving poultry have been banned.
- Table eggs may be transported from the holdings with laying hens to the point of packaging either in one-way packages or in containers that have been cleaned and disinfected after use.
- Poultry intended for slaughter may only be transported in lorries and in boxes or cages cleaned and disinfected after each use.
- Baby chicks may be transported only in one-way packing material to be destroyed after each use.
- The movement of people on poultry farms has been restricted, and appropriate protective measures have been adopted for people handling poultry.

Source: http://archives.foodsafetynetwork.ca/animalnet/2003/5-2003/animalnet_may_25.htm.

Birds and Influenza

One of the key drivers in the recent emergence and spread of influenza is the evolution of the poultry industry. The pandemics of the 20th century all have been attributed to influenza viruses originating in birds (Horimoto and Kawaoka 2001). Although influenza viruses can infect a variety of mammalian species, influenza infection has been recognized in birds for more than 125 years. Avian influenza was

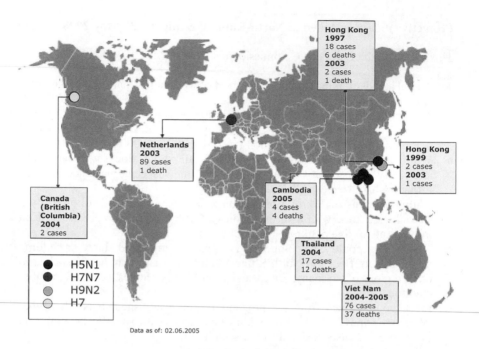

Data as of: 02.06.2005

Figure 3.4   Documented avian influenza infections in humans
Source: European Communities, 1995–2005, http://europa.eu.int/comm/health/ph_threats/com/Influenza/images/influenza.jpg.

first described in Italy in 1878 among chickens (Horimoto and Kawaoka 2001) and currently there are over 24 subtypes of the virus known to cause the disease (Capua and Alexander 2002). Migratory waterfowl and other aquatic bird species are the primordial or primitive reservoir of all influenza A viruses, and infections in these species are usually subclinical (Gorolinski, Hamburg et al. 2003; Swayne and King 2003).

Chickens seem to support a separate natural reservoir of influenza viruses, possibly acting as intermediate hosts in zoonotic transmission; while domestic poultry are not natural hosts for avian influenza viruses, new ecologic niches created by bird captivity and domestication, industrial agriculture, national and international commerce, and nontraditional raising practices have allowed pathogenic and nonpathogenic microorganisms to be transmitted within and between avian species and adapt to new host species (Swayne and King 2003; Stephenson, Nicholson et al. 2004). Such "convergence of factors" in the highly interconnected and readily traversed global village of our time has been pointed out by the Institute of Medicine as a mechanism of disease emergence.

Transmission of novel avian influenza viruses may thus occur when domestic poultry, such as chickens or ducks, come in contact with wild migratory waterfowl.

The virus replicates in the intestinal tract of waterfowl and can live in feces for months, allowing domesticated birds to contract the infection after eating contaminated soil. Domestic flocks and some mammals also may become infected with this virus through aerosol transmission from wild flocks (Capua and Alexander 2002). Of the avian influenza subtypes, the H5 and H7 strains have historically been responsible for all of the highly pathogenic avian influenza (HPAI) outbreaks (Horimoto and Kawaoka 2001). HPAI can cause mortality rates approaching 100 percent in some bird populations (Capua and Alexander 2002), and in recent years, HPAI outbreaks have had a dramatic global impact, both in developed and developing countries, in human and animal health sectors, with enormous international trade and societal consequences.

Commercial poultry raising around the world ranges from cottage industries to mass production operations. It has become increasingly intensified, with higher and higher concentrations of fowl living in crowded conditions. In the developed world, industrial poultry farming generally adheres to the accepted guideline of 10 birds per meter square. In wealthier countries that compete in the global marketplace, intensification is driven by the search for economies of scale. In the developing world, intensification has occurred primarily as a result of human crowding, and the demand for food in the growing human population. Figures 3.5 and 3.6 show the population density for humans and poultry worldwide; the most intense concentrations of both are found in China.

Europe, on the other hand, has both a more modest human density and poultry density per square kilometer. Thus, when the World Health Organization expressed concern in 2003 about the potential spread of avian influenza among people in Europe, "international food and animal health authorities dismissed the idea," according to a Reuters news article (Reuters 2003). Alex Schudel of the OIE's scientific and technical department was quoted as saying, "There is no way this could turn into a human virus like SARS" (Reuters 2003). Nonetheless, human cases of conjunctivitis (eye infection) did occur, and one health veterinarian in close contact with chickens died of apparent bird flu.

In Asia, authorities have not appeared as sanguine regarding the broad geographic waves of highly pathogenic avian influenza that have surfaced over the last several years. In fact, the coincident crowding of humans and birds has begun to raise questions about the structure of the whole poultry agricultural sector in Southeast Asia. As the illustrations above indicate, there are more people and more poultry per square kilometer in China and Southeast Asia than anywhere else in the world. The Food and Agriculture Organization of the United Nations expressed concern about the situation in a January 2004 press release, stating, "The spread of avian influenza from Pakistan to China may have been facilitated by the dramatic scaling up of pig and poultry production and a massive concentration of livestock in China, Thailand and Vietnam ... The poultry sector may need to be substantially restructured" (Food and Agriculture Organization of the United Nations 2004).

In addition to feeding the population of Southeast Asia, this area also is a major export source for poultry. There has been an explosion in the tonnage and value of poultry products from the region entering the global marketplace in the past two decades. The world poultry trade has increased fivefold in 20 years, reaching a value

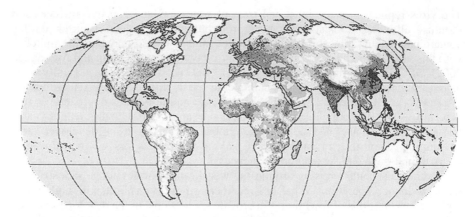

Figure 3.5   Global population density, 2000
Source: Center for International Earth Science Information Network (CIESIN), 1997.
Accessed using DDViewer [online application],
http://plue.sedac.ciesin.columbia.edu/plue/ddviewer/, May 1, 2004.

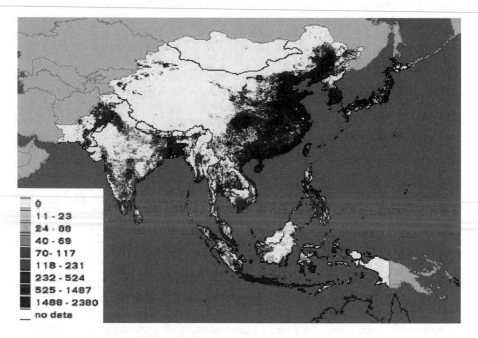

Figure 3.6   Poultry density in Southeast Asia
Source: FAO. http://www.fao.org/ag/againfo/subjects/en/health/diseases-cards/avian_bg.html.

of nearly US$10 billion annually. Far East Asia, a late entrant into the marketplace, saw the value of its exports multiply 25 times in three decades from $10 million in 1971 to $234 million in 2002, a phenomenal growth. In tonnage, the exports rose from 14,266 tons in 1972 to 1,805,152 tons in 2001 (Figure 3.7). Thailand alone experienced a fivefold increase in live chicken exports by value during this time. In contrast, the European Union, another region that has experienced growth in this market, saw a more modest increase; the value of poultry exports rose from approximately $246 million in 1971 to $4.4 billion in 2002 and the tonnage from 324,873 tons in 1972 to 2,706,053 in 2001.

So as countries like China and Thailand have geared up their poultry industries to feed their people and serve the global marketplace, a new influenza affecting birds and humans has emerged. It was first noted in the small cluster in 1997. It is believed to be related to the occurrence of avian influenza or bird flu in flocks of domesticated birds. Domesticated birds are highly affected while wild birds are not. The threat of a long overdue pandemic influenza, capable of much greater societal and health disruptions, underscores the urgent need to improve the prevention and control measures during the current interpandemic period. Coordinated planning and transparent communication between the human health and veterinary health communities should be one of the core activities.

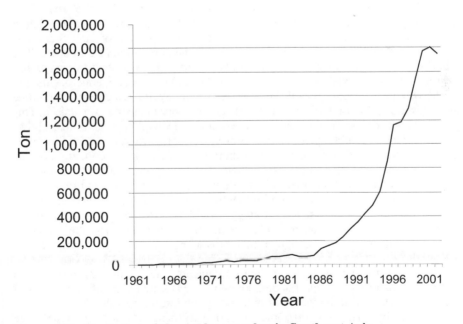

Figure 3.7   Explosion of the poultry market in Southeast Asia
Source: FAOSTAT 2003. Constructed by author.

Pandemic Fears and Magic Bullets

Indeed, the sustained nature of the poultry outbreaks and the growing toll of human cases have caused alarm throughout the world. WHO has formally warned of the threat, as has the CDC. In preparation, countries in the region have been working with WHO to create preparedness planning. WHO has recently published its own global plan (World Health Organization 2005.4). Meanwhile, various vaccine responses are under investigation. There is an antiviral agent that is effective against bird flu, oseltamivir phosphate, or Tamiflu. If taken at the first signs of flu, this medication reduces the duration and severity of symptoms. It is a "neuraminidase inhibitor," in other words, it inhibits the ability of the neuraminidase portion of the virus to bind to the cells of the infected host. There is a second drug of this type that is not effective against H5N1, unfortunately. The drawback to the effective medication is that it is made only by Hoffmann-La Roche & Co. at a single production facility in Europe and it is under patent protection. The company does not stockpile the medication but produces to demand. If the company does not wish to gear up and produce more medication for the protection of Asian populations, it cannot be compelled to do so.

WHO has written the use of this drug into its guidelines for workers who become ill with flu after culling poultry. Tamiflu was used extensively in the outbreaks in the Netherlands discussed above. The UK has begun stockpiling the drug, and other governments are in negotiations to do so. The fear is that the neediest countries have the least access, and the lowest stockpiles of Tamiflu. A recent *Wall Street Journal* report noted that currently available doses (based on doses ordered from Hoffman-La Roche) could cover 24 percent of the population of the UK, 22 percent of the population of France, one percent of the US and just 0.0024 percent of Vietnam and 0.0021 percent of the population of Cambodia. The Tamiflu production process takes 12 months and it is clear that "demand has overtaken supply" (Naik and Hookway May 18, 2005). If a pandemic occurs, the world will face a public health emergency. At the WHO Executive Committee meetings in January of 2005 the specter of "compulsory licensing" was raised. This is a provision of the World Trade Organization's "Doha Agreement" that allows countries facing a public health crisis to produce their own versions of lifesaving medicines despite patent ownership by others. Needless to say the mention of this option was not welcome among some delegations, especially the US delegation where the protection of pharmaceutical patents has been of overriding importance. Beyond the political distaste for this among many major pharmaceutical exporters, it is not at all clear that such a strategy would be effective since compulsory licensing requires the country declaring an emergency to have the technical competence in country or through partnerships with other countries to produce the needed drug.

There are actually two other, older antiviral agents (amantadine and rimantadine) that use another mechanism of action, known as "M1," that were effective against the virus in 1997. But the virus has mutated in the interim and these drugs are no longer effective. This is worrisome but not surprising. As we will emphasize throughout this book, RNA viruses are uniquely adaptable because of their inherent genetic instability. This ability can be a real problem in developing vaccine strategies.

On March 23, 2005 the National Institutes of Health announced that it was sponsoring clinical trials for vaccine safety and efficacy of a new H5N1 vaccine. The trials will enroll 450 volunteers in Baltimore, Los Angeles and Rochester to test the new vaccine, which is produced by pharmaceutical company Sanofi Pasteur in Pennsylvania. This is new for NIH, which usually focuses on basic biomedical research and leaves such testing to the pharmaceutical industry. In an April 2005 lecture at the University of Washington, Dr. Anthony Fauci, Director of the National Institute of Allergy and Infectious Diseases, calls the move "unprecedented". The new vaccine is made in human cells, rather than in egg cells since the virus is pathogenic for poultry and therefore cannot be grown in the egg cell system. If successful, production would require redirecting the entire influenza vaccine effort into this new technology, which is no small undertaking. We will discuss the prospects of such "magic bullet" solutions more fully in Chapter 6. It is not at all clear that a vaccine solution will be available if and when the influenza pandemic strikes. In the meantime, a number of governments are stockpiling Tamiflu.

China: Building Pressures

It is important to consider the setting in which these two new viral agents (SARS and bird flu) have emerged: China and Hong Kong respectively (which in fact have been part of a single country since 1999). China is the most populous nation on earth. The country includes 1.2 billion inhabitants, more than four times the population of the US. This population lives on a land mass with about 40 percent of the arable land of the US. Thus the ecological pressure of people and their activities on the biosphere is intense. China traces its history of public health practice to the 1920s and 1930s with the pioneering work of Professor Zhiqiuan Chen in Ding County of Harbei Province (Lee 2004). Primary prevention of infectious disease has been a longstanding objective of the Chinese public health system, and the rates of mortality dropped remarkably between 1949 and 2001, from 20 in 1,000 to 6.43 in 1,000 (Lee 2004). Life expectancy has leaped from 35 to 71.4 years during that same period (Lee 2004).

But the population of China is aging, with the fraction over age 60 exceeding 10 percent, the level that constitutes the international standard for an "aging population". The absolute number of the elderly in China is one fifth of the world's total elderly, and one half of the total of Asia's elderly. As humans age, their ability to fight infection wanes as their immune systems become less vigorous. Thus in China, there is a large population with less immunity than in many developing countries.

Dr. Liming Lee, an epidemiologist and professor at Beijing Medical University, observes "The ecosystem destruction and globalization together with antimicrobial resistance make the emergence and epidemic of infectious diseases inevitable" (Lee 2004 p. 331). In fact, some surmise that the SARS coronavirus probably had caused outbreaks in China before. As microbiologist Dr. Kenneth Shortridge notes from his Hong Kong vantage point:

> Such outbreaks may have been just as severe as the recent episode but probably would have died out because of limited opportunity for the virus to spread from village focal points. Bringing exotic mammals, presumably stressed and shedding increased levels of virus, into densely populated centers contrives an artificial setting ideal for exposing animal handlers and the public to the virus. *Burgeoning national and international travel* exposed the existence of the SARS disease and its causative agent.
>
> (Shortridge 2003 p. 1417, emphasis mine)

Southern China is an area where live markets of a variety of exotic animals exist to please a population with specific tastes. The best parts of the best animals are often sold or traded, leaving the remaining pieces of the animal to be consumed at the family table. One traditional belief is that "like heals like," so cooked brains may be fed to scholars, or feet to athletes. And, as discussed above, the poultry markets continue to grow in size and density. The United Nation's Food and Agricultural Organization laments the lack of good biosecurity and hygiene practices in poultry raising in these enormously crowded places. But when this new intensification of agriculture is superimposed on an inadequate sanitary infrastructure, it is hard to know how to reinforce practice unless the raw materials – clean water, sanitation and elimination of poverty – can be put into place. Over the last decade, with the "reform" of the Chinese economy and the building of a social society, life has changed rapidly. Urbanization is extremely rapid and uncontrolled. At the same time, "investment in health services has been given low priority for many years," according to most observers (Breiman, Evans et al. 2003 p. 1040). The UN estimates that just over one third of China's people have access to adequate sanitation. Thus, as the world's largest population rides through rapid shifts in lifestyle, land use, and living space, it is plagued by the emergence of new unknown pathogens.

Meanwhile, China, which joined the World Trade Organization in 2001, has recently blossomed into the fourth largest trading nation in the global marketplace; foreign trade exceeded $850 billion in 2003. The Chinese people also have become avid travelers. The Chinese Aviation Authority estimated that 2.5 million Chinese will take to the air for the national holidays in October 2003, primarily for domestic destinations. Recent survey results projected that fully 70 percent of Guangzhou families intended to travel within China by all transport means: a massive migration of 3.56 million people.

These ingredients – crowding, intensified food production, poor sanitation, increased travel and trade, pose a growing threat. More remarkable than the recent emergence of SARS and the H5N1 virus, perhaps, is the fact that we have not seen more of such events in this region.

Study Questions

1. When speaking of "speed" of global infection there are two possibilities: speed of illness from time of infection, and speed of "hitchhiking" and global spread by air traffic. Which of these was most important with SARS? Which would be most important with influenza?
2. Influenza is an "old" agent, and epidemics of influenza occur annually. What new factors of emergence are affecting the threat of influenza?
3. Why was the threat of avian influenza causing a pandemic illness in humans dismissed in Europe? In contrast, why is it taken so seriously in Asia?

Chapter 4

Stealth Agents – Slow and Deadly

Working as Regional Advisor for HIV/AIDS at the Pan American Health Organization (ΓΑΗΟ) in 1988, I was impressed that in virtually all of our reporting member countries, large groups of hemophiliacs already had clinical AIDS. The hemophiliacs were the epidemic's "canaries in the coal mine" – the first to be infected and the first to die. Latin America was seeing the same tragedy as Europe and North America, where between one third and two thirds of hemophiliacs were infected with HIV. The hemophiliacs' plight was one of devastating coincidences; an unfortunate nexus of treatment innovations that used harvested blood and the emergence of a blood-borne disease. Our response was to send consultants to inspect and work with our member countries to ensure that the blood supply was safe. We did this in each country, and in every case we successfully assured ourselves and our colleagues in-country that the supplies were screened and safe. The only exception was Bolivia, where the existence of illegal blood bank operations at the time made the task beyond our collective reach.

Much has been written about HIV/AIDS, arguably the largest challenge to modern public health and medicine ever, affecting every inhabited continent on the globe and claiming 40 million victims to date. But despite the extensive scientific and popular literature on HIV/AIDS, the story of its journey though the global trading system and the profound repercussions is only partially known. The literature has focused primarily on sexual transmission via humans; the non-sexual transmission through the global blood trade has been less completely examined. However the story of the spread of HIV through the blood trade is equally compelling, and a harbinger of just how risky our current global trading ventures can be.

The retrovirus HIV and the prion of Bovine Spongiform Encephalopathy (BSE, or "mad cow disease"), which will be discussed later in this chapter, pose a particular threat in global trade because they spread silently and widely in products before they are detected through the occurrence of clinical illness. These two "stealth" agents are both difficult to diagnose and have a very long incubation period – as mentioned in Chapter 3, this is the time between the entry or infection of the individual and the beginning of clinical disease. In the case of HIV, infected persons are largely without symptoms for a decade or more. Similarly, with new variant Creutzfeldt-Jakob Disease (nvCJD, the human version of BSE), it seems that clinical illness occurs years after infection, possibly 15–30 years or longer. This has enormous implications in a trading system in which thousands of miles can be spanned in hours. The pace of detection is necessarily late, and may follow the time period of circulation by many years. The length of incubation period is, in the detection of new infections, directly related to the size of the eventual human epidemic, i.e., the longer the period, the greater the number of eventual cases.

Adding to the danger of these diseases is the fact that they have been relatively recently discovered and are still being described and understood by microbiologists and virologists. The HIV retrovirus, for instance, was not known when the clinical symptoms were first reported, and only through vigorous research have the characteristics of the agent, its mode of operation in the human and the clinical characteristics of the illness it causes become better understood. This work was done from the mid-1980s through the 1990s, and continues to the present day.

Neither the HIV retrovirus nor the BSE prion is a "bug" (bacteria), biologically speaking. They cannot live independently: They require their hosts, human or animal, to survive and replicate. In the case of retroviruses, the virus takes over the machinery of the cell of the host and hijacks that factory to create copies of itself. Such agents literally possess their hosts, and eventually, in the case of AIDS and nvCJD, invariably cause the death of the host. With both these diseases, the pace of scientific discovery was outstripped by the changes in the manufacturing world that contributed to their spread. In other words, the risk of the HIV agent was being studied and defined by science even as that risk was being actualized through increased production of a blood-based product to treat hemophiliacs. The gap in time between when innovation and scaling-up of products occur and when the risk of those products is completely known through scientific work is the "science gap." Repeatedly, as in these cases, the advance of science has been outpaced by commercial enterprise.

HIV/AIDS: Global "Blood Brothers"

Over the past 30 years, people around the globe have unwittingly become "blood brothers" through the increasing global trade of blood and products created from blood. These products are life saving. Most women in poor countries die in childbirth not from contaminated blood but from the lack of ability to receive blood during a hemorrhage or bleeding crisis. In wealthy countries death from acute blood loss can be prevented through the infusion of blood, a practice that has been used for at least a century in medicine. Among those who have relied on those infusions are hemophiliacs.

Hemophilia A is a bleeding disease that has long been the source of suffering in the human community. Known as the "Royal Disease," it is a genetic disorder carried as a silent trait by mothers, with clinical illness only affecting their sons. Queen Victoria was a carrier of the trait and her daughters, through marriage, brought it into the Czarist families in Russia. The frequent hemorrhages in some of the sons are well documented in history and some believe this distraction within the royal house of Russia led to the rise of Rasputin. Without treatment, hemophilia causes painful bleeding crises and can lead to early death. Hemophilia is estimated to affect 400,000 people worldwide. The critical problem is the absence of normal blood clotting factors because a missing gene eliminates the body's ability to make these key biological proteins. The normal clotting of blood depends on the presence of a number of proteins, or "clotting factors." When these are not present, the blood will not clot, and so bleeding from injury (even minor injury) is prolonged. To address such problems, since the 1940s, evolving technology has enabled the creation of treatments in the form of new products from human blood. The blood is separated into its components, and the necessary elements are extracted, concentrated and developed into stable, shippable products for use in clinical care. These products, such as factor VIII (a blood clotting factor) allow people with hemophilia to avoid painful and dangerous bleeding crises, and live their lives with a higher quality of physical functioning. Today this area of product development continues as an active and exciting research arena, with great promise for new discoveries and therapies. Safeguards now are in place to prevent the spread of HIV/AIDS through these products. But this was not the case in the 1980s, when the development of some of the blood products rolled out just as the world was beginning to detect and understand the AIDS virus.

The first cases of clinical AIDS were reported in the US Centers for Disease Control and Prevention's (CDC) *Morbidity and Mortality Weekly Report* (*MMWR*) in 1981 (CDC 2001). This was a cluster of a new illness in homosexual men. At the time this illness was known by a variety of names, and its cause was not known. Doctors in central and east Africa had been noticing changes in the illness patterns there for some time. However in those poor settings the ability to test and diagnose, and even to report to the international literature, were substantially below those in San Francisco, where the first cluster of cases noted by the *MMWR* occurred. Only later would the significance of the increasing incidence of so-called "Slim's disease" in the countries bordering Lake Victoria be known.

HIV/AIDS is caused by a retrovirus that cannot live on its own, and requires human cells to replicate. Its origins remain murky; however it is closely related genetically to viruses found in monkeys. Most scientists now believe that a "species jump" occurred from monkeys to men. In fact studies suggest it occurred more than once. How this happened is not clear, but the first human sample with HIV was drawn in 1959 during a Lassa Fever outbreak investigation in Zaire. The sample was taken out of its storage in deep freeze to be tested in the 1990s. The HIV virus is not casually infectious. Care takers and family members of people with AIDS are rarely infected. The virus travels through the exchange of bodily fluids: blood, semen, breast milk, saliva. It is estimated that sexual intercourse with an HIV infected partner carries a risk in the range of one in one thousand of infection. But an HIV tainted unit of blood carries with it a risk of 90 percent for the recipient (Varghese, Maher et al. 2002). Despite this huge difference in risk, sex is much more frequent than blood transfusion and the World Health Organization (WHO) estimates that the majority of HIV transmission in the world is through sex.

The retrovirus responsible for AIDS has two distinct types, HIV1 and HIV2. The virus found in the 1959 blood sample mentioned above was HIV1. HIV2 appears to have been present for much longer in populations in West Africa and also seems to be less likely to cause AIDS or to be transmitted from mother to child. HIV1 is the epidemic strain of the retrovirus. Retrovirus literally means a virus that works backward, and this name describes the way the infectious agent actually works in the process of infection. The genetic material of the virus is RNA, and it enters the cell and takes over the machinery of the cell to cause replication of itself. The virus attacks "CD4" cells that are part of the body's normal immune defense system.

HIV1 infection first may cause no symptoms, or a mild flu-like illness that resolves on its own. The virus then sets about attacking the target lymphoid cells, and replicating itself, during which time the host or human involved feels nothing. After a variable period from one to 15 years or more (usually about seven to eight years in settings of developed country populations), the infected patient develops AIDS.

AIDS is actually a group of signs and symptoms that indicate the virus has done its work in destroying the body's defense against infection. The infected person will begin to have unusual infections that normally the body would defend against, such as thrush, pneumocystis carinii pneumonia, or, in the setting of developing countries, tuberculosis. They also may develop unusual cancers. Gradually the intensity of the infections progressively weakens the body, which eventually can no longer continue to successfully fight, and death occurs. Prior to the development of antiretroviral drugs, death was always the case about one or two years after AIDS was diagnosed. While great strides have been made treating AIDS with a cocktail of drugs that interrupt the replication of the virus and prolong survival for years, AIDS is still a very serious illness. The drugs do not work for everyone, and in poorer countries the costs of drugs and treatment have been unaffordable to the vast majority of people suffering with AIDS.

Concurrent with the dawning recognition of the AIDS epidemic in the 1980s was a period of innovation in the area of blood products for therapeutic use. Prior to the 1970s, fresh frozen plasma was the mainstay of treatment. This involved transfusing the patient with plasma that included the missing factors and therefore could provide the needed elements to allow the patient's blood to clot. Plasma transfusion required a closely supervised clinical setting, often a hospital. The product itself was bulky and required continuous refrigeration to retain its short-lived effectiveness for treatment. Otherwise, the proteins' coagulation factors, or blood clotting factors, would "spoil" or degenerate and not do their job in the patient's blood.

The essentials of blood

Blood is pretty amazing. It is really a bunch of cells and pieces of cells floating in a liquid. Red blood cells, white blood cells, and platelets circulate around the body in the liquid, plasma. When you cut a finger, the bleeding eventually stops; this is because blood clots. Platelets (which are bits of bone marrow cells) help plug the leak, but the plug only works if there is also an ability to clot. Clotting takes place when a number of different proteins act in sequence to create the glue to stop the bleeding. These proteins float free in the plasma. When plasma is frozen, it concentrates these proteins. Blood does a lot of other things as well, but key points to know to understand the crisis in the blood supply are that (1) you can take the cells out of the blood and have only plasma, (2) you can concentrate the proteins in the plasma to give to people who need them to help with clotting.

By the early 1980s science had provided a better therapeutic option. Instead of using plasma from two or three donors to treat a hemophiliac in crisis, medical technology had advanced to allow the isolation of just the clotting factor in a preparation that was much more biologically effective. The essentially pure preparations of the missing factors had enormous therapeutic advantages. The patient received just the "business end" of what he or she needed from outside of their own systems to effectively clot their blood. So all of the other proteins and other compounds in plasma that were not essential to clotting could be removed, reducing the volume that needed to be transfused, and the risk of allergic or immune reactions to the transfusion in the recipient. The first commercial production of factor VIII, the key factor missing in hemophiliacs, became available in 1968. While expensive, it was effective and hemophiliacs could use the product much more easily, although it was still given intravenously. But this new therapy required thousands of units of plasma to be processed to provide one unit of the clotting factor. Because each unit of plasma had only a small amount of clotting protein, lots of units had to be pooled to harvest this precious bit. And factor VIII required constant refrigeration.

A markedly increased demand for the building blocks of clotting factor (units of blood, or plasma, from donors) ensued. Plasmapheresis, the process of harvesting plasma from blood, had become, by 1980, a thriving commercial enterprise. The process involves a visit of some hours to a collection center where the blood of the individual undergoes separation at the bedside as it is run through a machine. Previously, blood concentrates had mostly been manufactured from blood plasma that was harvested from donors at blood banks, which rely heavily on volunteers. But with plasmapheresis, subjects were often paid for their blood. In Seattle, as in cities all across the country, people were offered about $70 per unit. The centers for harvesting were sited in poor communities, where $70 could mean the difference between making it or not making it between welfare checks. While plasma also could be taken from blood donated by voluntary (unpaid) donors, as mentioned above, that practice, called secondary, was less widely used because the supply was less predictable than it was with paid donors.

In the 1980s, new techniques for preservation of biological products were coming on line that would profoundly affect the global marketing of the clotting factor. Key among them was freeze drying, known as lyophilization, which freezes a material in a vacuum quickly. After the material has been freeze dried, it can be transported without the continuous refrigeration that biologically active compounds normally require to retain their activity. Freeze drying was a boon to the food industry as well, as any camper who has taken freeze dried food in his or her backpack knows. To reconstitute the food, which can be anything from eggs to fettuccini Alfredo, all one needs to do is add the water back in. In much the same way, the new blood factor products could be transported relatively inexpensively over long distances and reconstituted on site for use by the patient and his or her physician to end or to prevent a bleeding crisis.

Meanwhile, there were some indications that problems were on the horizon for the new blood products. Hepatitis, which is a liver disease caused by infection with a virus, was associated with the new products. Hepatitis is caused by several kinds of virus, and by the early 1980s it was clear that hepatitis B, commonly known as serum hepatitis, and hepatitis C, which was then known only as "non-A, non-B," were associated with the use of products from large pools of donors. While it had long been known that hepatitis could be transmitted in blood, and thus persons with active hepatitis were not allowed to donate blood, it was only becoming apparent that the new technology of pooling thousands of products ramped up the risk significantly even if the donors themselves had no signs, symptoms or history of hepatitis disease. Hepatitis, like HIV, is often not clinically apparent even to the infected patient, even at times when the patient may be infectious to others if he/she donates blood.

Ongoing concern about the safety of pooled factors due to the risk of hepatitis had spurred producers to search for a means of screening their product for hepatitis virus. But while hepatitis can be fatal, and hepatitis C in particular has a high mortality rate, the risk of hepatitis was weighed against the beneficial uses of the blood products, such as facilitating lifesaving surgery in hemophiliac patients. Consequently, the perception of risk was muted. Much later, the Krever Commission Report, a landmark scientific study of blood safety, would cite the lack of general awareness of this risk as a key facilitating factor in the subsequent tragic events with HIV (Krever Commission 1997).

The Krever Commission of Health Canada, founded in 1993, carried out an extensive inquiry to determine the exact nature of the calamity that had befallen hemophiliacs and others receiving blood products the decade before. The Commission reviewed more than 1,000,000 pages of documents, and held extensive hearings. Its findings were challenged in the Canadian courts prior to their final publication. Thus this Commission Report outlines much of what is known, and calamity is not too strong a word. We now know that half of the hemophiliacs in the US and an untold number of hemophiliacs worldwide were infected with HIV through blood products. In some countries such as Japan, this was probably the primary route of entry of HIV into the population. The large amount of units of blood that went into each product and the relatively high rates of infection among donors, many of whom gave blood in exchange for money, proved a tragic combination. Most of these products were produced in the US, where the commercial sector for the production of blood factors is most developed. As of the time of the Krever report, there were 400 commercial centers for plasmapheresis operating in the US. The centers that employed paid (and typically higher-risk) donors as opposed to volunteer donors provided 60 percent of the worldwide requirement for plasma. Figures on the trade in blood products while the US and other producing countries had a contaminated blood supply are difficult to get. But the available data show the growth of blood factors trade in the 1980s was remarkable; overall trade in blood products more than doubled.

According to the report, there were four major producers in that decade: Alpha Therapeutic Corporation, Armour Pharmaceutical Corporation, Hyland Therapeutics division of Travenol Laboratories, and Cutter Biological Division of Miles Laboratories Inc. The latter two corporations are now known as Baxter and Bayer Corporations, respectively. In each case, the growth of production during the 1980s was rapid. The industry was regulated by two sources: an industry association and government. The American Blood Resources Association, founded in 1971, assists in the development of manufacturing standards and guidelines and certifies centers. The US Food and Drug Administration's Center for Biologics Evaluation and Research licenses the interstate shipment of blood products, carries out inspections, and develops standards. Its activities benefit from the advice of a committee of experts from the industry, public health, laboratory medicine and other medical disciplines.

By mid-1982 the possible link between AIDS and the blood supply was reported in the CDC's *Morbidity and Mortality Weekly Report* (Centers for Disease Control and Prevention 1982). The following year, this connection was widely known and accepted in light of the occurrence of cases in hemophiliacs living in geographically dispersed areas. That year, the CDC recommended that certain groups of people be excluded from the blood donor pool in the US. The difficulty in retooling the fast growing factor production industry was substantial. This was because (1) the science of HIV/AIDS disease was evolving, and the data were not therefore clear-cut, (2) the paid plasmapheresis donors (in other words, the majority of donors) included largely the very groups that appeared to be experiencing the highest level of infection, and (3) the group most heavily impacted by HIV, homosexual males, were watchful for discriminatory measures. The initial self-exclusion strategies, for example, did not ask donors about homosexual sexual practice for fear of discrimination.

By early 1983, both the voluntary and commercial sectors had taken some measures to reduce the participation of high risk donors in plasmapheresis. But, the Krever Commission report notes, "There is evidence, however, that the voluntary sector refused to stop collecting in high risk areas, though its blood donor recruiting officials no longer targeted high risk individuals, and that the commercial sector also continued to operate in such areas" (Krever Commission 1997 p. 748). Viral inactivation methods had been in development since the early 1970s to try to cut down on hepatitis transmission in blood. These methods are steps in the manufacturing process that are specifically targeted at killing potentially infectious viruses before the product is transfused into the patient. However, the industry leaders considered such steps part of the proprietary secrets of production and so the work towards successful strategies was not shared across the corporate competitors. In late 1984 and early 1985 the major producers had all been licensed to distribute heat-treated products to cut down on the threat of hepatitis and AIDS infection.

It was not until 1985 that a reliable laboratory test to screen for the HIV retrovirus was developed, tested and available for use. But before the diagnostic test was available, there were efforts to assess the risk to the global blood supply. The Krever Commission report states that in 1983, Dr. Michael Rodell, the vice president of Armour Pharmaceutical, outlined the potential for widespread contamination at a meeting of the blood products advisory committee of the Center for Biologics Evaluation and Research.

> Dr Rodell said that, on average, persons who were paid for their plasma had it collected forty to sixty times per year. He then estimated that, at that rate, and given the pool sizes used in the United States, four infected persons could contaminate the entire world supply of factor VIII concentrate.
>
> (Krever Commission 1997 p. 370).

That risk is determined by two factors: the number of units of blood pooled in the production of a single unit of coagulation factor and the prevalence of the infection among donors. In other words, since production for factors VIII and IX entailed the pooling of tens of thousands of units of blood from donors, the potential for a single contaminated unit to be mixed in, and to therein infect the entire lot, was large. This is a general concept and can be described in a simple binomial equation. The results of this calculation are shown below for HIV (Table 4.1); the vulnerability of this new lifesaving product to contamination was clear.

The process of pooling biological materials also is employed in the production of ground beef, gelatin and seeds. This gearing up of production, in which many individual biological units are combined into a larger whole, is going on all over the world to create the food and biological products destined for the voracious global marketplace.

As with any product, blood products can be subject to recall. A recall is initiated when the public's health is at risk due to contamination of the product. This option was available to the FDA as soon as the risk of HIV transmission in blood factors was known, or in March of 1983. An Institute of Medicine Study convened years later to review the history was critical of the absence of a cogent, strong recall policy on the part of the Food and Drug Administration.

Table 4.1   Probability that a plasma pool contains plasma contributed by one or more infected donors

Prevalence of infection among donors	Number of donors contributing to the pool						
	2,000	5,000	7,5000	10,000	20,000	50,000	100,000
1:5,000	33	63	78	86	98	100	100
1:10,000	18	39	53	63	86	99	100
1:20,000	10	22	31	39	63	92	100
1.50,000	4	10	14	18	33	63	80
1.100,000	2	5	7	10	18	39	63
1:200,000	1	2	4	5	10	22	39
1:500,000	0	1	1.5	2	4	10	18

Notes:
1. Probability is calculated as a function of the prevalence of infection in the population of donors and the number of donors contributing plasma to the pool (percent).
2. Risk calculated using the standard formula for the operation: probability that a pool contains plasma from one or more infected donors is $1 - (1 - p)^n$ where p = the prevalence of infection among donors and n = the number of contributors to the plasma pool.
Source: Krever Commission 1997.

The committee believes it is not possible to conclude that the FDA made a decision that was clearly in the interest of public health given available information as of July 19, 1983. A close reading of the data suggests that a policy, not only of automatic recall, but of delicensing AHF [antihemophiliac factor or Factor VIII and IX] concentrate until further information was available concerning its role in the transmission of AIDS might have been justified on public health grounds. This would have included, of course, a recall of all stocks of AHF then on the market and withdrawal of all AHF concentrate in the inventory of producers.

(Institute of Medicine 1995 p. 151)

By 1985, a screening test called an ELISA (enzyme-linked immunosorbent assay) was developed and had become available. ELISA technology is relatively straightforward, but the development of such a test for AIDS was not. The agent, an RNA retrovirus, was unusual in its biology as we discussed above, and this created additional challenges in the laboratory. Two groups, the US Centers for Disease Control and the French Institute Pasteur, were both striving for the holy grail of a test for HIV/AIDS. Cooperation and collaboration were less characteristic of the relationship between these efforts than competition. The ELISA that US scientists developed was ready for market by Abbott Research Laboratories after its approval in 1985. By then, the global trade in blood products had been burgeoning for some time. It is not possible to track production and export of particular products very exactly, because these data are considered proprietary. However, legal proceedings have obtained some of the information in the process of settling compensatory claims in countries all around the world, revealing that the pharmaceutical companies had indeed gone global with their products.

Tracking importation of blood with the guidance of industry data would allow us to know the rate of infection per exposure, what risk occurred with what level of exposure and over what time periods the infection occurred. In essence, we could more precisely describe the potential path of global contamination if this information were shared by industry. Most authorities recognize that thousands of hemophiliacs were infected through this route, but the percentage of those deaths that were preventable cannot be known exactly without complete information. Pharmaceutical companies were not the only ones who were reticent to talk about blood product distribution and HIV. A number of national governments are thought to have withheld or simply turned away from important information.

The Risks of Denial

China and India represent the most rapidly expanding HIV epidemics in the world today. These populous countries have been late in their organized response with prevention and control programs for HIV. The disease is extremely stigmatized, and politicians have avoided discussing the epidemic. In policy jargon, this is called a "lack of transparency" – a theme that runs through disease disclosure, and also, as we shall see, through trade negotiations. In the mid-1990s Chinese peasants were infected with HIV through donating blood and plasma (Volkow and Del Rio 2005). Blood is seen as important to health in China, and blood harvesters, called "blood heads," were in the business of reinfusing blood. After components of the blood had been harvested for processing, using unclean equipment, which had often been used on numerous donors, the donor received back his own blood. This allowed the individual to donate more frequently – a sorely needed source of cash as the rural economy in China was collapsing. Today whole villages in the interior of China are "AIDS villages." It is not known how much of the tainted blood from the "blood heads" harvesting in China was destined for the export market and in what form and how it was processed. Because the most dangerous operators were, according to the government, clandestine, information about this potential global threat is not available. What we learned from the early 1980s is that tainted blood products are central to the international spread of the epidemic. India continues to struggle with the challenge of assuring a safe blood supply in its enormous and diverse population. The persistence of unsafe blood harvesting practice is not only a very efficient means of assuring new domestic AIDS cases for a country, it can constitute a potent ongoing source of infection for unwitting vulnerable populations dependent on blood derivatives who live thousands of miles from the source of infection. Modern methods of treating blood derivatives in processing have largely mitigated this threat in legitimate, above-board commercial enterprise, but blood products from other sources can go untreated.

Japan also had been characterized by some as reluctant to be transparent about HIV. In retrospect, that characterization was unfair. The insistence by Japanese authorities that HIV was introduced in the blood supply was seen as an attempt to deny the importance of "sexual tourism" in the introduction of the virus. But the virus did in fact initially hit Japan through the blood supply. According to the World Federation of Hemophilia, the majority of Japanese hemophiliacs are thought to have been infected from 1983 to 1985 by non-heat-treated factor concentrates imported from the US. By 1985, the US was providing 90 percent of imported factor concentrates in Japan (Krever Commission 1997), and the Japanese AIDS Research Group reported that the causative agent of AIDS was found in factor VIII concentrates (Krever Commission 1997). Of 5,000 hemophiliacs in Japan, approximately 2,000 had been infected with HIV/AIDS by 1997, according to the Krever Report. The occurrence of HIV/AIDS through factor concentrates became known in Japan as "Yakugai" AIDS (meaning AIDS due to the harmful effect of medicine).

It is difficult to reconstruct the thinking and events that set the stage for HIV's journey to Japan. However, the Ministry of Health of Japan may have unwittingly assisted. In 1983, the Japanese AIDS Research Group, which was the central technical group advising the Ministry on prevention and control policy, reportedly considered a proposal from the US fractionator Travenol to allow the importation and sale of heat-treated (virus-inactivated) factor VIII in the country. At that time, a new product could receive regulatory approval without undergoing clinical trials if it could be classified as a "change to manufacturing method having no effect on the effective ingredients" (Krever Commission 1997 p. 748).

The Ministry rejected the idea, apparently mistrusting the reliability of the US FDA tests and fearing side-effects from heat-treated concentrates (Krever Commission 1997). Thus, while US reports in 1983 showed that HIV could be contracted from contaminated factor concentrates, the Ministry continued the import of non-heat-treated factor concentrates, with the stipulation that they be accompanied by a certificate that they did not contain plasma from donors at high risk of contracting HIV/AIDS. The use of imported non-heat-treated concentrates increased in 1984 and peaked in 1985. Although heat-treated factor concentrates were approved for use in 1985, because the Ministry recommended that physicians continue to prescribe non-heat-treated factor concentrates (and blood product manufacturers continued to distribute them without warning labels about the risk of AIDS), many hemophiliacs continued to use non-heat-treated concentrates through 1986. A further exacerbating problem was the fact that some health care providers neglected to inform their hemophiliac patients of their HIV infection, allowing their sexual partners to become infected. Several high ranking officials have been indicted, and a class action lawsuit has been filed against Bayer on behalf of victims in Asia and Latin America. Trials in the "Yakugai AIDS" scandal in Japan continued through 2004.

The Risk for the Very Poor

In the Americas, two countries that were not in the trading community because of political embargoes, Cuba and Nicaragua, were as a result spared the sudden incursion of HIV infection into their populations of hemophiliacs. They remained relatively HIV-free during the mid-1980s. In the case of Cuba, the first HIV infection detected was in a returning veteran of the Angola conflict. Sanitaria were set up and HIV positive people were forcibly hospitalized. The sanitaria effort may have had some effect in limiting HIV, but the evidence suggests that being off the trade route for blood products from the US in the 1980s also had a major protective effect.

But other nations that have not been major players in global trade have suffered from the spread of HIV through blood transfusions nonetheless. Their plights resulted not from international trade in tainted blood products but from poverty. In Romania in the early 1990s a large AIDS outbreak at an orphanage was tracked to blood transfusions given to boost nutrition in a setting of heartbreaking hunger. The outbreak, arguably the largest iatrogenic (caused by medical intervention) outbreak in the history of the AIDS epidemic, was uncovered through the application of the new ELISA test to the population. A seroprevalence of 11 percent was found in the first group of children under five tested in large-scale testing of the Romanian population by the Romanian Institute of Virology. This was many times higher than the rate of infection seen in other age groups. Soon it became apparent that institutionalized children were at particular risk. Byzantine policies had imposed a pronatalist agenda on the people of that very poor nation, resulting in the birth of many unplanned and unaffordable infants. Parents gave up their extra children for care by the state. These children were placed in large state orphanages, but the state was unable to feed them adequately. Blood transfusions were used to stave off anemia, the result of dietary deficiencies. The state facilities at that time often used glass and metal injection equipment that was not sterilized between use on individual residents. The result was an efficient transmission of HIV, which had been detected five years earlier in the country, probably entering through its busy port on the Black Sea. Thus the application of new surveillance technologies revealed a hidden but disastrous infection with the new virus.

In Zaire, children also suffer from anemia. In this setting, an old scourge of humankind, falciparum malaria, is the cause. Again, microtransfusion to prevent the debilitating anemia was used. Again, the present and circulating HIV virus was a passenger in the process of transfusion. In Africa, sexual transmission is the major mode of HIV spread, however injections and transfusions also play a part. The problems in very poor countries with HIV transmission by injection or blood transfusion have little to do with the global trading system, with the possible exception of recent events in middle China. Nonetheless, these outbreaks underline the risk from a route that should not persist given the technologies in our hands today.

New Variant Creutzfeldt-Jakob Disease (nvCJD) – A Complicated Name, an Emerging Threat

As with the spread of HIV through blood products, the emergence and dissemination of new variant Creutzfeldt-Jakob Disease (nvCJD), through beef products was due in part to global trade pressures and opportunities and in part to a lack of detection and scientific understanding of the disease. Similar to HIV/AIDS, nvCJD has a long incubation period, estimated at up to 15 to 30 years (Ghani, Ferguson et al. 2003), adding to the detection challenge. The incubation period of Bovine Spongiform Encephalopathy, the related disease in cattle, is also in the order of years, further complicating interventions (Wells, Scott et al. 1987).

In 1986, cows in the herds of the UK began to drop. BSE, or "mad cow" disease, was spreading from farm to farm. Eventually, it became evident that the disease was related to the consumption of meat and bone meal (MBM) products derived from the slaughtering process, which had recently changed. Since World War II, feeding practices in the UK for cattle and dairy cows had included adding bits of other animal protein to the feed. This practice is thought to have arisen when soybean availability and price became prohibitive during the war. The Far East, a major producing region for soybeans, was not able to export during that global conflict. British herders began to recycle bits of sheep and other animals to supplement the protein content – a role previously served by soybeans.

So what changed? During the 1970s and 1980s, three trends came into play in the UK. First, energy became more expensive. The process of slaughter and rendering cattle had traditionally included an energy-gobbling step called a solvent and extraction procedure. After all the edible or usable cuts of meat were removed, the carcass essentially was cooked at very high temperatures with a solvent that takes the remaining animal and renders it so that it can be further processed into the end products of bone meal and tallow. This required very high sustained temperatures, and the two products, bone meal and tallow, were used in other manufacture. However, the market for tallow, which is similar to wax, had been waning for decades. Tallow candles are a thing of the nineteenth century, and the waxy tallow, which includes animal protein, became increasingly a product for disposal rather than recycling. Bone meal, on the other hand, remained a popular protein supplement in animal feed, as well as a product used in other manufacturing processes, and even in modern fertilizers. The change in the marketability of the rendering products, coupled with the mounting costs of the energy required to produce those products, led to a shortcut of sorts. In the UK, the step of solvent and extraction was changed – temperatures were lowered and the production of tallow through extensive extraction was largely curtailed. An initial theory was that something in the change of rendering practice had allowed the TSE agent scrapie to enter the bone meal supplementation of beef and cause infection. Later, it become evident that the BSE agent probably had always been present to some degree and that unlike with the earlier cooking process, with the new cold vacuum extraction method, the resulting meat and bone meal was not effectively disinfected for prions. (For more on the changes in rendering and the market forces behind them, see Chapter 6.) Meanwhile, in 1989, the first banning of mixing "offal" (various bits of the slaughtered animal unfit for human consumption) from slaughter into feed for animals or humans was put into place in the UK to contain the epidemic.

At the time of these changes, veterinary science had already described a number of diseases similar to mad cow disease in a variety of other animals. These diseases, collectively known as the Transmissible Spongiform Encephalopathies, or TSEs, affect a broad spectrum of vertebrates including monkeys, mink, deer, and elk. A similar but very rare human disease called kuru in New Guinea is only found in groups in the Highlands who historically practiced cannibalism. The fatal neurological disease was found primarily among the women who were accorded the brain of the deceased, and was related to the consumption of human brain tissue from an infected individual. This practice was arrested decades ago and the disease kuru disappeared. Research into how these diseases were related, how they were transmitted and how they were caused was in the early stages when BSE emerged. One such disease, scrapie, had been known for centuries to sheepherders. This form of TSE is named for a symptom it causes in sheep, which is the vigorous and damaging rubbing the animals do prior to their demise. Scrapie had long been known clinically but what caused scrapie had not been known. It fell, as did the other TSEs, into a group of diseases called "slow virus diseases," which reflected how they appeared to scientists. They looked infectious, but very slowly infectious with long periods of time from infection to illness, and a relatively protracted course of illness.

Thus in the 1970s and 1980s researchers were seeking to close the science gap in the area of neurological degenerative diseases of animals. In 1966, the idea was first advanced that the unit of TSE transmission was a specific protein whose folding was unusual and caused disease (Alper, Haig et al. 1966). In the late 1970s, this line of hypothesis was further pursued and in 1982 neuroscientist Stanley B. Prusiner coined the term "prion" or "proteinaceous infectious particle." The "prion hypothesis" is now the central understanding of how these diseases are transmitted and cause disease, but that understanding remains very controversial and incomplete. The hypothesis turns our understanding of how infection can occur on its head in that it does not rely on the introduction of genetic material from the infectious agent to the host. We do not know how the infectious proteins become infectious, or why. It seems that a genetic trait in about 40 percent of people make them susceptible to nvCJD, and there are no cases in people without this trait, methionine homozygous. Thus just as retroviruses were relatively unknown at the dawning of the HIV epidemic, so prions have been at the dawning of the nvCJD crisis.

The large outbreak of BSE in the UK in 1986 prompted further research. The UK has generally excellent surveillance of disease of both humans and animals, and the toll of BSE was closely counted. Fortunately the outbreak in cattle also spurred prudent surveillance by the British public health authorities of the human population to detect if the consumption of cattle would have deleterious effects. In 1997, 11 years after the onset of the BSE epidemic in the UK, the first cluster of new variant Creutzfeldt-Jakob disease cases in humans were noted there. Twenty one cases of this rare disease were reported in young people in three years. Creutzfeldt-Jakob disease, the most common type of human TSE, was first described in the 1920s. It is responsible for about one death per million per year, and occurs in older adults (average age of onset is 60). The course of the disease is about four months from diagnosis to death, and includes a variety of symptoms of brain dysfunction, including psychological, visual and intellectual changes. The patient suffers uncontrollable muscle movements which typically include violent jerking. The "brain tracing" or EEG of the patient is typical; diagnosis can only be confirmed through brain biopsy or postmortem examination of the brain. There is no therapy. The new cluster of cases reported in the United Kingdom, a variation ("new variant") of Creutzfeldt-Jakob, were remarkable because they all occurred in people less than 50 years old. The clinical course was 14 months, not four months. Unfortunately all of the cases were fatal. All 21 had exposure to potentially infected beef products in the 1980s before the risk of contamination was known.

The science of making the link between the mad cow disease of the 1980s and the cluster of new variant CJD in the 1990s was complex. The key methodology in understanding the linkage between beef exposure and illness has been the work-horse of epidemiology, the case control study. In these studies, the exposures of people who have a disease are compared to the exposures of people who do not to determine what factors may be associated with developing the illness. (For more details on case control studies, see Chapter 7.) The studies, which cover observations as far back as 1964, gradually brought into focus the characteristics of CJD, a longstanding, well-described disease of humans, as well as the association between consumption of beef in the years of the BSE epidemic and the subsequent occurrence of nvCJD, the newer illness in younger people. Hillier and Salmon (2000) summarized these findings in a recent report (see Table 4.2).

The case studies are an example of trying to track the emergence of a new illness against the background of a known, although quite rare disease; it illustrates how epidemiologists go about solving the puzzles presented when the nature of an infection fundamentally changes. CJD normally is at once the most common TSE of humans, and also quite rare. Its sporadic incidence rate of occurrence is between 0.06 and 1.06 cases per million population. Thus if one were watching a population of one million people (the approximate size of the city of Seattle) for one year, one

Table 4.2   Case control methods for BSE studies

Study	n	Case selection	Control selection and method of information collection
1. Bobowick *et al.*, USA, 1973	38	Biopsy- or autopsy-proven cases diagnosed since 1966 were requested by writing to all members of American Association Neuropathologists in USA and Canada plus all cases referred to NINDS	Nearest relative of the deceased asked to participate in structured interview and asked to select friend of the patient of the same age and sex to serve as control. All families visited in their home by same doctor and nurse
2. Kondo *et al.*, Japan, 1982	60	902 neurological clinics asked to report cases between 1975–7. Criteria of Masters used. Only definite and probable cases included. Study area: all Japan	Nearest relative of the deceased asked to participate in structured interview and asked to introduce a neighbour of the same age and sex as the patient. When necessary public health personnel allowed to serve as 'neighbour'
3. Kondo, Japan, 1985	88	CJD cases retrieved from annual or pathological autopsies in Japan, 1964–1978	From the same register autopsies from craniocervical injuries, myocardial infarction and pulmonary tuberculosis were selected as controls. Recorded information compared
4. Davanipour *et al.*, USA, 1985	26	Cases ascertained from records submitted to the Laboratory of Central Nervous System Studies between 1970–1981. Study restricted to Pennsylvania and surrounding mid-Atlantic states	Two control groups were selected. Hospital controls matched for age and sex were selected by writing to medical record departments. Ten case notes of people admitted at the time of the patients admission were selected. Random number tables were used to select one of these cases. The other control group was family members. A questionnaire was administered by telephone
5. Harries-Jones *et al.*, UK, 1988	92	Cases obtained from regional neurological centres in England and Wales by direct referral after repeated written requests for cases. In addition copies of all death certificates on which CJD or spongiform encephalopathy were mentioned were obtained from the Office of Population Censuses and Surveys (OPCS)	Two groups of hospital controls were selected by questioning ward staff and accepting the first proffered matched subject. One control had a 'neurological' diagnosis different from CJD and the other a non-neurological 'medical' diagnosis
6. van Duijn *et al.*, Europe, 1998	405	Cases were obtained from the European national registers (19) which had been compiled by targeting professional groups including neurologists, neurophysiologists and neuropathologists and asking for direct referrals	Control participants were recruited from the hospital where the patient who had CJD had been diagnosed. Data was collected by a structured interview. Next of kin of the control was interviewed wherever possible
7. The National CJD, Surveillance Unit, UK, 1990, ongoing	473	Cases were obtained from direct referral by hospital physicians, neurologists, neuropathologists and neurophysiologists.	An age- and sex-matched hospital control was selected. Where possible the relative of the control was interviewed.
8. Collins, Australia, 1999	241	Cases were obtained from the Australian CJD registry 1970–1993 retrospectively and from 1993–1997 prospectively.	For every case, three community controls were recruited and interviewed through a random dialling telephone survey and data collected using a questionnaire.

Source: Hillier and Salmon 2000.

would probably see at most a single case of this illness. Over two years one would expect to see one case occur. Most of these cases would occur in people over the age of 65.

The actual structure of the case control studies examined in the Hillier report varied. One issue with studies of devastating illness such as nvCJD is recall regarding past exposures. Given the fatal nature of the illness, the person who had the disease – the case – generally was not available for interview. So the studies instead relied on information collected by health providers or interviews with close relatives to determine the cases' exposures. The studies also faced challenges with the controls, or unaffected people included for comparison. First of all, unlike the cases, they were available to be interviewed directly, which may mean their information about exposures is more accurate or at least different from that received from the sources interviewed for the cases. Some studies address this potential problem by using the same source regardless of the subjects' availability, for instance using doctors' records for information on both cases and controls. Another challenge is selecting cases and controls that are demographically comparable but not too similar. From a study design point of view, the danger is that if controls are too closely associated with the case, they might not be different enough to distinguish important exposures related to the illness. For example, if all of the family members worked on a dairy farm and ate beef regularly but, since the disease is quite rare, only one person (the case) fell ill, it would be hard to define what was different in the diet of the various family members. On the other hand, if the controls are from a very remote place, they might have very different exposures in their environments and diets, and that also could obscure a risk factor.

Once the information on cases and controls is gathered, imperfect as it may be, statistics are used to analyze the information and sort out chance associations between exposures and illnesses from those that are more likely to be real, or significant. The stakes are huge in this work. If in fact there is an association between eating certain things and illness, it carries enormous implications, as we will see with nvCJD. The results of the extensive case control studies are shown in Table 4.3.

The key observation is the odds ratio, or the likelihood of getting the disease if you have a certain exposure compared to the likelihood if you do not have that exposure. Basically if there is an increased risk of the illness being linked to an exposure, the odds ratio goes up. An odds ratio of one means that all is equal, there is no increased risk. An odds ratio of less than one means that the exposure is actually associated with a lower risk of disease – and may even protect against the disease. Another critical value in these studies is the "p-value," which measures the possibility that chance alone, rather than a true association, accounts for the study results. A p-value of 0.05 means that there is less than a 5 percent probability that chance alone explains the observation.

Looking at the table of findings in Table 4.3, the highest odds ratios and lowest p-values are seen for long animal exposure; consumption of animal, including weekly consumption of beef; and exposure to other animals such as squirrel, monkey, deer and rabbit. The epidemiologic studies do not stand alone, but further work in the laboratory in the UK has convincingly demonstrated that the agent that causes BSE is linked as well to nvCJD. It is thought that the agent lives within the infected animal's neurological tissue, so eating brain or nerve tissue from infected cows is risky. In terms of the slaughter procedure we talked about earlier, the nerve and brain tissue is usually removed during carcass processing, but techniques were imperfect and it has been well demonstrated that meat often contained such material. The importance of this risk, eating beef when BSE was affecting food animals, has also been emphasized in an ongoing case control study being carried out by The National Creutzfeldt-Jakob Disease Surveillance Unit in the UK.

When the linkage between British beef and nvCJD was published in 1998, a tsunami hit the British beef industry. The impact of the outbreak was devastating economically, with whole herds sacrificed when a single case of mad cow disease was detected on a farm. It is now estimated that more than 200,000 potentially infectious cattle were slaughtered and entered the food chain during the epidemic years. Trading partners began filing "urgent notifications" with the World Trade Organization advising that they would be embargoing beef and beef products of all sorts from the UK. On the WTO notification forms, there are a number of rationales a notifying country can give to justify urgent trade limits. One of these is protection from human disease, and this rationale was the most frequently cited in the notifications for blocking beef products related to BSE in the UK. (For more on the notification system, see Chapter 8.) My colleagues and I did a careful cost analysis to quantify the actual dollar amount of the UK's lost trade in beef in the year 2000 (Figure 4.1).

Table 4.3   Significant findings from BSE case control studies

Exposure	Study (from Table 3)	Odds ratio, 95% CI	P
Dietary—fish			
Raw Seafood	1	4.02 (1.3 12.9)*	<0.05*
Raw oyster/clam	4	3.3	<0.10**
Dietary—meats			
Roast lamb	4	3.6	<0.10**
Roast/smoked pork	4	2.6	<0.10**
Scrapple	4	4.0	<0.10**
Pork chops (high vs. never)	4	6.6	<0.10**
Ham (deli/canned)	4	12.1	<0.10**
Liver (ever vs. never)	4	5.9	<0.10**
Meat (rare vs. well done)	4	8.0	<0.10**
Raw meat	6	1.57 (1.1–2.2)	0.05*
Brain	6	1.63 (0.9–2.9)	0.1*
Beef (weekly)	7	2.37 (1.2–4.7)	0.01
Veal	7	1.69 (1.1–2.8)	0.005
Brain	7	3.1 (1.4–6.9)	0.005
Venison	7	7.9 (1.8–34.9)	<0.005
Zoonotic: hobbies and sports			
Involving fish	4	4.5 (1.6-)***	<0.005
Involving squirrel, skunk	4	4.4 (0.9-)***	<0.10
Deer (frequent vs. none)	4	6.8 (1.1-)	<0.05***
Rabbit (frequent vs. none)	4	6.0 (1.0)	<0.05***
Zoonotic: occupational			
Ever lived or worked on a farm or market garden, or employed in an abattoir or butcher	8	2.6 (1.8–3.7)	<0.001
Animal exposure (long vs. none)	4	*8.6 (1.8-)*	*0.001*
Deer, monkey, squirrel	4	*9.0 (0.9-)*	*< 0.005****
Cow (male exposure)	4	*5.7 (0.8-)*	*< 0.10****
Zoonotic: pet exposure			
Keeping cats	5	2.0 (1.2–3.6)	<0.01
Pets other than cats and dogs	5	4.4 (1.5–12.7)	<0.01
Ferret contact	5	2.1 91.0–4.2)	0.05 .
Squirrel	4	*12.3 (1.1-)*	*<0.05****
Mink contact	5	*8.6 (0.9 –77.9)*	*0.08*
Zoonotic: animal product exposure			
Frequent exposure to leather products	6	1.9 (1.1–3.3)	<0.05*
Exposure to fertilizer containing hoof and horn	6	2.3 (1.3–3.9)	<0.005*
'Iatrogenic '			
Surgical operation	2/3	3.48 (1.3–9.4)	<0.01
Physical injury	2/3	2.53 (1.0–6.4)	<0.05
Organ resection	2/3	2.78 (1.0–6.5)*	Fishers exact, <0.05
Head-face-neck trauma or operation	4	3.5 (1.0–13.5)*	<0.05
Other trauma	4	4.0 (1.2–14.6)*	<0.01
Suture	4	2.9 (0.9–9.9)*	<0.10
Zoster in adult life	5	2.6 (2.4-)	<0.005
Dementia in family	5	3.6 (1.8–7.1)	<0.0005
Surgical procedures (×2)	8	1.7 (1.0–2.7)	<0.05
Surgical procedures (×3)	8	2.1 (1.3–3.4)	<0.005
Tonometry (within 2 years of disease onset)	4	*9.2 (1.2–424)*	*Fishers exact, 0.02**
Cataract/eye surgery	8	*6.1 (3.2–11.9)*	*< 0.001*
Carpal tunnel surgery	8	*9.2 (2.5–34.1)*	*0.001*

Notes: Odds ratios are for 'case vs. all controls' unless specified. Cases where OR>5 are shown in italics. *OR and *p* value calculated from original data using StatCalc (EpiInfo 6 version 6.04a), **OR and *p* provided in original data but without sufficient data to calculate CI. ***OR, *p* and lower limit of 95% CI provided in original paper, but insufficient data provided to calculate upper limit.
Source: Hillier and Salmon 2000.

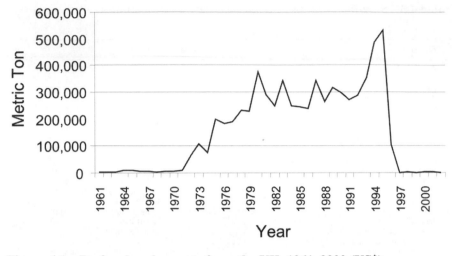

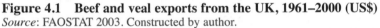

Figure 4.1   Beef and veal exports from the UK, 1961–2000 (US$)
Source: FAOSTAT 2003. Constructed by author.

We were able to use a trade dataset to actually look product by product at what did *not* get shipped to which importing country. Our minimal estimate of lost exports for the UK in 2000 is $5.6 billion. Meanwhile, beef exporters from other nations saw a rise of trade of $1.5 billion. Thus, in economic terms, making the link between consumption of British beef product during the BSE epidemic and human nvCJD was costly indeed. When the beef epidemic is superimposed on the human epidemic, we can see more easily the time course and relation between the two (Figure 4.2).

Since the epidemic in the UK, there has been a disturbing coda in France, which maintained a trade embargo on British beef products long after other European Union countries had lifted theirs. It has since been discovered that France apparently failed to recognize or report a major outbreak of BSE that occurred within its own borders during the 1980s and 1990s. According to a recent report, a passive surveillance system put into place by the French government in the 1980s counted only 103 cases of BSE, while researchers now believe there were more than 300,000 cattle affected (Supervie and Costagliola 2004). This enormously complicates the picture of BSE and nvCJD. France has recently reported its seventh victim of nvCJD. The irony of blocking allegedly risky goods from abroad while a major domestic epidemic of BSE was underway is a grim one. Unraveling the story of BSE and identifying where exposure to potentially risky feed and animal products has occurred elsewhere in the global trading marketplace has, with the addition of the French epidemic, become enormously more complex. Again, a lack of awareness and transparency has trumped the best prevention and control efforts of science.

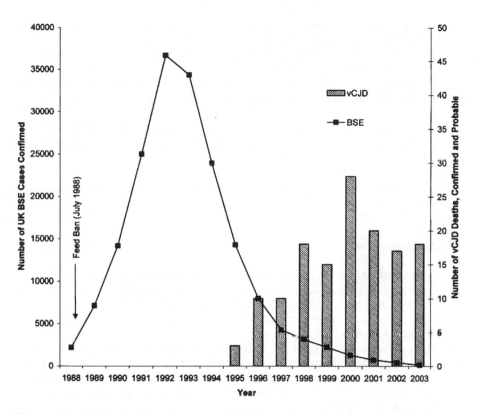

Figure 4.2   Total confirmed cases of BSE in cattle and of human variant Creutzfeldt-Jakob disease (vCJD), UK, 1988–August 2003
Source: Beisel and Morens 2004.

Unknown, Far-flung Hazards

While they are very different diseases, HIV and nvCJD share several important similarities in the ways that they entered into and spread through the global marketplace.

1. Both were inadvertently introduced into products as a result of innovations designed to respond to the pressures and opportunities of international trade. In each case, those innovations involved using untested processes on large quantities of material from animal (vertebrate) sources. In the case of HIV, the pooling of many units of blood to create one unit of factor VIII derivative increased risk. In the case of BSE the longstanding practice of pooling was not the risky step; it was the change in the processing of the rendering itself which probably led to the risk.
2. HIV and nvCJD both involve infectious agents that were largely unknown when

they began to cause disease in humans, and testing for safety of processing of product was therefore necessarily uninformed by the risk of disease.
3. The diseases were broadly transmitted around the globe through the international trading of products.
4. And finally, the eventual epidemics they caused have had extremely high costs in terms of human lives and suffering and economic loss.

Both of these tragic episodes were unknown hazards that industry and trade bumped into in the night. Science was not in a position to inform decision makers about the risks involved in manufacture and distribution of product. In later chapters we will consider if this always has to be the case or if there are new ways of addressing such threats that can increase our safety as trade and development advance.

Study Questions

1. What characteristics of HIV/AIDS infection are analogous to new variant Creutzfeldt-Jakob disease in humans? How do these characteristics play into the global transmission of these infections?
2. How did innovation in product manufacturing play into the globalization of these infections?
3. Does science have the answers to prevent similar infections?
4. What were the commercial issues raised in factor VIII and IX sales and marketing by the emergence of HIV/AIDS in the global blood supply? For consumers? For blood banks? For pharmaceutical manufacturers? For governments?

Chapter 5

The Global Express and Intentional Harm

On a Monday afternoon, a traveler collapses at the Vancouver Airport in British Columbia with a high fever. Responding emergency workers advise that the man has a suspicious looking rash and a quarantine officer issues an international alert. The man is hospitalized with a diagnosis of meningococcemia, a dangerous, contagious bloodstream infection, and his companion and other travelers are detained in the customs and immigration waiting area. Eventually, medical authorities conclude that the sick man in fact has highly infectious smallpox. Soon, the man's companion becomes ill and confesses that they are members of a terrorist group dedicated to the fall of capitalism who have infected themselves with smallpox and dispersed to 14 target countries just as their infectivity is peaking. Canadian authorities post another international alert and a frenzy of communications ensues among affected countries. Health authorities scramble to find contact numbers for their overseas counterparts. A key computer server at Health Canada crashes for four hours, blacking out electronic communication. French authorities exhaust their supply of English-speakers as the 48-hour crisis unfolds. In Italy, teleconferencing capabilities falter.

While participating nations deemed the so-called "Global Mercury" drill a success, they also acknowledged that the exercise conducted in September 2003 highlighted significant vulnerabilities in the international response to bioterrorism, chief among them communications infrastructure and cross-border coordination. As the various affected nations hustled to tamp down the outbreak in their countries, an international strategy failed to emerge. The exercise, designed with meticulous attention to biological plausibility, highlighted that work remains in preparing for the possibility of bioterrorism – that is, the use of infectious microorganisms to attack humans, plants or animals (World Health Organization 2004). While Mother Nature is providing ample challenges to global public health in anticipating, detecting, and controlling outbreaks of new infectious diseases, intentional outbreaks caused by deliberate human acts of aggression also have increasingly become an area of concern. This chapter will review that threat.

The Global Mercury exercise, which focused on communications capacities, is one of a handful of bioterrrorism preparedness drills organized in response to growing concerns about the prospects of such an attack. In the "Dark Winter" scenario, conducted in June 2001, former US officials grappled with a covert smallpox attack that began in Oklahoma and spread rapidly. By the end of the drill, which simulated a two-week period, 16,000 cases of smallpox had been reported in 25 states and suspected cases were reported in 10 additional countries. Vaccines were in short supply, food was running out and Canada and Mexico had closed their borders to the US (O'Toole, Mair et al. 2002). In the May 2000 "TOPOFF" exercise, US health officials struggled with a plague epidemic unleashed in Denver, Colorado. At the end of the tabletop exercise, which simulated four days, thousands of people had contracted pneumonic plague and death estimates ranged from 950 to 2,000. Health care facilities were beyond capacity, stores were closed and civil unrest was simmering. One participant concluded,

> Many previous bioterrorism exercises dealt with non-contagious diseases. It is just beginning to dawn on us how dramatically different this was as the exercise ended. It terminated arbitrarily and many issues were left unresolved. It is not clear what would have happened if it had gone on ... There were ominous signs at the end of the exercise. Disease had already spread to other states and counties. Competition between cities for the NPS [National Pharmaceutical Stockpile] has already broken out. It had all of the [characteristics] of an epidemic out of control.
>
> (Inglesby, Grossman et al. 2001 p. 443)

As evolving scientific and political developments have conspired to make bioterrorism a greater possibility, health and emergency officials increasingly have scrutinized national and international capacities to handle such an event, and repeatedly concluded that current capabilities and preparedness plans come up short.

After the 9/11 attacks on New York's World Trade Center, few remain sanguine about the potential of terrorist attacks. Still, the notion of bioterrorism for many remains the stuff of science fiction novels – terrifying, hideous, and highly unlikely. But biological attacks, in fact, have a long history, dating at least from the 14th century, when the bodies of people with bubonic plague were essentially transformed into weapons as they were vaulted at the enemy, to the 21st century, when anthrax-dusted missives made their way around the northeastern US in the months after 9/11. Over the years, armies, terrorists and dissidents have employed biological agents to taint water and food sources, damage livestock and crops and attack humans directly (see Table 5.1).

The Geneva Protocol of 1925, signed by 108 nations, banned bacteriological weapons for use in warfare, but did not prohibit research and development, and World War II spurred more of both. The US, which did not ratify the treaty for 50 years, launched an offensive biological weapons research and development program in 1942, conducting experiments with anthrax and Brucella (Christopher, Cieslak et al. 1997). The program expanded during the Korean War in the early 1950s and experimentation with military and civilian volunteers began in 1955 (Christopher, Cieslak et al. 1997). Between 1949 and 1968, secret experiments testing aerosolized agents were conducted in a handful of US cities, provoking public health concerns when the experiments came to light in the 1970s (Office of the Surgeon General 1997) (see Table 5.2).

During the Cold War, the US and Soviet Union traded accusations regarding biological weapons use and international concern continued to grow over the menace of biological warfare. Ongoing international disarmament discussions raised the prospect of destroying biological stashes, but it was not until the issue was

Table 5.1 Selected biological warfare and terrorism incidents in history

Kaffa (today Feodosiya, Ukraine) 1346	Attacking Tatars catapulted bodies of bubonic plague victims over the walls of Black Sea port town of Kaffa.
Fort Pitt (Pittsburgh) 1763	During the French and Indian war, British Lord Jeffrey Amherst dispatched smallpox-laden blankets to the Native Americans, who had little previous exposure or immunity.
World War I	Evidence suggests Germany exported contaminated livestock and animal feed through neutral countries to the Allies.
World War II	The Japanese army infected prisoners in Manchuria with biological agents and the Nazis infected prisoners in Germany. The British experimented with anthrax on Gruinard Island off the coast of Scotland.
Chicago, Illinois 1972	Members of the "Order of the Rising Sun" were arrested for possessing typhoid bacterial cultures they allegedly planned to use to contaminate water supplies.
Dalles, Oregon 1986	Rajneesh cult members plotting to influence election results spiked salad bars in local restaurants with *Salmonella*, poisoning more than 750 people.
Tokyo, Japan 1990–1995	Aum Shinrikyo cult members launch a series of failed attacks in public places with aerosolized botulism and anthrax spores.
Washington, DC; New Jersey; New York 2001	Anthrax-laced letters infect 23 people and kill five in the wake of the September 11 attacks. Thousands of others are placed on antibiotics as a precaution, and US Postal Service and Congressional offices are closed.

Table 5.2 Biological agents weaponized and stockpiled by the US military (destroyed 1971–1973)

Lethal agents*
  Bacillus anthracis
  Botulinum toxin
  Francisella tularensis
Incapacitating agents*
  Brucella suis
  Coxiella burnetii
  Staphylococcal enterotoxin B
  Venezuelan equine encephalitis virus
Anticrop agents†
  Rice blast
  Rye stem rust
  Wheat stem rust

---

*Weaponized
†Stockpiled, but not weaponized

Source: Christopher 1997.

untethered from chemical weapons that it gained traction. In 1972, the US, USSR and 101 other nations signed the Biological Weapons Convention (BWC) prohibiting the production, stockpiling and acquisition of such weapons. The Convention was ratified three years later. While the treaty has survived three decades, concerns over compliance have been a chronic issue. Questions have persisted, for instance, about the degree to which Russia has been open about its past bioweapons programs. Before it disbanded, the Soviet Union had a vast biological weapons research network – at one time encompassing more than 200 field offices and employing 60,000 people – and scientists trained in the discipline remain scattered throughout the former republic, along with stores of dangerous pathogens (Chaffee, Conway-Welch et al. 2001; Potter 2004). In 1979, at least 66 civilians in Sverdlovsk, Russia (now Yekaterinburg) died after the accidental release of anthrax spores from the Soviet Institute of Microbiology and Virology. The Soviets initially denied the incident was tied to biological weapons research, but in 1992 Russian President Boris Yeltsin acknowledged the link. Today, US officials believe more than a dozen countries are attempting to develop biological weapons (Bolton 2002). The US accused Iraq and North Korea of BWC violations in 2001 and Cuba in 2002.

Biological weapons possession is difficult to police. Unlike more traditional weapons that require huge storage and production facilities, biological weapons capable of significant damage require relatively little of either. Further complicating the matter is the fact that many of the agents used to produce biological weapons also can be used for legitimate purposes, such as vaccine development, disease investigation and biodefense, which is allowed under the BWC treaty. Member states have grappled with ways to make compliance verifiable, from impromptu inspections to required reporting of "dual-capable" facilities, or those that can produce both legal and illegal biological products. The US has balked at some of the proposed provisions, however, claiming that they would be ineffective and intrude on the privacy of pharmaceutical and biotech research companies. The issue has been tabled until the treaty is up for review in 2006.

Residual Cold War stockpiles and nation states with biological weapons represent only part of the problem. Rivaling concerns of biowarfare waged among nations is the prospect of bioterrorism attacks by individuals and groups. Biological weapon development is not limited to sophisticated laboratories. In fact, some agents are available in nature, such as anthrax and botulism, or possible to cultivate in basement laboratories. The same equipment used to brew beer or to spray pesticides on crops could serve to manufacture and deploy biological weapons (Office of the Surgeon General 1997). In its 2004 report, *Public health response to biological and chemical weapons*, the World Health Organization noted that since its earlier report on the subject in 1970, "the accessibility of biological agents on a militarily significant scale has been substantially increased by advances in industrial microbiology and its greater use throughout the world" (World Health Organization 2004 p. 2). The report also cited the advent of genetic modification techniques in recent decades that potentially enable the creation of new biological agents. Similarly, the British Medical Association published a 2004 report urging prompt action to curtail the development of biological and genetic weapons. The report, *Biotechnology, Weapons and Humanity II*, warned of the potential development of imitation and synthetic viruses that could defy current medical treatments and even biological weapons that could target certain ethnic groups (British Medical Association 2004). While a new bioweapon could be developed with current technology in two to three years, it would take eight to 10 years to develop a drug or vaccine to combat that agent (Institute of Medicine 2001; Knobler, Mahmoud et al. 2001).

Biological agents can be deployed through ordinary, easily accessible channels. As earlier chapters have discussed, depending on their individual properties, pathogens can be conveyed via contaminated tanks and processing equipment; in blood and on surgical instruments; in soil, water and food. They can be passed on by infected travelers, animals or insects, or scattered through the air (Venkatesh and Memish 2003). With ever more goods and people moving further and faster, distribution channels are only enhanced. Moreover, relatively small amounts of biological agents can wreak significant damage. A single plane drop of 50kg of aerosolized anthrax could kill and injure hundreds of thousands of people (Office of the Surgeon General 1997). But the physical toll represents only a portion of the damage. A 2003 Institute of Medicine (IOM) report concluded that given the unpredictable and malicious nature of terrorism, an attack, or even the threat of one, "will have psychological consequences for a major portion of the population" (Stith Butler, Panzer et al. 2003 p. 5). The handful of anthrax attacks in the US after 9/11 caused significant disruption, closing Congress, postal facilities and businesses, depressing the stock market and generating a run on antibiotics as panicky Americans attempted to stock their medicine cabinets. The IOM report, *Preparing for the Psychological Consequences of Terrorism: A Public Health Strategy*, concludes that the current US public health infrastructure is unprepared to address the psychological needs of the population in the event of ongoing threats of terrorism.

Despite these alarming assessments, acquiring and disseminating just the right agent at the right time and place remains a complicated endeavor that few would desire to or attempt to undertake, much less manage to accomplish. Working with biological agents is risky for potential attackers as well as their targets, and is fraught with unpredictability due to uncontrollable environmental circumstances and varying, sometimes lengthy, incubation periods (Office of the Surgeon General 1997). In fact, most reported biological incidents to date involving terrorist groups or individuals have been hoaxes. According to the Center for Nonproliferation Studies, hoaxes accounted for all the 70 reported biological weapon attacks by "non-state actors" in 2002, 600 of 607 in 2001, and 22 of 26 in 2000 (Turnbull and Abhayaratne 2003).

Assessing the Risk

The threat of a biological attack varies considerably based on the properties of the agent used and the environment in which it is released. Biological weapons targeting humans have at least four routes of potential entry:

- inhalation
- ingestion
- injection
- absorption.

Some agents, such as anthrax, can attack through more than one route, with decidedly different results. For instance, while anthrax absorbed through the skin is sometimes fatal, inhaled anthrax is almost always fatal. In assessing the danger of particular pathogens as potential bioterrorism weapons, health officials consider the following characteristics to determine what kind of damage they might inflict – both physically and psychologically:

- Availability – how easy or difficult is it to obtain or cultivate the pathogen?
- Transmissibility – how does the agent spread? Can a small amount go a long way?
- Stability – is the pathogen a hardy one that can readily survive and spread in the environment?
- Lethality or virulence – how much harm will the agent wreak on people, animals, crops?
- Pathogenicity – what portion of people exposed to the agent develop the disease?
- Incubation period – how long after exposure does the disease surface?
- Fear factor – how much alarm will the infection generate?

Public health, veterinarian and agricultural experts all have identified agents of greatest concern to their various disciplines. These "A" lists serve to focus detection and response strategies so they are better prepared in the event of an attack. US efforts have focused on the CDC's "Category A" Agents, or those that the CDC has identified as posing the greatest concern for biological attacks on humans (see Table 5.3).

Table 5.3   CDC "Category A" Agents

Agent	Transmission	Symptoms, incubation, fatality rates	Prevention/ treatment methods	Important features
Anthrax (*Bacillus anthracis*) Gram-positive, encapsulated, spore-forming, nonmotile rod	Inhalation, ingestion or cutaneous (95%) Person-to-person rare	Incubation: 1–6 days depending on mode of exposure Symptoms: vary by exposure; can include fever, acute respiratory distress, skin ulcers, nausea, vomiting Case fatality rate: skin exposure rarely fatal; inhalational almost always fatal	Vaccines, antibiotics, antitoxins	Very stable Previously used as a weapon – proven risk
Botulism (*Clostridium botulinum toxin*) Spore-forming obligate anaerobic bacillus	Ingestion in food, beverages; inhalation No person-to-person	Incubation: 12 hours to several days Symptoms: double or blurred vision, drooping eyelids, slurred speech, difficulty swallowing, muscle weakness and ultimately paralysis descending from the shoulders Case fatality rate: with treatment, 5%–10% fatal	Antitoxins, vaccine under development	Easy to produce and transport Highly potent and lethal

Plague (*Yersinia pestis*) Bubonic, Septicaemic, Pneumonic Bacillus	Infected vectors such as fleas; direct contact; inhalation; and rarely, ingestion	Incubation: 1 to 4 days Symptoms: fever, chills, headache bubonic (most common) includes swollen lymph nodes; primary pneumonic (rarest and most dangerous) severe pneumonia and respiratory failure Case fatality rate: very high if untreated, low if treated	Isolation, antibiotics, vaccine in some countries	Weaponized in former USSR Requires lengthy hospitalization and isolation Pneumonic highly contagious among people Caused pandemics in 6th, 14th and 20th centuries
Smallpox (*Variola major*) Variola virus, a species of *Orthopoxvirus*	Inhalation; contact with infected bodily fluids or contaminated objects	Incubation: 7–19 days Symptoms: rash, high fever Case fatality rate: among unvaccinated populations, 20–50% or more	Vaccine	Very stable Eradicated in 1979, therefore low clinical recognition and most people very susceptible Highly contagious among people
Tularemia (*Francisella tularensis*) Gram-negative nonmotile coccobacillus	Inhalation; bites from vectors such as ticks; ingestion of contaminated food or water No person-to-person	Incubation: usually 3–5 days Symptoms: flu-like, possibly skin ulcers Case fatality rate: 5%–15%, primarily due to untreated respiratory forms; lower with antibiotherapy	Antibiotics, vaccine (effectiveness not clear)	Weaponized in US and USSR, engineered for vaccine resistance Highly infectious

Viral hemorrhagic fevers (such as, Ebola) Virion member of *Ebolavirus* genus in the family *Filoviridae*	Person-to-person via contact with infected blood, secretions, organs or semen	Incubation: 2–21 days Symptoms: severe acute viral illness, fever, followed by pharyngitis, vomiting, diarrhea and rash Case fatality rate: ranges from 50% to nearly 90%	Drug therapies and vaccines under development	First identified in 1976 Linked to large epidemics in Africa

Source: Rotz, L., Khan, A., Lillibridge, S.R. et al., "CRC – Public Health Assessment of Potential Biological Terrorism Agents," published as report summary in EID, Vol. 8, No. 2, February 2002, available at http://www.cdc.gov/ncidod/eid/ vol8no2/01-0164.htm.

The OIE's "List A"

The Office International des Épizooties (OIE), charged with leading global efforts to control animal disease, classifies the following animal diseases as posing the greatest socio-economic or public health threats. The Terrestrial Animal Health Code requires member countries to report incidences of these diseases to the OIE:

- Foot and mouth disease
- Swine vesicular disease
- Peste des petits ruminants
- Lumpy skin disease
- Bluetongue
- African horse sickness
- Classical swine fever
- Newcastle disease

- Vesicular stomatitis
- Rinderpest
- Contagious bovine pleuropneumonia
- Rift Valley fever
- Sheep pox and goat pox
- African swine fever
- Highly pathogenic avian influenza

Another component in assessing the threat of particular agents, as well as that of biological attacks generally, is the target population's ability to detect and respond to outbreaks. Intentional infections are in many respects just like any other kind of outbreak. But certain distinguishing features can make the detection and response even more challenging. Bioterrorist attacks, for instance, may involve foreign or genetically modified pathogens never before detected in the region. Intentional transmission may generate infection where it is least likely to be expected or detected rather than in the usual places or products. The infection may originate in multiple sources scattered in different areas rather than, say, one infected chicken coop, thus making detection more difficult. And, considering its emotional freight, bioterrorism may elicit more panic from the public. In fact the psychological factors are probably key in making this route attractive to terrorists. Preparing for these factors adds another layer of complexity. Since the mid-1990s, in response to growing concerns about the possibility of bioterrorist attacks, billions of federal dollars earmarked for preparedness efforts have flowed to state and local health agencies. As a result, most jurisdictions have developed response plans and invested in enhanced surveillance and laboratory capabilities. Innovative pilot programs have been launched, such as syndromic surveillance systems, which automatically detect clusters of disease from computerized data collected from hospitals, clinics and labs. Similarly, vaccines have been developed to combat anthrax, smallpox and plague. But a number of the vaccines initially were developed for use by military troops and have not been tested on people who might be more vulnerable, such as the very young or old (Knobler, Mahmoud et al. 2001). Progress is limited, since economic incentives for testing existing and developing new vaccines are slim, given their uncertain market. Moreover, the logistics of distributing vaccines from the National Pharmaceutical Stockpile, along with most other preparedness provisions, such as coordinating among the nation's 3,000 local health agencies, remain largely untested.

Sadly, the investment in bioterrorism preparedness has come at the expense of other public health efforts that may well be useful in the event of a bioterrorist attack. The US Council of State and Territorial Epidemiologists' 2004 nationwide survey, for instance, found that while the number of epidemiologists dedicated to bioterrorism preparedness has increased, the number of epidemiologists focused on areas such as environmental and occupational health has decreased or remained stagnant. In addition, the report found that the infusion of federal funds targeting bioterrorism has fostered a dependence on federal monies, threatening the states' abilities to plan and act independently in response to their specific needs and concerns (Council of State and Territorial Epidemiologists 2004).

Agroterrorism

Although bioterrorism may conjure visions of airborne pathogens unleashed on packed stadiums or, post 9/11, dangerous packages shipped through the mail, an area of rising concern is imported and domestic agricultural products. The agricultural sector is at once particularly vulnerable to attack and effective in dissemination, offering a cheap, accessible avenue for biological attacks. Upon announcing his resignation in December 2004, former US Health and Human Services Secretary Tommy G. Thompson declared, "For the life of me, I cannot understand why the terrorists have not attacked our food supply because it is so easy to do" (Pear 2004). Similarly, in a November 2003 statement to the US Senate Committee on Governmental Affairs, the General Accounting Office (GAO) reported that "serious questions remain about whether the agriculture sector and the food supply are sufficiently prepared for deliberate acts of terrorism" (US General Accounting Office 2003). In a more recent report issued in March 2005, the GAO concluded that while improvements had been made in agroterrorism preparedness and prevention since the 9/11 attacks, shortcomings persist, including problems with diagnostics, prompt animal vaccine deployment, and communications (US Government Accountability Office 2005).

Agroterrorism could take one of two tacks – spoiling crops or livestock, which would exact a primarily economic toll, or alternatively focusing on contaminating food products, and harming humans directly. The first approach is in some respects more feasible, since agents that attack plants or animals tend to be more available, durable and contagious – plus easier to handle, since they cannot be transmitted to humans (Chalk 2004). Either way, the potential damage is substantial. The agriculture sector, symbolically and economically, is part of the national fabric. It contributes about 13 percent of the gross domestic product and 18 percent of domestic jobs (US General Accounting Office 2003). Depending on the nature of the disease, an attack on the food system could have enormous repercussions, from compromised food supplies to embargoes on international exports and even drops in tourism. The 2001 foot-and-mouth outbreak, for instance, cost the UK some $14.5 billion (Chalk 2004b). Direct costs of a similar outbreak in the US are projected to run as high as $24 billion and entail the slaughter of about 13 million animals (US General Accounting Office 2003). In addition to economic costs, tampering with food can cause psychological and political damage, creating a jittery public concerned that its food sources are unsafe.

Securing the food system is a huge, arguably impossible undertaking, especially as our food sources continue to expand around the world. The US relies on imports for 20 percent of its fresh produce and wholly 60 percent of the seafood consumed (US Food and Drug Administration 2004). More than six million food shipments cross US borders each year and only a small portion of this cargo is physically inspected upon entry. Historically, less than 5 percent of cargo arriving at US ports has been inspected. Similarly, just 2–3 percent of fresh produce entering the US is inspected (Cupp, Walker et al. 2004). Instead, importers are expected to vouch for the safety of their products.

But imported goods are not the only concern. Agricultural operations in the US are similarly vulnerable, in part due to the recent changes in the industry illustrated in earlier chapters. The consolidation of the food industry has produced conditions in which livestock are more susceptible to infection – and in which that infection spreads more rapidly. Massive dairy operations contain anywhere from 1,500 to 10,000 head of cattle at any one time, typically in very close quarters, presenting the opportunity for rapid spread of disease (Chalk 2004b). Similarly, some feedlots house upwards of 30,000 head. Moreover, farm-to-table pathways span vast distances, with each stop along the way serving as a potential access point for pathogens – from the fields and barns to the processing and distribution plants, storage and retail facilities and transport vehicles. On average, in the US, a pound of meat travels about 1,000 miles from the point where it was produced to the point at which it is consumed (Chalk 2004a). Farms, by their nature, are open and reasonably accessible. Food processing and packing plants also tend to lack security measures and commonly employ a transient workforce (Chalk 2004a). And at retail operations, food is once again subject to tampering by the many employees who have access to products for legitimate purposes. In 2003, a Michigan supermarket worker was charged with contaminating 200 pounds of meat with Black Leaf 40 insecticide, causing 92 people to fall ill (Centers for Disease Control and Prevention 2003). Since most food is perishable, the time available to detect contaminated products before they are consumed is limited.

While opportunities for agroterrorism are abundant, the mechanisms for detection and response are limited. Farmers, ranchers and veterinarians are attuned to the diseases that regularly affect or threaten their crops and animals. But their knowledge of and ability to identify non-endemic infectious diseases is less extensive. Similarly, vaccination strategies for foreign diseases still are under development. And, given the tremendous costs of a potential outbreak, farmers are understandably reluctant to report concerns unless they are certain they have a problem. A suspected outbreak could force the slaughter of hundreds of cattle and cost millions in lost present and future business. In 2001, a report of tongue lesions among cattle in a sale barn in rural Kansas spurred foot-and-mouth disease fears, causing the cattle futures market to dive. In the 48 hours it took lab tests to confirm the fears were unfounded, the cattle industry lost some $50 million – the lesions, it seems, came from thorny hay (Gips 2003). In an attempt to allay fears about the consequences of reporting outbreaks, the USDA has committed, along with the states, to providing some compensation to livestock owners for animals slaughtered as part of a disease control effort.

Despite the many vulnerabilities of the food system, since 1912, only 12 cases have been documented of substate use of agents to infect plants or animals, and only two of those could be considered acts of terrorism (Chalk 2004a). While the US, the Soviet Union and Iraq all developed agents to use against plants and animals, they have never been deployed in any major attacks (Franz 2004). Peter Chalk, a political scientist with the RAND Corporation, theorizes that attacks on plants and animals, which tend to have delayed impacts, are perhaps from a terrorist's perspective too "dry" in comparison to other, more dramatic possibilities (Chalk 2004b p. 144).

US Government Response

Nine months after 9/11, calling biological weapons "potentially the most dangerous weapons in the world," US President George Bush signed the Public Health Security and Bioterrorism Response Act of 2002. The act's provisions for protecting the nation's food supply include a beefed-up presence at the borders and a series of networks to improve communications between federal and state food testing laboratories. The Food Emergency Response Network (FERN), for instance, links state and federal laboratories registered to test food samples in the event of an outbreak. The FDA, which oversees all food products except meat, poultry and processed egg products, hired more than 650 new field inspectors to monitor imports and increased inspections at entry ports from 12,000 in fiscal year 2001 to 68,000 in fiscal year 2003 (US Food and Drug Administration 2004). The Bioterrorism Act also included four regulations designed to better trace food from farm to table and to detect and respond to problems:

1. Food facility registrations – requires registration with the FDA of all owners and operators of domestic and foreign facilities that manufacture, process, pack or hold food for human or animal consumption in the US.
2. Tracking records – requires importers, manufacturers, and processors to record where they receive food from and where they send it.
3. Prior notice – requires importers to notify the FDA of food shipments before they arrive at US ports. The ports receive some 25,000 notices daily.
4. Detention – authorizes the FDA to detain suspicious food shipments for up to 30 days.

Meanwhile, the USDA, which oversees livestock and poultry, has taken similar measures, increasing surveillance at entry ports, enhancing communication networks among state and federal laboratories, and investing in the development of rapid tests to ensure timely detection of outbreaks. The USDA also has focused on expanding veterinarians' recognition and understanding of foreign animal diseases. Nonetheless, the fragmented structure of federal agencies overseeing food safety seriously compromises officials' ability to effectively police potential hazards (for details, see Chapter 7).

Product Sabotage

As we look at the global express, with its increasing diversity of international goods, growing dominance of multinational corporations, and widening gap between poor and rich, it is entirely possible to visualize a biological attack employing a vehicle other than food. Increasing offshore production of a growing number of goods provides both the opportunity and in many cases, the motive, with poor factory workers toiling in sweatshops to produce products destined for the US. Even if only partially successful, if a widely used product such as brand name textiles were infected with a biological agent, havoc would ensue in that market segment within the US. Biological weapons require less financial investment than conventional weapons, and they are more easily concealed than tanks, planes or bombs. A North Atlantic Treaty Organization handbook states, "Biological weapons are unique in the ability to inflict large numbers of casualties over a wide area – with minimum logistical requirements and by means that can be virtually untraceable" (North Atlantic Treaty Organization 1992). Thus the attraction of offshore production of goods that the American consumer will ingest or wear closely against his or her skin might wisely be tempered with realistic concerns for biosecurity at production sites. Biosecurity in turn will depend in part on the allegiance of the line worker to the company and to safety of that company's product. In today's world, there are other powerful countervailing allegiances among poor factory workers abroad. This will increasingly be a risk as the gap between incomes in the global community continues to widen. The most effective security measure, then, may be fair compensation and working conditions.

Conclusion

The vast majority of infectious disease outbreaks are unintentional, and the world is working in concert to curb those events. A smallpox outbreak anywhere in the world is cause for an international concern (Knobler, Mahmoud et al. 2001 p. 17). Deliberate incidents are very rare, and when they occur, they are typically the work of an individual or dissident group rather than that of a nation. Nonetheless, concern is growing over the prospect of a bioterrorist attack. Harmful biological agents are more generally available. At the same time, technological developments are enabling the production of new pathogens capable of evading current safeguards. And our food system, with its centralized production and far-flung distribution is becoming increasingly more vulnerable. In response, local, state, national and international agencies are working together to better detect and respond to potential threats, from sophisticated surveillance to systems that track food sources from hoof to plate.

Study Questions

1. When and what was the earliest example of biological warfare?
2. What four routes of entry into humans are potential paths for biological weapon attacks?
3. Why are potential biological attacks on animals of concern to the human community? What are the four regulations within the Bioterrorism Act that seek to address these risks?

Chapter 6

Primary Prevention

As we discussed in Chapter 1, we can apply the conventional levels of prevention – primary, secondary and tertiary to the way we think about protecting the world from infectious diseases. The first, or primary, level is preventing a disease from emerging; the second level is preventing a local outbreak; and the third is preventing international transmission, or a pandemic. In the next three chapters, we will explore each of those levels in greater detail, beginning at the most basic level: the factors contributing to disease emergence. All of the factors linked to emergence are in essence created or caused by humans; some of them are more feasible for humans to correct than others. One element is the increasing burden on the planet, with its limited resources. Another is a new ecosystem of sorts that we have created through burgeoning trade and travel – a world of high mobility and no boundaries. Also factoring into the equation is intensified food production practices. And finally, we have a growing array of medical practices with unknown consequences, such as xenotransplantation and widespread antibiotic use. Figure 6.1 adds such mechanisms to our original prevention pyramid.

Exhausting our "Ecospace"?

Typically, diseases emerge when an agent crosses over from another vertebrate species to humans. The mechanisms of that crossover are largely unknown, but some factors seem to facilitate the process, such as poor sanitation, the encroachment of humans on animals' habitats, maintaining food animals in crowded conditions, and extensive use of antimicrobials. The intensification of poultry agriculture in Southeast Asia has commuted bird influenza into a growing number of human cases – 161 at current count (Centers for Disease Control and Prevention 2005 p. 470). An off-shoot, cockfighting, has included practices that have contributed to further infection, such as humans sucking blood and mucus from the beaks of injured birds (Sipress 2005). Early in the HIV epidemic there was thought to be a transmission between monkeys or apes and humans. Whether this was through exposure of hunters and their primate prey in the rainforests or through bushmeat consumption or another route remains a mystery.

There is a consensus that most of the new pathogens that have emerged over the last twenty years have done so in response to ecological pressure rather than evolutionary change in the microbes themselves. Ecological changes such as new agricultural practices, urbanization, globalization and climate change seem to drive microbes from animals into new human hosts (Slingenbergh, Gilbert et al. 2004). These drivers are largely the product of human activity. Despite this certainty, there

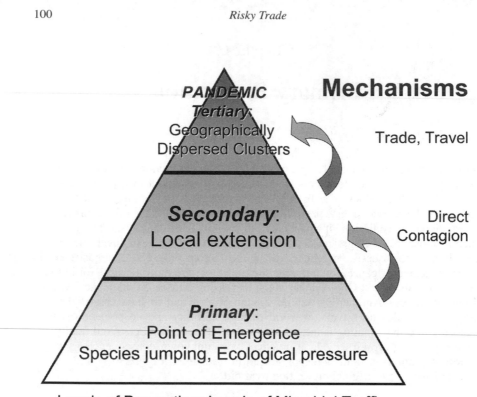

Figure 6.1   The mechanisms pyramid

has been little definitive work done to outline the threshold of various factors in the emergence of new human pathogens. For example, while most international authorities agree that intensification of the poultry industry is related to the emergence of fatal bird flu outbreaks in Europe and Asia (Food and Agriculture Organization of the United Nations), little is known about how or why this RNA virus jumps from birds to humans.

At the microbial level, recent studies of the highly fatal 1918 influenza virus suggest that the neuraminidase portion of the virus is responsible for its contagiousness in humans. (Recall from Chapter 3 that the short influenza RNA virus has two key binding sites – the "H" or hemagglutinin site and the "N" or neuraminidase site.) Scientists believe that the 1957 pandemic flu emerged after the virus moved from ducks to pigs or chickens that were infected at the same time by a human virus. After the viruses exchanged bits of genetic material during their reproduction in the pigs and chickens, the new virus was armed to infect humans. However, because of the state of science in 1957, this information is tentative.

Intensive study is now underway of the virus causing Asian bird flu, which has already hopped the species barrier in the 161 recorded human cases to date, causing 86 human deaths as of February 2, according to WHO.

At the macro level, we do not know the threshold number for poultry intensification. How many birds per square meter can be handled safely? How many is too many? What role do ducks that migrate from farm to farm play in disease transmission? The US Department of Agriculture (USDA) stipulates that no more than 10 chickens can be housed per square meter. Contemporary practice in the US is for these 10 chickens to inhabit a three-square-foot space for their entire lives, often with their beaks and talons removed to prevent injury. Intense poultry practices such as this are correlated with the susceptibility of such birds to highly pathogenic avian influenza, as described in Chapter 3. That susceptibility, thought to be related to stress and crowding, has been demonstrated all over the world.

What role does sanitary practice play in the transmission to humans? What are the critical variables in keeping cages clean, providing safe water to poultry, or clean and safe feed? What is the compromise between the most efficient and profitable poultry raising practices and safety among poultry workers? When the Food and Agriculture Organization of the United Nations (FAO) discusses restructuring the increasingly intense poultry industry in Southeast Asia, the best design of that restructuring is not clear – we have no scientific blueprint. The US' experience with bird flu, in fact, suggests that USDA guidelines do not prevent the disease in poultry

We have quantitative tools we can use to answer some of these important questions. A group of scientists recently analyzed the impact of the "livestock revolution" on the ecology of infectious diseases. The revolution, or the growing demand for animal protein, has been incited by the planet's increasing human population and the rising incomes of the larger and larger urban populations. This demand is met in Asia primarily with poultry, much of which is raised in crowded conditions just outside urban centers. The authors outline four major areas of risk in this process that need to be carefully considered in terms of the emergence of new infections:

1. Production intensification.
2. The host "metapopulation," which means a population that experiences microbial traffic and therein experiences the spread of disease (in this case the poultry).
3. The transmission pathways other than those within the animal population; that is, the entire food chain from feed to live animals, processing, marketing/distribution, food preparation and consumption.
4. The nature of the pathogen (for example, its virulence and the ease with which it spreads) (Slingenbergh, Gilbert et al. 2004 pp. 470–71).

While crops can only be intensified within the bounds of arable land, the livestock revolution is not so constrained. A key feature is the "severance of the traditional links between the amount of available local land and feed resources" (Slingenbergh, Gilbert et al. 2004 p. 470). Poultry intensification in Latin America, the Near East, North Africa, East Asia, and South Asia is taking place close to the exploding markets of the urban megacities in these regions. It is estimated that by 2015, half of the world's human population and 35 percent of the global meat production will take place in Asia. Working with data from the FAO on the agricultural population and chicken meat output, the scientists plotted the information on a graph, as shown in Figure 6.2.

It appears that Asia has seen relatively little increased productivity in chickens despite a rapidly increasing density of the agricultural population, including both small farms and large industrial scale enterprises. This mixture of large and small enterprises in close proximity has served as a potent combination for the outbreak of bird flu. The small farms probably served as the first points of illness, but the large commercial farms then played an important role in extending the outbreaks with their vulnerable populations of fowl and high volume traffic of birds and products over large geographic areas.

A New Environment, New Rules?

There has been extensive scientific work done that suggests that the human community is outstripping the planet's ability to accommodate it. While not yet as crowded as chickens on factory farms, with 6.2 billion human inhabitants, the balance within natural systems is increasingly affected by "anthopogenic"

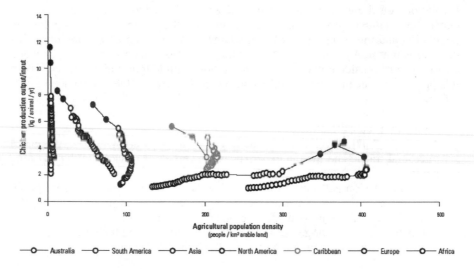

Figure 6.2   Changes in chicken meat output/input and agricultural population density by continent, 1961–2001

Note: Void circles denote actual changes; filled-in circles indicate predictions for 2015–2030.
Source: Slingenburgh, Gilbert et al. 2004.

(manmade) activity. In his landmark 1993 book *Planetary Overload: Global Environmental Change and the Health of the Human Species*, Anthony J. McMichael outlines the human-generated stress on natural systems. He posits that the availability of food will become increasingly problematic for the human community. The macroecologic effects of human activity on climate, water, food, agriculture, pollution and human health are well described, but the systematic link between the macro, or what we can see, and what is going on at the micro level remains an important area of research. To address the emergence of new pathogens, we need more knowledge about exactly what mechanisms form the critical pathway to emergence.

While there is a finite amount of space on the surface area of the globe, we have in some senses created a new dimension of space – the mobile environment. In considering the human environment, increasing emphasis has been placed on the "built environment." For example, the creation of roads and paving of land has hardened the land, and created challenges for disposing of water and human pollutants. The construction of buildings has created spaces that are studied for their effects on human health, from secondhand smoke to "sick building syndrome."

In the pursuit of trade and travel, new manmade spaces also have been created that have yet to be described in terms of how they act on the life processes of microbes, and how they affect infection. But we are beginning to see some signs. Human travel, for instance, seems to have the potential to affect seasonal disease patterns. Many "biological" aspects of life appear to be seasonal – births, deaths, a variety of chronic diseases, and of course infectious diseases all peak during certain parts of the calendar year. At least this is the case in temperate climates, where such phenomena have been the most extensively studied. This is a well-described aspect of infectious disease, including respiratory infections such as colds and flu, and more serious infections such as pneumonia (Dowell, Whitney et al. 2003). Interestingly, this seasonality has remained a constant even as human beings have modified their natural environment in remarkable ways, building shelters, designing heating and cooling systems and inventing new protective clothing among others. This well-described but poorly understood phenomenon has enabled us to plan vaccine development and prevention efforts at certain times of the year in anticipation of upcoming outbreaks. But as we saw in Chapter 3, when people travel between hemispheres, where the seasons are reversed, they can introduce viruses off-season, potentially throwing this historically reliable system of vaccines and prevention out of balance.

Another instance that illustrates the potential influence of the new mobile environment on the microbial world is the transportation, via food products, of a pathogen from one region, where it may be endemic, to another area where it is not. In our processing, shipping, packaging and preparation of food, we are bringing into our homes and our alimentary canals food and microbes that may come from thousands of miles away. We experience some of this microbial traffic as illness, when microbes pathogenic to humans infect us and make us sick. But this is an exceedingly small percentage of the microbes being moved about; these are the microbes we have gotten to know because they make us ill. Recall Chapter 1's description of the millions and millions of species of microbes found in the Sargasso

Sea. It is not that we are actually creating whole new hosts for pathogens to live in, at least not yet. It is rather our new mobile manmade ecological space has an impact on the rapidly evolving microbial world, and we are flying blind about what that impact could be.

The work of bringing ecological science into the study of how microbes change or adapt within their microscopic world is the focus of evolutionary biologist Paul Ewald and his colleagues. They have posited that a microbe's mobility is linked with its virulence (how seriously ill it can make us). The argument is that the basic value of "ecological fitness" is central for populations of microbes. This is simply the ability to pass their genetic material from one generation of their species to the next through replication. If the microbe can easily move from host to host (that is, if it is highly infectious), it invests more energy moving in mobile hosts and less on developing high virulence. On the other hand, some species such as anthrax lie in wait for extended periods of time and then immobilize their hosts by making the host moribund or dead, counting on the immobilized host to serve as a point of infection for other hosts. Ewald has coined the term "cultural vectors" to describe this transmission that takes place independent of typical mechanisms such as flagellae, which allow the microbe to swim, or mosquitoes, which transport the microbe to another host (Ewald 1996). These strategies have developed within the plethora of microbe species over thousands of years of their evolution. It is beyond the scope of this book to try to explain in detail the extensive work and thinking done to date in this area. However, it is central to consider how the modern creation of new mobility spanning thousands of geographic miles may impact microbial evolution over time.

Extending Production Chains

Systems of production of food and biological products have changed dramatically over the last twenty years. In the era of our grandparents, our food came from local farms. The produce and products were often uneven in quality and supply because the production system depended upon many variables – there were good years and bad years. This is no longer so. Now production chains are thousands of miles long and often intercontinental. This is true for biological products that we eat, such as meat, eggs and milk, and increasingly also for biological products that we use as pharmaceuticals – medicines to cure the sick.

The global marketplace is driven by the market – the consumers and their purchasing power. This is basic. As one senior official at Nestlé explained, the fundamental driver in that company's reform efforts of the dairy sector in Pakistan has been that there is an eventual market of consumers, in Pakistan and abroad, that will bankroll the enterprise. The second driver is competition for that market among corporate interests. This is the underlying force that market devotees claim will spur reform within the corporate enterprise. The belief is that the pressure of the competition for the market will of necessity force the enterprise to "do it right." Competition will increase efficiency and quality in production and, according to market fundamentalists, assure the best possible management of the corporate endeavor. According to economist Joseph Stiglitz and others, market fundamentalists are those who believe the market forces alone, without human interference, should guide the evolution of global enterprise. This will be addressed further in the concluding chapter.

But globalization and the consolidation of corporations has changed the playing field. The example of Bovine Spongiform Encephalopathy (BSE) demonstrates one aspect of this. As discussed in Chapter 4, the UK beef industry had historically been a relatively stable one. The industry was, as economists would describe it, "fragmented" among many smaller farms across the British Isles. To protect this industry, the government maintained a tariff on the imports of competing products from abroad. With the explosion of global trading in beef after World War II, coincident with refrigerated transport, and the movement towards global "free" trade, Britain negotiated a timetable under the General Agreement on Tariffs and Trade (GATT) to scale down these tariffs on beef. This reduction in tariff brought heightened competition to the British beef industry and with it, pressure to increase the efficiency and lower the cost of production.

It was against this backdrop that an innovation in rendering was introduced and implemented in the slaughterhouses of Britain. For centuries, after slaughter, the carcasses of cows and other animals have been "rendered," or processed once all the edible and usable bits of flesh and meat have been cut away. And for decades, British farmers had been using the meat and bone meal (MBM) that resulted from this rendering as a protein source for beef cattle. Historically, the rendering process was similar to pressure cooking – it entailed applying very high temperatures for a very long time so that eventually even the bones broke down into powder. It was an expensive, fuel- and time-consuming process. Then a new cold vacuum extraction method was introduced that required lower temperatures (that is, less energy) and less time for rendering. (The interested reader is referred to Boyle's law in physics, which describes how removing all gases from an environment should enhance the efficiency of energy transfer which is, essentially, what rendering is all about.) It seemed a win-win in light of the increasing pressure on the British beef industry, which was now facing global competition for British domestic markets.

But when this new rendering practice was introduced, the prion disease known as mad cow disease emerged. It turns out that with the new process, the resulting meat and bone meal was not effectively disinfected for prions. The very existence of prion disease was unknown prior to its dramatic emergence, first in cows and then in people. The context of this emergence is important to appreciate. Somehow, the streamlining of the rendering process played a role. The agent could have been present for decades, just not in meat and bone meal products because the earlier rendering process removed it. British scientists have tested the new process by deliberately introducing animals with mad cow disease and assaying the resulting MBM product. They have indeed found that the newer rendering process does not remove the infection, whereas the older process did.

There are three key points to take away from this story:

1. Changes in production and processing of products based on animal or human material can spark the emergence of new human infectious pathogens.

2. Such changes can be hastened in a global marketplace in which enterprises adopt strategies to increase efficiency in production either for competition or profit seeking.
3. The new agent can be globally distributed before the problem is fully recognized and public health measures can be implemented.

Getting Really Up-close with Microbes – Xenotransplantation

We have seen how pathogens can jump from their usual animal habitat to a new human habitat when macro pressures cause extreme crowding, as with poultry keeping, or when infected animal products enter the human food supply, as with BSE. But sometimes the leap is really just a short step across cells. This is the case when humans actually implant the microbes directly into their bodies through transfusion or transplantation. We saw this in our earlier discussion of HIV/AIDS in Chapter 4, which illustrated that the virus is transmitted far more efficiently via a blood transfusion than it is through other means, such as sexual contact. While this serves as a cautionary example of the dangers of exchanging body parts and products, another instance involving HIV/AIDS illustrates the attraction of transplants – even the riskier, cross-species variety. Before antiretroviral therapies became effective, HIV/AIDS was a fatal disease. When the infection progressed to the clinical stage of AIDS, the individual died within two years. About nine years ago, a radical untested therapy was tried on one desperate young man in Pittsburg. Because baboons, unlike many other primates, are resistant to HIV, the man and his doctors decided to attempt to replace his bone marrow with that of a baboon. The man's own marrow, comprising the stem cells that produce white blood cells, which defend against infections, was no longer working. The HIV virus had riddled his body and he had no natural defense against disease. The bone marrow transplant succeeded. Today he survives, and baboon cells are still detectable in his system. This is an example of "xenotransplantation" – the use of organs from other species to replace faulty organs in humans.

With more than 50,000 Americans waiting for organ transplants in the US, the demand for new parts is outstripping the supply. Animal parts offer the promise of additional organ supplies and, as we saw with the man in Pittsburg, in some cases other species also have abilities to resist fatal diseases that humans do not. Animals seem to many like the logical next source of transplants, and scientific work is underway to access this source. In the US, the Food and Drug Administration (FDA) has not licensed such transplants. But other countries have, and they are attracting what the press calls "medical tourists." Take Howard Staab, a 53-year-old carpenter from North Carolina who traveled to New Dehli, India, for a new heart valve in 2004. Press accounts tell us that Mr. Staab "outsourced" to India the surgery that would have cost the uninsured carpenter $200,000 in the US (Lancaster 2004). In India, the bill totaled $10,000, including the airfare, hospitalization and procedure – plus a side trip to the Taj Mahal. Savings aside, Mr. Staab underwent some risks beyond those that typically accompany the procedure: risks of hospital acquired infection, and of the potential transmission of new viruses from the pig that donated his valve.

Mr. Staab is probably not the usual medical tourist, but with the increasing costs of medical care in the US, he may represent a trend. Since the founding of the venerable Mayo Clinic in Minnesota as a mecca for international medical tourists, well-heeled "carriage trade" clientele have traversed the globe in search of the very best in health care. Mr. Staab represents the extension of this trade to the uninsured, who, while having modest means in the US, nonetheless are wealthier than 90 percent of people on the planet, and consequently may seek out more affordable surgeries in poorer countries, including those that may permit procedures the US prohibits, such as xenotransplantation.

When an organ from a pig or baboon is transplanted into a human, four things happen: (1) the human defenses recognize the foreign material and militate a response, (2) this vigorous immunological battle that would normally cause the rejection of the foreign material is treated with a variety of powerful drugs to stop it, so the patient becomes immunosupressed, (3) any viruses or prions in the animal donor immediately become residents in the human donor, and (4) the new organ slowly begins to pick up the physiological functions of the organ it has been brought in to replace. Clearly, the second and third parts of this scenario introduce potentially dangerous conditions for disease transmission.

The "What We Don't Know" Problem

The uncertainties surrounding xenotransplantation and infectious disease transmission are evident in two articles published in scientific journals in 2004. One was positive that scientists and industry were able to predict, identify and deal with the risks of pig (porcine) donors (Fishman and Patience 2004). The other was much more cautious and mixed (Boneva and Folks 2004). The disclosure statements of the authors of the first article are peppered with their relationships with industry, whereas the more cautious appraisal by the other team are not. This observation is not to impugn in any way the integrity of the first team. The truth is that scientists remain largely ignorant of the ecology at the microbial level despite their swagger. Another truth is that there is a nascent industry in xenotransplantation just waiting for the green light from the FDA.

Some very strong, compassionate arguments exist for xenotransplantation: there are not enough organs available for transplant and people with kidney failure or liver failure or pancreatic crises can wait years for a donor who might be dead or alive. The wait is difficult and can be life threatening. Renal dialysis, for example, which replaces the function of a working kidney, makes patients feel increasingly ill as they undergo repeated treatment. According to Matching Donors, a Massachusetts-based non-profit organization that matches donors with recipients, an estimated 17 people a day die waiting for transplants in the US alone.

The pig has become the preferred candidate for donating organs to humans. Primates, the other most promising potential candidates, are expensive to acquire and keep, more likely to provoke ethical objections, and are perceived as risky because HIV is a simian (monkey) virus. Pigs can be bred to genetically erase their "foreignness" to humans by manipulating the genetic coding for the glycoproteins on their cells. And they are about the right size for their organs to fit the human body. However they also carry new porcine (pig) retroviruses. Recall that HIV is a retrovirus, albeit of a different type. These retroviruses are actually embedded in their genetic material, so although pigs can be bred in sterile surroundings, there is no way to remove these retrovirus agents from their make-up. They are, in the language of microbiology, "endogenous."

Much work is ongoing to overcome the various obstacles to using pigs as donors for human organs. The problem of the endogenous retroviruses caused the FDA to arrest early clinical trials in the US. But scientists are working hard to study what the risks are and how to overcome them. As we saw with Mr. Staab, caution in India is not as pronounced and pig donated organs are being transplanted into humans there. Those humans then return to the US to recover, and presumably will seek care if and when they become ill, potentially exposing other patients. If there are risks from pig retroviruses, eventually they will be known, but the incubation period may be as long as the decade of quiet infection that precedes clinical AIDS in those with HIV. Potential risks lurk on two biological fronts. One concern is that the retroviruses from the pig could infect the human host and in turn, the infected person's contacts and community. Another is that the retroviruses might incorporate genes from the human (0.1 percent of the human genome contains endogenous retrovirus sequences) and the resulting mixed organism would prove infectious to the human and that human's contacts and community.

A final area of concern, which is general for animal organ donation to humans, is the transfer of antibiotic-resistant infections from the animal. As we will see later in this chapter, animals of many types are receiving antibiotics in great volumes in their feed and in treatment. While guidelines are very strict for how donor animals for human organ transplantation trials are raised in those nations carrying out such experiments (including the UK and Australia), the guidelines in other countries may not be. So medical tourists who travel in search of the cheaper transplant bear close watching, and their close contacts should also be made aware of these potential risks of unknown infections.

The Lyodura Story

While the risks of disease transmission from animal transplants are generally less known, and consequently more difficult to guard against, human-to-human transplants also can cause unanticipated problems with infection. One unfortunate example is the consequences of procedures employing Lyodura, a product developed in Germany in the early 1980s for use in neurosurgery. To work on the brain, neurosurgeons necessarily work inside the *dura mater* – Latin for hard layer. But it is not really hard. It is basically a soft pliable sheath that surrounds the brain and the spinal cord and acts as a crucial protector. So when surgery is extensive, making sure this critical lining is put back in place is important. The company in Germany came up with a new product to do this tissue grafting. Taking the "dura" from the carcasses of other humans, the company processed the material into tissue for grafting in human neurosurgery. The product, Lyodura, was created by B. Braun

Melsungen AG and distributed worldwide. However, in 1986 a 28-year-old woman in the US developed the stumbling gait of Creutzfeldt-Jacob Disease (CJD) 17 months after undergoing surgery that employed Lyodura. She died within the year.

She was not alone. The product had entered the global express and was marketed in a number of countries. Most notably, Japan imported 100,000 grafts between 1982 and 1991, and a total of 93 cases of fatal CJD were traced to these imports. The period of time from the implant to the onset of clinical illness was as long as 17 years (Centers for Disease Control and Prevention 2003). Clusters of disease also occurred in Thailand and Spain (Centers for Disease Control and Prevention 1993). While safety adjustments in processing were carried out early, there was no effective recall of the product. Its production was eventually discontinued in 1996, a decade after the danger was known. Thus the arena of organ transplants is fraught with the same potent dangers as that of plasmapheresis. Whenever biological tissues from human or animal sources are introduced into a new human host, infectious risks occur that are difficult to predict and therein difficult to prevent.

One We Know

Another type of emergent threat has a clearer path: evolution of resistant microbes in response to exposure to antibiotics. Antibiotics act as a selective pressure for resistance by killing off the susceptible microbes in each generation, leaving only those that have developed a strategy to resist them. Since microbes reproduce so often, this pressure assures the emergence of a fair number of resistant microbes in a relatively short period of time.

Mother Nature in motion – microbial strategies against antibiotics

Antibiotic resistance genes   These genes are "borrowed," moving from microbe to microbe by genetic means such as *plasmids* – transporting genes from one kind of bacteria to a second that may be very different (that is, gram positive to gram negative).
Bacteriophage (like a simple virus attacking bacteria)   Can transport plasmids or chromosomes from one bacteria to another.
Naked DNA   Released when bacteria die, these can be picked up by other bacteria and spliced into their genetic material through *transformation*.

Source: Levy 2002.

The selective power of microbes in response to antibiotics has been well demonstrated, starting with a classic experiment conducted by microbiologist Stuart Levy and his colleagues in the latter half of the 1970s:

> In the mid-1970s, we performed a study that involved raising 300 chickens on a small farm outside Boston. We provided 150 newly hatched chicks with oxytetracycline-laced feed and another 150 without. We followed the effect of the antibiotic-laced feed on the

animals and people on the farm. As we began the study, the control group had little or no
resistant organisms. In the group receiving low levels (200 ppm) of oxytetracycline,
tetracycline resistance began to emerge among the faecal *Escherichia coli*. What was
surprising was that, within 12 weeks, we detected as much as 70% of all *E. coli* with
resistance to more than two antibiotics, including ampicillin, sulphonamides and
streptomycin. The resistances were all on transferable plasmids that emerged following
use of just tetracycline.

(Levy 2002 p. 27)

While antibiotics were designed to fight off infections in sick people and
animals, they were approved for use as "growth promoters" for animals in the US
in 1949, and in the UK in 1953. Meanwhile, in the 1960s, scientists began to
understand that the presence of antibiotics in the microenvironment of bacteria
caused "transferable antibiotic resistance." This means that populations of microbes
not only become resistant to the antibiotic over time, but also can pass the new,
adaptive characteristic resistance around to other populations of microbes – their
biological extended family as it were. Antibiotics fed to animals are not deactivated
in the animals' digestion process. In fact they remain largely biologically active
when they are excreted by the animals on fields, into waterways or elsewhere. Other
vertebrates, including humans, begin to be colonized with the resistant organisms if
they share an environment with animals in which the resistant strains are
developing. In areas where animals and humans are crowded together with poor
access to sanitation, this aspect of antibiotic usage in animals becomes even more
dangerous.

The two microbes for which the most is known are *Campylobacter* and
Salmonella. These organisms have been shown to acquire new resistance while in
animals, and to transfer that resistance to humans through the consumption or
handling of contaminated meat. In the case of campylobacter, the practice of
intensive poultry production plays a role. Most chickens are colonized by
campylobacter – they carry them in their gut. The chickens are not sickened by these
microbes; the campylobacter are part of the normal gut flora. When chickens are
raised in very close proximity, with thousands in a single facility, they are more
prone to disease threat, as we have seen with the bird flu virus. They are also more
prone to bacterial disease. Thus, chickens are often treated with antibiotics,
including fluoroquinolones – a particular type of antibiotic that also is important in
treating human infections. According to the US Centers for Disease Control, the rate
of resistance to this important class of antibiotics in human infections with
campylobacter rose from 13 percent in 1997 to 19 percent in 2001. In Minnesota,
fluoroquinolone-resistant strains were isolated from 14 percent of chicken products
in retail markets. When molecular level comparisons were made, these strains
exactly matched those isolated from human infections in the surrounding
communities.

As these rising resistance rates indicate, one obvious strategy to prevent the
emergence of drug-resistant strains is to limit the antibiotic exposure of microbes
living in humans and food animals. Possible strategies would include limiting or
discouraging the use of antibiotics by veterinarians, pharmacists, physicians and the
public through legislation and/or international policy and law. But this is actually

not at all straightforward in today's world. The use of antimicrobials to fight disease in humans and animals and promote growth in animals is a well-entrenched practice.

It is estimated that in the US alone, some 23,000,000kg (50,000,000 pounds) of antibiotics are used annually. While surprisingly little information is available about the usage of antibiotics in food animals in most countries, the World Health Organization estimates that roughly half of all antimicrobials produced are used to treat humans, and most of the rest are used in animal feed – primarily for pigs and poultry – to either fend off infection or enhance growth (World Health Organization 2002). The practice has become even more important with the rise of intensive agriculture, in which animals are kept in crowded conditions that make them more vulnerable to infectious diseases. Subtherapeutic use of antibiotics in these settings not only reduces outbreaks of illness but also has been shown to increase the overall weight of the animal by 4 or 5 percent, which adds to productivity and eventually to profitability of the enterprise. The tension between ecological caution and business profit is noted in a recent report by the US General Accounting Office (GAO); "While antibiotic use in animals poses potential human health risks, it also reduces the cost of producing these animals, which in turn helps reduce the prices consumers pay for food. Antibiotics are an integral part of animal production in the United States and in many other countries where large numbers of livestock are raised in confined facilities, which increases likelihood of disease" (US General Accounting Office 2004 p. 1).

The degree to which the drugs are used as growth enhancers (rather than to combat disease in sick animals) is subject to debate. According to the Animal Health Institute, an industry group that represents US antibiotic manufacturers, some 10.2 tons of antibiotics a year are used on the eight billion food animals produced annually in the US – 87 percent of which is for "treating, controlling and preventing disease" (Animal Health Institute). In contrast, the Union of Concerned Scientists, an environmental group, in 2001 estimated that US animal producers administer 12,300 tons of antibiotics a year for "nontherapeutic" (that is, growth-enhancing) purposes.

National legislation and guidelines for antibiotic use in animal husbandry vary among countries, as does the level of surveillance. In the 1990s, amid growing concerns about the emergence of drug-resistant bugs, the World Health Organization identified the issue as one of global public concern. In 2001, WHO, together with the Food and Agriculture Organization of the United Nations and the Office International des Épizooties (World Organization for Animal Health), drafted a set of "Global Principles" to address the use and abuse of antimicrobials in animals. Included was a strategy to ban drugs that are important for treating human illnesses for use as growth promoters in animals.

But as the WHO initiative acknowledges, given the world market, any successful effort will have to be global in scope. The strategy that WHO disseminated in 2001 is not a regulation but a series of recommendations "to both persuade governments to take urgent action and then to guide this action with expert technical and practical advice" (World Health Organization 2001). As a non-binding recommendation, the strategy may fail to galvanize sufficient international action, particularly in areas that are strapped for public health resources (Fidler 1999). Indeed, a workshop in 2002 examining the degree to which the recommendations were implemented found significant gaps. The workshop summary concluded: "The extent of implementation of the Global Strategy was very variable, both across and within Regions. Where priority interventions were in place, in many instances these were nominal only, since compliance was not enforced" (World Health Organization 2002 p. 1). Among the obstacles identified were limited resources, unregulated use of antimicrobials in food-producing animals, and "lack of inclination to enforce existing regulations."

In most developing countries, where agricultural exports are a potential source of critically important foreign currency, there are few regulatory barriers for using antibiotics as growth promoters and those that do exist are weakly enforced. In many cases, veterinary services have been transferred in recent decades from the government to private hands, and the livelihood of veterinary workers now depends on the ability of the farmers to pay for the service. If a practice such as subtherapeutic use of antimicrobials is judged potentially profitable, the chances are that it will continue relatively undisturbed.

But the use of antibiotics as growth promoters is not confined to resource-challenged regions. If fact, it has been a longstanding practice in the US, where a host of microbes have developed resistance, most likely as a result of the drugs in food animals, including *Salmonella*, *Campylobacter jejuni*, and *Escherichia coli*. A senior official from the Office International des Épizooties (World Organization for Animal Health) recently confided to me that he was "appalled" by the levels of antibiotics found in US exported beef arriving in Japan.

A number of other industrialized nations have been more diligent about monitoring and curbing the use of antibiotics in animals. The European Union has prohibited lacing the feed of animals with antibiotics that might also be useful in human disease, with the intent of preserving the effectiveness of such antibiotics as long as possible. The scientific evidence for this move is powerful, and comes largely from the UK, Denmark and Germany, where there has been careful monitoring of feed practices and resistance patterns over the last decade. Research suggests the bans can lead to a corresponding drop in drug-resistant bacteria. One study showed that the rate of resistance to the antibiotic avoparcin declined in Germany and in Denmark after that drug was prohibited for use as a growth promoter (Witte 2000). Scientists studied the disease patterns by using molecular genetic techniques to fingerprint specific gene groups that characterize both animal and human resistance to particular bacteria. These characteristic patterns were then tracked in different populations of animals and humans to trace the changes in their frequency of occurrence. Research demonstrated that the decline in resistance was correlated in time with the proscription of the use of avoparcin as a growth promoter and that the decline in the characteristic gene cluster took place in numerous animal and human systems coincidentally.

By 2006, all antibiotics will be banned from use for growth promotion in European Union member countries. Many producers and others have questioned the science behind these bans. Indeed some have called for a quantitatively based formal risk assessment. But others point out that conducting such an assessment would require waiting until the potential negative health consequences had played out in terms of human therapeutic failures (Witte 2000). Then, once deaths or other health consequences had begun to occur, we could count them and do calculations to demonstrate risk. Awaiting this outcome, when the science from the bench, the lab and numerous animal systems is clear, seems unconscionable. Thus the precautionary principle moved the European Union to implement the ban. (For more on risk assessment and the precautionary principle, see Chapter 8.)

As the recent GAO report indicates, the European Union's impending implementation of more stringent bans of antibiotics is being watched closely by the US as a potential source of future trade embargoes (US General Accounting Office 2004). The US is beginning to benchmark its own system of monitoring the problem with efforts in other countries, particularly the European Union. But as the report also points out, to date, public authorities in the US have lacked sufficient access to reliable industry information on the use of antibiotics, making it difficult to assess the current situation and what actions may be appropriate. Here science has no gap in its knowledge. The risks of increasing antibiotic resistance are clear. However, in terms of information needs for policy, the GAO report states flatly that "Although they have made some progress in monitoring antibiotic resistance, federal agencies do not collect the critical data on antibiotic use in animals that they need to support research on the human health risk" (US General Accounting Office 2004 p. 7). So at present, the US, a major meat exporter in the world marketplace – with exports of $2 billion in 2002 – appears to lag behind the global community in this aspect of food safety, running a risk of trade embargoes that eventually could drive it to regulate the practice without key information from industry practice.

Around the globe, in developed as well as developing countries, the research base and national policies regarding antibiotic use are uneven. While there is no reason to believe that the biology and ecology are fundamentally different with regards to the use of antibiotics as animal growth promoting agents in Europe, Asia or Africa, national policy makers historically have made decisions based only on studies related to their own particular situations. Meanwhile, on a daily basis, additional resistance is being "stockpiled" through the consumption by humans of resistant strains of pathogenic microbes. As noted earlier, these antibiotics do not disappear from the environment when their use is halted. While there is information in Europe that resistant strains will become sensitive again when the selective pressure of antibiotic use is removed, that information is not nearly as complete or compelling as it should be to justify the persistence of risky practices in animal husbandry. Antibiotic residues and active compounds are not only found in the food we eat. Increasingly they are found in ground water and in the soil, begging a serious question. Is there a point after which we have accumulated enough active antibiotics in the human environment to permanently alter the equilibrium of nature? Is this prospect a real threat to us?

Antibiotics in Human Prescriptions

In many developed countries in Europe and North America, antibiotic prescription authority has been vested in health care workers since the mid-1900s, and usually is limited to physicians or nurse practitioners. In many other countries antibiotics are available without a prescription from a pharmacist. The US Centers for Disease Control and many state health departments have launched programs to educate the public and physicians about prudent use of antibiotics. Antibiotics are, of course, only useful in infections where bacteria (or mycobacteria such as tuberculosis) are involved. They have no effect whatsoever on human infections caused by viruses. Viruses cause the majority of infections seen by doctors, including sore throats, cough and fever, and diarrhea. However, when patients come to the doctor, they expect to be treated, not just advised to rest, take fluids and "two aspirin and call me in the morning." This is even more the case in the current health care practice milieu in the US, where visits to health care providers are difficult to schedule, short and expensive. Patient demand for antibiotics is noted as a major driver of inappropriate use.

In other developed countries, antibiotics are often not controlled by prescription. In most Asian, Latin American and some European countries they are available from pharmacists over the counter – without a doctor's prescription. This has become an issue in antibiotic resistance. It might best be apparent in the case of tuberculosis. Tuberculosis is a slow moving but devastating infection which begins in the lungs. It requires long-term treatment (six months to a year) with three active antituberculosis drugs. In some countries, such as the Philippines, compounds available in pharmacies to treat "cough" may contain one active antituberculose agent mixed with vitamins. This will help with symptoms, but not cure the infection. Instead, as we have seen, resistant organisms will be selected and thrive in the patient. Most of the drug-resistant tuberculosis seen in Seattle and other West Coast cities in the US is among people from countries where this is the standard practice. According to the CDC, the majority of drug resistance in tuberculosis in the US originated in the Philippines and Vietnam.

Poorer countries present different challenges in antibiotic control. There are extensive informal networks of traffic in medicines in sub-Saharan Africa, for example. When researchers first sought antibiotic sensitivity information on microbes in hospitalized patients in the Central African Republic 15 years ago, they were surprised to find high resistance to tetracycline, a common antibiotic. However, if the researchers had gone to the corner where vendors sell cigarettes and other small household items out of suitcases, they would have found stocks of small plastic bags with about 20 black and red capsules. The vendors, who were supplied by traffickers traveling south over the Sahara called "boubangari" (pronounced boobangerry), would have told the prospective clients that these were good for treating cough in children. The pills would carry no label or directions, so the instructions on how to take them would be given verbally to the clients. Thus tetracycline, known in many parts of the world simply as "black and red," was pervasive in the wares of street vendors, and wide resistance developed.

Creating prescription authority and regulation of antibiotic use internationally is not a simple matter. The majority of pharmaceutical corporations are transnational in their marketing and production. Like their counterparts in the meat industry, they have financial incentives to avoid government regulation of their product sales. While industry has increasingly come to understand that widespread, inappropriate use of antibiotics will shorten the effectiveness of their products, that inevitability is likely to occur well beyond the life of the drugs' marketing plans, so this consideration may not be as central to decision making as safety would dictate. Misaligned financial incentives also are evident in Asia Pacific. Physicians in the region have historically been marketed with financial incentives to prescribe antibiotics. Drug salesmen, known as "detailers," call and visit physicians in practice to promote their products. In Asia, some hospital systems actually compensate physicians according to the number of prescriptions they write. This has resulted in profound overuse of antibiotics and very effective selection for drug resistance in a number of medical centers.

In developed countries where there is consumer ability to purchase drugs, there are incentives for drug producers to limit the regulation they work under and to promote the drugs they produce. In the US, for example, the past decade has seen the emergence of direct marketing to the consumer. This trend includes high investment by pharmaceutical companies in media advertisement campaigns to promote certain brand names of drugs. This trend has not included direct marketing of antibiotics to consumers, rather it has focused on the promotion of pain relievers, antidepressants, medications for sexual dysfunction and antihistamines and cold remedies. This relatively new media approach includes medications available by prescription only, often advising the public to "ask your doctor" for the pill by name.

Primary Prevention – The Role of Shoe Leather

The actual emergence of new microbes is difficult to prevent. In the case of antibiotic resistant organisms, the selective pressure is well known and characterized, and yet it is apparently difficult to remove. The promiscuous use of antimicrobials in humans and animals seems destined to continue in the near term, and thus every law of nature suggests the emergence of new resistant microbes will also continue. Similarly, medical forays into xenotransplantation and other procedures with unknown risks for disease emergence are inevitable. Meanwhile, the human population will continue to grow and increasingly tax the planet. International travel and trade will continue to expand, all the while tweaking the microbial world in unexpected ways. The challenge of preventing the emergence of new microbes is daunting and our resources and knowledge for doing so are limited.

So it is important to turn our attention to the next, or secondary, level of prevention – keeping a disease from spreading among local populations. In the following chapter we look at the tools available for local prevention and control: so called "shoe leather" epidemiology.

Study Questions

1. How many people today live without access to clean water and adequate sanitation? What percentage of the total global population does this represent?

Risky Trade

2. Give two examples of how consolidation and changes in process of biologically based products have contributed to primary emergence of new human pathogens.
3. The United States, as noted in the GAO report, is not collecting some key information about antibiotic use in animal feeds. What kind of information is missing and why is it important?

Chapter 7

Technical Armor

Accompanying the emergence and spread of trade- and travel-related infectious diseases are advancements in our ability to identify and respond to these infections. As we have seen in earlier chapters, we have managed to track the source of foodborne infections – sometimes thousands of miles across multiple borders – to the farms where the contamination originated. We identified and contained the first bout of the deadly worldwide SARS epidemic within months. And we have developed a series of treatments that significantly prolong AIDS patients' lives.

Unfortunately, the success stories we hear reflect those relatively rare occasions when we are able to tap the techniques, expertise and technology required to produce the kind of definitive result that merits publication in a scientific journal. A study of 336 foodborne outbreaks reported in the US in 1998 and 1999 found that investigators were able to pinpoint the food linked to the infection in less than half (46 percent) of all cases and confirm the culpable microbe in less than a third (29 percent) of cases (Jones, Imhoff et al. 2004). Consider that these success rates involve cases that were actually detected and reported, and that occurred in the US, which has comparatively robust public health expertise and technology resources.

While we are seeing the beginnings of a global infrastructure that will improve the safety of worldwide trade, the component tools, systems, agreements and regulations are nowhere near the scales they need to be to approach the growing threat. The next two chapters will look at existing resources and systems and examine some of the most significant gaps that merit prompt attention.

The Promise of Science – New Tools

In the Laboratory

Today, we are more adept than ever at identifying and characterizing the many strains of foodborne pathogens. Through techniques such as pulsed-field gel electrophoresis (PFGE), we can examine the DNA of isolates to determine if infections have a common source. The process entails splitting open the microbes and releasing their genetic material, which is then highlighted by applying stain and electronic charges that reveal the microbe's molecular patterns. Whole banks of molecular tracings are stored in computer databases, enabling investigators to link bugs from discrete geographical areas. PFGE slides such as the one shown in Figure 7.1 enable investigators to establish such relationships.

PulseNet is one such database which electronically connects state laboratories around the US, allowing them to compare PFGE results. Launched by the Centers

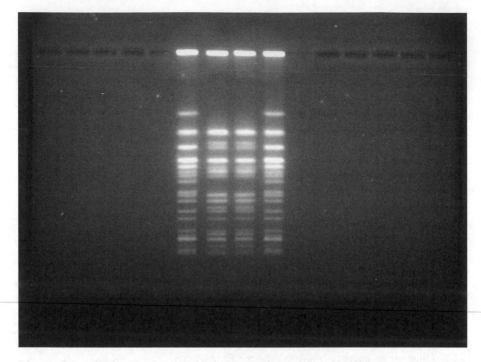

Figure 7.1   Example of a pulsed-field gel electrophoresis slide
Source: Callaway Packing PFGE Data Recall Release #RC-00-006
http://www.fsis-pfge.org/FOIA03-250-6.HTM. USDA, Food Safety and Inspection Service,
http://www.fsis-pfge.org/PFGE-Samples.html.

for Disease Control in 1998, the network now contains more than 100,000 DNA
fingerprints of various strains of *Salmonella*, *Escherichia coli*, *Shigella* and *Listeria*.
In recent years, PulseNet also began collecting data on *Campylobacter jejuni*,
Clostridium perfringens, *Vibrio parahaemolyticus/cholerae*, and *Yersinia*
enterocolitica. The network enables health officials to perceive clusters of cases and
examine their DNA patterns to see if they may be related. If common patterns
indicate the cases appear to have resulted from the same source, investigators can
then begin to explore what that source might be and take steps to prevent additional
infections. The European equivalent, Enter-Net, began as Salm-Net in 1994. The
surveillance network links some three dozen countries (mainly in Europe), enabling
them to share data and detect cross-border outbreaks of *Salmonella* and *E. coli*
infections. In 2001, the network surfaced 500 cases of *Salmonella Oranienburg* in
seven countries that ultimately were linked to chocolate made in Germany (Werber,
Dreesman et al. 2005). In 1996, it revealed more than 4,000 cases of *Salmonella*
Agona in four countries that investigators concluded were associated with a peanut
snack food (Killalea, Ward et al. 1996).

In the Field

As in the lab, the emergence of trade- and travel-related infections has highlighted both promising advances and significant obstacles in epidemiology. While some epidemic diseases, such as meningitis in West Africa and influenza in temperate zones, tend to occur seasonally and therefore present the opportunity to plan and prepare, most are unpredictable. So the work of epidemiologists – detecting, investigating and responding to outbreaks – tends to be ad hoc; in response to events. Programmatically, this is difficult for local health authorities. Their capacity – both in money and people – has to expand, often dramatically, in the face of a crisis.

Epidemiologic Investigations: Shoe Leather

Shoe leather is a prized component of epidemiological investigations. It is how epidemiologists refer to the extensive fieldwork involved. Good field epidemiology occurs not in an office, but at every location where the culprit microbe may have stopped en route to creating an outbreak. Given the length of production and distribution chains in the modern global express, epidemiologists need more than just shoes, of course. Epidemic investigations involve five basic steps: (1) the detection of a new problem, (2) the characterization of disease occurrence, (3) the systematic study of how the problem is perpetuated in the population, (4) the implementation of control strategies, and finally (5) the evaluation of those control strategies. In other words, epidemiologists determine what is going on, how to stop it, and how to be sure we have succeeded.

The epidemic techniques and methods vary, but successful investigations share several key features: the ability to know something unusual is happening in the population; the integration of clinical, laboratory and epidemiologic information to define the problem; and the capacity to carry out appropriate analytic studies to identify the source, most often with a "case-control" study, which will be described below.

Detecting the problem My students are always surprised to learn that the US does not have federally mandated disease reporting requirements. In fact, in our country, the requirement to report disease occurrence is a state function and varies widely by state. The Centers for Disease Control (CDC) make recommendations to the states and these recommendations are sometimes reinforced by states' desire to qualify for federal grants. In other words, state health departments may need to show they are compliant with disease reporting recommendations to be competitive for federal funding by CDC. But even if they attempt to comply, the reporting may not fully reflect what is happening in the region. States typically only require reporting on those diseases that tend to occur or are most threatening to the health of their populations. Successful disease reporting requires resource investment in diagnostic expertise and technologies, information processing and enforcement. These investments often come from the citizens living within a given state through tax and other revenues. Policy makers appropriately seek to limit unnecessary reporting in part because of the expense involved.

Public health students traditionally are taught that detection relies on surveillance of reported cases of illness: the ongoing collection, compilation and analysis of disease trend information in a population. In the US alone, some 3,000 local health departments, 59 state and territorial health departments and 180,000 laboratories contribute to surveillance efforts (US General Accounting Office 1999). In theory, surveillance information informs health officials about what is usual and therein allows the detection of the unusual. For instance, a large *E. coli* outbreak in 1997 was marked by unusually high rates of young children hospitalized with renal failure in Seattle's Children's Hospital & Regional Medical Center. But surveillance is rarely the means through which public health is alerted to epidemic occurrence. Routine laboratory-based surveillance typically does not include diagnostics for new agents in emerging infections, such as SARS. Moreover, while surveillance is potentially sensitive enough to reveal a change in patterns, it is generally not sufficiently specific, meaning it tends to create false alarms that are not warranted by the real occurrence of disease.

In fact, accurate alerts are more often generated through informal communications between clinicians and public health authorities than through formal disease reporting. While systems of national diagnostics might pick up unusual patterns (see the sprouts and *salmonella* case study below), clinicians often are in a position to provide earlier alerts of public health threats when they perceive unusual cases of disease. For the detection of new agents, both systems clearly contribute to the effort. Clinicians are unlikely to note subtle shifts in the identity of an agent if there is no accompanying change in clinical symptoms or in the type of person affected (for instance, people of a different age or gender). Formal systems of case reporting, on the other hand, have an inherent delay because of the time required to compile information, carry out diagnostics and compare results to baseline occurrence. For instance, in the summer of 2003, the Netherlands experienced about 50 percent more *Salmonella* enteritidis infections than it had in previous years – or an estimated 7,500 extra cases (Van Pelt, Mevius et al. 2004). But it was not until well after the fact that investigators were able to confirm the unusually high rates and assess potential sources. Eventually, they surmised that the likely cause was an unusually high portion of imported poultry as a result of an avian influenza outbreak in Dutch chickens that had curtailed the local supply. Had they known earlier, the imports could have been scrutinized more carefully. This delay can be short circuited if there are strong working relationships between health care providers and local public health. This was evident in the *E. coli* case mentioned above, in which it was actually an astute clinician at Seattle's Children's Hospital, not a surveillance system, who noticed an unusual number of children admitted with serious renal disease and alerted local health authorities. In the case of SARS, it was the insistence of local clinicians in Guangzhou, China, that the pneumonia they were seeing was not usual and not treatable that eventually created awareness of the epidemic.

But clinicians generally are not diligent reporters. They are busy and often unfamiliar with the public health context in which they are working. The CDC's Foodborne Disease Active Surveillance Network (FoodNet) attempts to address this problem by actively surveying laboratories in an effort to monitor foodborne disease trends. But the network, launched in 1995, is by no means comprehensive – as of 2004, it included 10 participating surveillance areas covering about 14 percent of the US population. Alternatively, Canadian health officials administer a global system that electronically monitors hundreds of news outlets, Internet discussion groups and other sources in English and French to detect potential outbreaks. The core technology is a Web-crawling software that operates 24/7, scouring the Internet for key phrases that might denote a new epidemic. The Global Public Health Intelligence Network (GPHIN), which is expanding to other languages, is a key source used to alert officials at health agencies worldwide, including the World Health Organization (WHO).

Ultimately, the dream of many in public health is to automate surveillance to cover a broader spectrum of the population and overcome delays in formal reporting. Generally, this involves automating the collection of diagnostic information from clinical records and the analysis of that compiled information to detect unusual occurrences. In addition to clinical diagnostics, the automated systems may incorporate reports of other indicators, such as school absenteeism, unexplained deaths, and emergency dispatches (Lober, Karras et al. 2002). The elevation of bioterrorism to a public health priority in the US has provided new impetus for developing these automated systems. This makes sense, since in the kind of crisis that a bioterrorist attack would precipitate, clinicians would be overwhelmed with caring for the ill and have little time to file reports to local health authorities. Consequently, several health organizations have begun to build automated alert systems. But establishing these systems entails a host of challenges. The patient confidentiality provisions of the US Health Insurance Portability and Accountability Act (HIPPA) of 1996, for instance, require system designers to strike a balance between collecting enough information to identify trends while at the same time protecting patients' identities. Another hurdle is incorporating data from diverse systems and analyzing the heterogeneous data in a meaningful way. For example, diseases may be categorized differently depending on individual institutions' coding and diagnostic systems, which are developed with many considerations in mind, from insurance billing purposes to historical practices. Some "syndromic surveillance" systems have addressed this problem by clustering cases by symptoms rather than by specific disease codes (Lober, Karras et al. 2002), enabling alerts when there is an unusual occurrence of a particular symptom, such as respiratory problems. Additionally, organizations may have different software and protocols for transmitting the data. Still another challenge is developing technology that is sophisticated enough to recognize phenomena such as seasonal surges (winter flu, for example) as expected occurrences rather than abnormal outbreaks meriting an alert. System designers must cope with all these elements and at the same time make the programs as unobtrusive and easy to use as possible (Lober, Karras et al. 2002).

Characterizing the disease Once an unusual surge of symptoms or disease occurrence is detected, the next step is establishing a "case definition." This definition is the cornerstone of the epidemiological investigation: what is a case and what is not? Making that call is somewhat of an art, especially when it involves a new agent that may not be readily identified in a laboratory. In that instance, it is important to keep a case definition "open" – to include cases that might have some, but not all, of the characteristic symptoms. At the same time epidemiologists can get confused if too many "noncases" are included.

In international epidemics, defining a case becomes even more complex, given the range of diagnostic capabilities, political and economic considerations. The early stages of the discovery of HIV/AIDS serve as an example. The HIV diagnostic test was not available until 1985. Even then, it was not generally available in some poor, heavily-impacted countries such as those in sub-Saharan Africa. In the late 1980s, three separate case definitions were in use: the "Bangui Definition" written by a group of experts convened in the capital of the Central African Republic, the "Caracas Definition" written by a group of experts in Venezuela and the "CDC Definition" devised by the US Centers for Disease Control. The Bangui definition was written to enable AIDS diagnoses where laboratory testing was not available, Caracas was for clinicians with access to HIV testing but not rigorous diagnostics for opportunistic infections, and the CDC definition was used by clinicians in wealthy countries where full diagnostics were available. Over time, as diagnostics became more available and more was known about the characteristics of AIDS, it became possible to generalize these definitions during the 1990s. Even today, different access to clinical and laboratory diagnostics exists for workers in rich and poor countries, a fact that profoundly complicates the ability to treat and prevent disease. In the 30 years of the global AIDS epidemic, generalizing (or equalizing) access to diagnostic tools has been only modestly successful. More recently, during the SARS outbreak in 2003, all of the countries involved employed the WHO's case definition – except the US. As a result, the number of SARS cases tallied by US officials and the WHO differed, creating a discrepancy that was not only confusing to the public but that also potentially undermined health officials' credibility.

Studying the problem   Once the case has been defined, the next step of the epidemic investigation is describing the epidemic or outbreak in terms of person, place and time. In other words, who is affected, where (geographically) cases are occurring and when in time the cases have occurred. The epidemiologist collects information from clinicians and other community sources and calculates a series of rates. Person, gender and age are key determinants – is it an outbreak in children? Is it in women or men or both? Historically, this has proven to be very important in understanding disease patterns, and not as straightforward as it appears. Returning to the example of HIV, during the initial stages of investigation in the 1980s, in the US, women were thought to be unaffected, because the first US cases affected men. But in Africa, AIDS was thought to be very different, because women and men were equally affected. Ultimately it became clear that both sexes are susceptible to HIV, and in fact in some instances women are more vulnerable to infection than men. So epidemiologists initially were misled about HIV in the Americas because the first cases in the US generally occurred in men who had sex with men and those with hemophilia, a disease that affects only men.

Data on the occurrence of the disease over time allows the construction of the "epi curve" (epidemic curve), which provides a clue about where the population is in the course of the epidemic. Classically, such curves are bell-shaped (Figure 7.2).

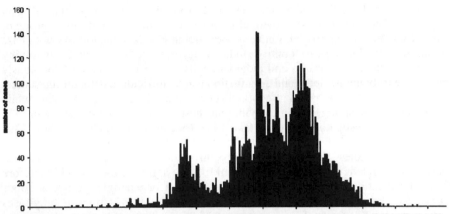

Figure 7.2   Probable cases of SARS by week of onset worldwide, 1 November 2002–10 July 2003

Notes:
1. n = 5,910.
2. This graph does not include 2,527 probable cases of SARS (2,521 from Beijing, China), for whom no dates of onset are currently available.

Source: http://www.who.int/csr/sarsepicurve/epiindex/index.html.

The epidemic growth at the front end can be sudden if there is a common source for the outbreak – such as a contaminated batch of ice cream – or more gradual if the transmission is from person to person. Usually, disease transmission ends and the epidemiologic curve tails off when all of the susceptible individuals in a population have become infected. The ill then either die or recover and have some immunity to reinfection. But public health interventions such as product recalls or isolation of infected persons also can hasten the end to epidemics and prevent additional illnesses and deaths. The nature of the intervention, of course, depends on the source of the outbreak. To discern this, health officials often rely heavily on case control studies, the workhorse of the epidemic investigation. This tool has been a centerpiece of the CDC's Epidemic Intelligence Service's success. Basically, it involves comparing a group of infected individuals (cases) with those who have remained uninfected (controls) to describe the differences in exposures between the two groups. If an investigation reveals that the infection is linked to a particular exposure (for instance, consumption of a certain batch of hamburger), then officials may be able to control the outbreak by ending or reducing that exposure (recalling the meat). The method made its dramatic debut in London during the great cholera outbreak of 1854. Pioneer epidemiologist John Snow mapped the city of London, noting where the cases occurred, along with the water districts. From this, he discerned that the neighborhoods where cholera was occurring were served by a single public pump, and that removing the pump handle would therefore eliminate the primary source of exposure.

Case control studies have since evolved from this very simple but elegant beginning. They involve taking meticulous histories from cases and from a group of carefully selected controls who have a comparable risk of infection. As with case definitions, conducting case control studies is again something of an art involving sometimes subtle distinctions and judgment calls. For example, controls obviously have to be truly uninfected – and an infection can be difficult to detect if the subject is incubating disease or has an infection that has not produced symptoms. And while there is typically an urgency in carrying out these studies to identify the source of the disease, investigators have to take time to construct reliable studies. This includes ensuring that the size of the study sample is adequate and addressing potential bias issues. For instance, case control studies must contend with recall bias, or the tendency of a person who is ill to have a greater interest and therefore better recollection of events leading to the illness (for example, particular foods consumed) than a person who is not ill. Another potential bias is overmatching cases and controls. For example, if controls are drawn from the cases' friends or neighbors, they may share characteristics that ultimately turn out to be potential risk factors for the infection, such as a shared water source. Obviously if the people being studied have all been selected because they share a common characteristic, then this characteristic cannot be examined in the study.

Sprouts and *salmonella*: a case study

The detection and investigation of an international outbreak stemming from the sprout trade reported by Mahon, Ponka et al. (1997) illustrates the potential of epidemiologic techniques.

Detection   In June 1995, a surveillance system newly instituted by the US Centers for Disease Control and Prevention picked up an increase in the occurrence of the *Salmonella Stanley* strain, particularly in Arizona and Michigan. The Salmonella Outbreak Detection Algorithm (SODA) compares electronic reports from the nationwide Public Health Laboratory Information System (linked to state public health departments around the country) and signals when an unusually high number of cases are reported in a particular region. Coincidentally, standardized serotyping within Salm-net (now Enter-Net), a laboratory-based surveillance system of the European Union and the European Cooperation in Science and Technology, picked up an outbreak of the same strain in Finland. European officials reported that the spread appeared to be associated with consumption of alfalfa sprouts.

Characterizing the disease   After the outbreaks were detected, health officials in Arizona, Michigan and Finland conducted case control studies. In each instance, cases were defined as people who had become ill in the specified timeframe (which varied by location) and had submitted samples that showed the presence of *S. Stanley* (see Figure 7.3).

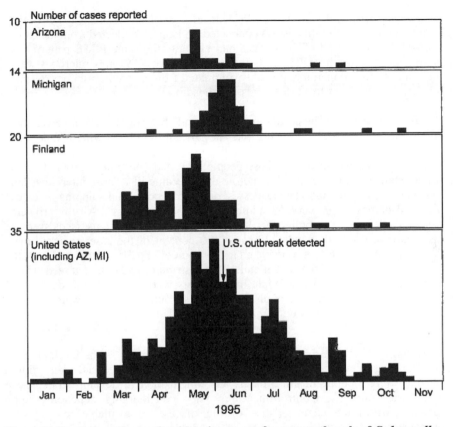

Figure 7.3 Comparison of epidemic curves for one outbreak of *Salmonella*, 1997

Note: The week of illness onset (Arizona, Michigan, US) or stool sampling (Finland) of patients with *Salmonella Stanley* infections, 1 January – 30 November 1995.
Source: Mahon, Pouka et al. 1997.

Studying the disease Investigators matched the cases they identified with controls who had not become ill. In the US investigations, cases and controls were matched by age and neighborhood. In Finland, family members and public health workers served as controls. Cases and controls were questioned about recent food and environmental exposures. In Arizona, 39 percent of the 19 cases recalled recently consuming sprouts, while only 8 percent of the 18 controls reported consuming sprouts. Similarly, in Michigan, 41 percent of the 29 cases and 10 percent of the 58 controls reported eating alfalfa sprouts. Finnish public health authorities found that fully 100 percent of the 25 cases remembered eating sprouts, compared to only 20 percent of the 25 controls. US investigators then contacted other states with recently-reported *S. Stanley* cases and requested them to explore possible links with alfalfa sprout consumption.

Conducting laboratory diagnosis   Pulsed-field gel electrophoresis (PFGE) and antimicrobial susceptibility assays conducted on isolates collected from the cases showed that almost all of the isolates had virtually the same PFGE pattern and antimicrobial resistances. The tests indicated that the *S. Stanley* microbes were the same strain and therefore probably originated from a common source, despite the fact that the cases lived thousands of miles apart.

Seeking the source   The next step was to find that source. US investigators employed a "trace-back" investigation. They began by interviewing people who had become infected and reported recently eating sprouts – 50 cases in six states. (The trace-back included only those people who had consumed sprouts from a single retail outlet in the five days before they became ill.) Those interviews led to stores and restaurants. The businesses' delivery records and shipping invoices provided names of growers, lot numbers and sprouting dates. All the growers were linked to a US supplier that had purchased nearly half its seeds from a distributor in the Netherlands; ultimately, 96 percent of the cases reported that they had eaten sprouts that were linked to this source. The Finnish cases also were linked to the shipper in the Netherlands. This distributor had obtained seeds from Italy, Hungary and Pakistan. While investigators were never able to determine which of these sources was implicated in these outbreaks, they were able to firmly link infections to sprouts from the Danish distributor.

Developing and evaluating control strategies   Concurrent with developing an understanding of whom a disease affects, how it is transmitted and identifying a probable source, public health officials are called upon to develop strategies to control the outbreak. Control measures vary considerably depending upon everything from the characteristics of the disease to available resources to government officials' willingness to recognize and tackle an outbreak. For instance, in the case of SARS, which is transmitted person to person and is highly contagious, infected patients are isolated and travel is restricted. As the understanding of HIV/AIDS has grown, strategies have evolved to include protected sex, needle exchanges and heat treatment of blood supplies. Arresting the spread of foodborne diseases, from BSE to *Salmonella*, often entails slaughters, recalls and embargoes. In this chapter, we will discuss some of the technical tools available for containing outbreaks in the context of foodborne disease. The following chapter will examine some of the international frameworks in place for containing and halting the spread of disease.

As illustrated in the *S. Stanley* case study in this chapter and the foodborne outbreaks featured in Chapter 2, tracking the source of an outbreak can be a labyrinthine and often futile process. Weeks, or even months, can elapse between the time a food is produced and the time it is consumed and signs of illness surface. Elements of a single infected cow potentially can be dispersed and incorporated into multiple products, from cosmetics to steaks to animal feed (Figure 7.4).

With products moving faster and further around the globe, systems that identify where food products originated and the routes they travel "from farm to table" are

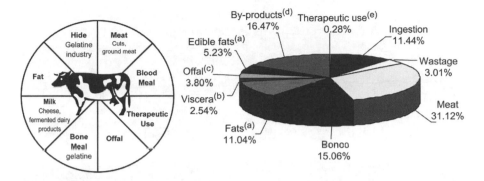

Figure 7.4   Composition and use of a bovine

Notes:

a) composed of: fats of head, heart, neck, tripe, intestines, pancreas, liver, kidneys, pelvic cavity, genitals, sacral canal
b) composed of: tripe, third stomach, rennet, reticulum, intestine, bladder, spleen, chitterlings, intestinal walls for sausages
c) composed of: tongue, brain, cheek, lung, heart, sweetbreads, liver, kidneys, stomach, tail, marrow, scrap meat
d) composed of: nerves, blood, leg bones, foot bones, skull bones, maxillary, horns, hide, hair, calcul, bile, industrial fat
e) composed of: pituitary gland, hypothalamus, parathyroids, thyroid glands, adrenal glands, epithelium, pancreas, prostate

Source: Barcos 2001.

becoming increasingly important. So-called traceability systems for animals and animal products have existed in some form in industrialized countries for decades. Livestock are identified by brands, tattoos, tags or implants, and that identification is used to track their movements and the other animals and herds to which they are exposed (Figure 7.5). Identification techniques must at once be convenient, durable, affordable and harmless to the animal (Barcos 2001).

Even more complicated than tracking the movement of livestock is tracking food products, which are blended with other batches, and potentially repeatedly processed and stored for varying periods of time (Pettitt 2001). Animal products typically are identified by "lots" that designate products that were handled, processed and stored under similar conditions, including time and place. Fruit and vegetable products historically have not been tracked as meticulously as animal products, in part because of the difficulty of labeling individual items, but those requirements are changing. The US Bioterrorism Act of 2002, for instance, requires records reporting the previous location and next destination of all food products from any enterprise that manufactures, processes, packs, transports, distributes, receives, holds, or imports food – although farms and restaurants are exempted (US Food and Drug Administration 2004). Meanwhile the European Union, concerned about potential health and environmental consequences of genetically modified foods, has explored traceability and labeling requirements for any genetically

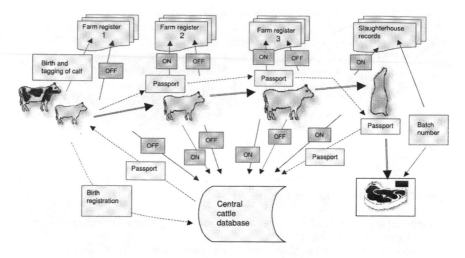

Figure 7.5   The cattle tracing system in Great Britain
Source: Pettitt 2001.

modified ingredients, a move that has been challenged as a trade barrier by the US, Canada and Argentina.

As with surveillance, the effectiveness of traceability systems relies in part on common definitions and procedures, from what is tracked to how it is categorized and labeled (Caporale, Giovannini et al. 2001). And once again, this standardization depends not only on common systems but upon universally available resources. Much work remains to create global systems that collect the necessary information to trace the many steps a product follows from inception to consumption, including rearing, feeding, slaughtering, rendering, packing, storing and shipping.

In cases in which a contaminated food source is identified, there remain the additional challenges of determining if the tainted food source cross contaminated other foods, and of notifying consumers who may already have purchased or consumed the infected products. In the US, the USDA's Food Safety and Inspection Service (FSIS) oversees recalls for meat, poultry and processed eggs and the Food and Drug Administration (FDA) regulates all other food products, including fruits, nuts and vegetables. Some 36 million pounds of meat and poultry were recalled in 2003. With the exception of infant formula, recalls generally are voluntary, although if the food distributors refuse to retrieve potentially contaminated products, the agencies can seize or detain those products. In a 2004 report, the US Government Accountability Office concluded that the food agencies need more clout to enforce recalls, and that in any event, they need to do a better job tracking the recalls that do take place (US Government Accountability Office 2004a). An analysis of 10 recalls under the purview of each agency between May 2003 and Aug 2004 showed that both agencies were slow to verify the recalls were being carried out, with the USDA averaging 38 days and the FDA 31 days – in some cases exceeding the recalled foods' shelf life. The GAO's survey of a sampling of 2003 recalls at both agencies indicated that well under half the recalled products were recovered – an average of 36 percent for FDA-regulated foods and 38 percent for USDA-regulated foods (US Government Accountability Office 2004a).

For the most part, the public is notified of the recall via press releases. Because food distribution channels are considered private business information (who sold what where), the FDA and USDA usually cannot publicly reveal the retail outlets that received the recalled products. Even if they could, the continual repackaging, mixing and processing can make it difficult if not impossible for customers to discern whether they are purchasing or consuming a recalled product (Figure 7.6).

"Generally distributors purchase beef from multiple sources, mix it in their inventory, and lose track of the source of the beef they send to the stores that they supply" (US Government Accountability Office 2004a p. 41). According to the report, this practice complicated the recall that followed after a single cow in Washington state tested positive for BSE in late 2003. Initially the recall targeted the 23 carcasses that were slaughtered on the same day and location as the infected cow, but those were shipped with 20 other carcasses, which were by then indistinguishable because their identification tags had been removed. So the recall then grew to include all 43 carcasses, which were in turn distributed to processing facilities, which blended their meat with that of other cattle; then distributors; then

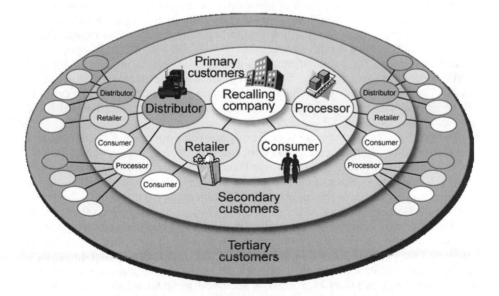

Figure 7.6   The food distribution chain
Source: US Government Accountability Office 2004a.

retail operations, some of which again mixed the potentially contaminated meat with other non-contaminated meat. Ultimately, an estimated 64,000 pounds of beef were recovered or destroyed, but it is unclear how much of the 10,400 pounds of initially targeted meat was included in that recovery (US Government Accountability Office 2004a). The enormous scope of this recall highlights the importance of understanding the magnitude of the potential problem before taking the drastic measure of ordering a recall. (For details, see the Risk Analysis discussion in Chapter 8.)

The Global Safety Net

The current techniques and technology available for identifying outbreaks and their sources represent significant strides in epidemiology, and promise still more for the future. But two important gaps remain. The first is the disparities in different nations' abilities to detect and respond to outbreaks. The second is the lack of communication across borders and disciplines about the growing dangers linked to globalization and the spread of disease.

Resource Gap

In traditional systems in the developed world, a local health department experiencing a major outbreak can call in national authorities to help, mobilize other resources in the community such as university or civic groups with expertise, or bring in assistance from neighboring jurisdictions. But in poor countries the task of mobilizing resources is more daunting. In the best of times, local health capacity is strapped. Basic public health services such as childhood immunizations, food vendor inspections, and environmental health regulation are lacking. Foodborne and waterborne infections are routine. When an epidemic of disease strikes, these fragile local systems are often overwhelmed. And their support network typically is limited; their national governments may also lack the people and technological resources such as laboratories to cope with the crisis.

The provision of medical care is extremely uneven from country to country, and the accessibility of health care is likewise uneven. In fact, the amount of dollars spent on "health" according to the World Bank ranges from $22.60 per person per year in low income countries to $2,841 per person per year in high income countries – a hundredfold difference. Access to a physician ranges from four physicians for every 10,000 people in poor countries to 28 physicians for every 10,000 people in wealthy countries. National systems of health services delivery are extremely varied in how they work, how trained or skilled their personnel are, how well supplied and supported the personnel are to do their job and how regularly and how much they are compensated for working. Hospitals are variously seen as places to avoid until one is near death, or places to go early in an illness to seek care, depending on the success of the hospital and the prevailing belief and confidence of the community in the institution. In many countries, access to health care is simply not adequate to detect the emergence of infections until dramatic loss of life occurs. This was evident in the famous Kikwit outbreak of Ebola. By the time the government sounded an alarm, the outbreak was more than two months in progress and had caused hundreds of deaths. The Kikwit hospital, which became the epicenter of infection, had no running water or barrier materials, making the containment of the infection all but impossible. While the outbreak was not trade-related, it illustrates the potential of disease to spread unchecked in countries that lack the resources for effective detection and response.

Moreover, the inability of a government to effectively deal with a problem such as a disease outbreak serves as a disincentive to accurately count the problem. Consider, for instance, the cyclical epidemics in sub-Saharan Africa of meningitis, a severe disease in which the lining that surrounds the brain and cushions it from the skull becomes inflamed. Without treatment, it is often fatal. Epidemics occur every four years in countries along the "meningitis belt" such as Burkina Faso, Mali, and Niger, claiming thousands of lives. While effective vaccinations against infection exist and the condition can be successfully treated, vaccinations have not been available in sub-Saharan Africa, and treatment is often not available either. Consequently, tracking and reporting cases is of limited benefit. So although some meningitis outbreaks in northwestern Africa are reported through the World Health Organization, they represent a profound undercount of the actual occurrence of the disease. This situation is changing as the necessary vaccines are becoming more available to poor countries. Another obstacle to detecting and reporting disease is the potential economic consequences of an outbreak. As the next chapter will illustrate, reports of infectious disease can result in economically devastating trade and travel embargoes.

Various global initiatives are under way to address the disparities. In an effort to enhance surveillance worldwide, the World Health Organization initiated the Global Salmonella Survey (GSS) network in 2000. The international surveillance program collects laboratory data primarily on *Salmonella* outbreaks from participating members from around the world. It also provides regional epidemiology and laboratory training, along with quality assurance and testing services. The network's members represent about 140, or 70 percent, of the world's countries. Still, as Figure 7.7 suggests, many member countries lack the expertise and resources to perform regular testing and surveillance. Collection techniques are far from uniform, making data comparisons problematic.

Similarly, the laboratory database PulseNet also has begun to branch beyond borders. PulseNet International has included PulseNet Canada since 1999, and work has begun to establish similar networks in Europe, Asia Pacific, and Latin America. The PulseNet database helped link two small clusters of *E. coli* O157:H7 infections that occurred six months and thousands of miles apart in Southern California and Okinawa, Japan (Centers for Disease Control and Prevention 2005). Like Salm Surv, PulseNet's successful expansion relies on standardized practices among participants – no small feat considering varying resources, training and systems. In this respect, it is sometimes easier for such networks to expand into developing countries without existing systems than it is into countries with previously established practices. Adding to the challenge is the likelihood that new, more sensitive molecular sequencing-based subtyping methods are probably in

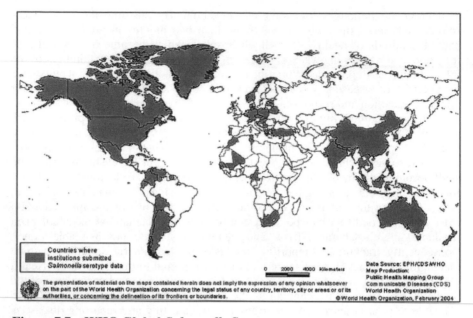

Figure 7.7   WHO Global *Salmonella* Survey
Note: Shading indicates countries where GSS institutions submitted *Salmonella* serotype data at any time between 1998 and 2003 (as of February 2004).
Source: World Health Organization Global Salmonella Survey, http://www.who.int/globalatlas/animatedmaps/gss/gssmaps.html#.

PulseNet's future. Ideally, these new systems will be designed to be compatible with the current program so that the existing databases remain relevant.

Also in 2000, the World Health Organization founded the Global Outbreak Alert and Response Network (GOARN), which provides assistance within 24 hours to governments facing potential epidemics. The network taps experts and technical resources from around the world to quickly identify and respond to disease outbreaks of international importance. WHO coordinates the response and rounds up the necessary resources. Teams "parachute in" with portable laboratories equipped to communicate around the globe from even the most remote areas. In its first five years of operation, the network organized responses to more than 50 events in some 40 countries, tapping more than 400 experts for assistance.

Along with WHO's program providing broader access to diagnostics and emergency assistance are efforts to standardize and improve epidemiological investigation methods. In the late 1970s, for example, the US Centers for Disease Control began to promote its epidemiologic investigation practices internationally by exporting its Epidemic Intelligence Service (EIS), a two-year, on-the-job training program for health professionals that focuses on detecting, investigating and responding to disease outbreaks. The effort included a number of US/European workshops and training courses. While European countries had routinely used many of the same tools as the US, they used them in somewhat different ways. These collaborative trainings helped to generalize the tools and their use in the developed world. The global EIS targeted countries somewhat haphazardly, based on the interest of national authorities and the political importance of the country to US interests. In 1997, the Training Programs in Epidemiology and Public Health Interventions Network (TEPHINET) was launched to support field-based training programs to further bolster global competence in epidemiology. TEPHINET includes "train-the-trainers" workshops in an attempt to broaden expertise in participating countries.

In addition to these efforts, the World Trade Organization offers training and technical assistance to help developing countries understand and meet the food safety requirements stipulated in the various trade agreements, which will be discussed at length in the next chapter. But the training is of limited value when there are inadequate resources available to make sustainable changes to safety systems. In an attempt to address this, the Food and Agriculture Organization (FAO), World Organization for Animal Health (OIE), World Bank, WHO and WTO have launched a grant program that provides some assistance for projects related to meeting the WTO's Sanitary and Phytosanitary standards. Among the challenges of implementing these projects is ensuring that they target the welfare of the country as a whole rather than focusing exclusively, for instance, on the safety of export crops.

In summary, while there are some programs in place to provide assistance on a global level, these efforts are inadequate to address the enormous gap in public health resources between poor and rich countries. The growing scope and pace of traffic and change in the global marketplace serves to accentuate and in some cases widen this gap.

Communications Gap

While trade and travel have rendered borders moot when it comes to the spread of disease, there is slim awareness of outbreaks in trade and travel partners' economies. Similarly, there is disturbingly little "cross talk" between the health authorities and their counterparts in the commercial and transportation sectors about relevant trends.

We need more international collaboration so that health authorities are alerted to our trading partners' health concerns. This process is hindered by more than just the logistical challenges discussed above. While we thoroughly document worldwide imports, exports, and travel patterns, missing from the records are reliable reports about the health of the populations within countries that constitute the market for travel or imported foodstuffs. An improved understanding of health conditions worldwide would help identify the populations most at risk from the importation of emergent diseases. However, my travels to the most remote regions of sub-Saharan Africa suggest such targeting might be misleading. Imports penetrate well beyond urban centers where health monitoring systems are more likely to be in place. Small roadside vendors along the most rudimentary dirt roads peddle all manner of imported cigarettes, medications and other products.

We also need more communication across disciplines. Trade in a new food or pharmaceutical commodity generally is not tracked by public health at the local level. In fact, local health authorities are no more aware of major shifts in how people make a living in their communities than anyone else. The driver for change in the nature of work is the private sector: the employer. In subsistence economies, the "employer" may be the crop and the harvest and the market rather than an organized entity. If public health is to become proactive in preventing the incursion of new infections through trade and travel, part of the task is to become informed about the shifts in those segments that affect the local population. While public health workers who live in their communities have a certain level of local knowledge, major changes often still surprise them. Public health is rarely consulted, for instance, in the planning process for a new factory, bridge, air route, or for importing food or pharmaceutical products. Systematic consultation in such decision making may not be efficient. But the current division in thinking and operation between public health, commerce and transportation at the local level is not working, either. Some initial efforts are under way to bridge these divides. PulseNet, for example, is partnering with VetNet, a new network comprising animal health and veterinary groups that study zoonotic infections, and collaborating with the food industry and with the Bioterrorism Prevention and Response Program, which focuses on intentional infections.

Even within disciplines, poor coordination hinders safety systems from working as effectively as possible. Indeed, the US system for monitoring food safety, which has developed organically as various concerns arise, is remarkably fragmented and in some cases even illogical. The system encompasses some 30 laws administered by 12 agencies (US Government Accountability Office 2004a). The regulation of eggs illustrates just one of the complexities. While the FDA oversees matters relating to eggs still in the shell, once those shells are cracked and the eggs are in some way "processed," responsibility shifts to the USDA's FSIS. Similarly, the regulatory agency responsible for a food product such as a pizza or a sandwich depends on the particular ingredients; "… federal responsibilities for regulating the production and processing of a packaged ham and cheese sandwich depends on whether the sandwich is made with one or two slices of bread, not on the risk associated with the ingredients" (US Government Accountability Office 2004a pp. 7 8). So open faced sandwiches are inspected daily by the USDA's FSIS while the FDA inspects manufacturers of closed-faced sandwiches about once every five years. A GAO analysis of 8,653 FDA inspections conducted in six states between October 1987 and March 1991 found that nearly 6 percent duplicated inspections performed by other agencies.

In essence, global safety systems do not approach adequacy to meet the challenge of trade and travel today. The scale of these systems, where they exist at all, is entirely insufficient to ensure safety. Under the Clinton Administration, the Secretary of Agriculture came and addressed my class on Emerging Infections. He stated that a new system, PulseNet, was operating in all 50 states to keep food safe for Americans. I knew the system, which at that time covered two states. The Secretary of Agriculture is not the only person to be duped by upward accountability in the public sector. It is endemic to international organizations, national governments and non-governmental organizations as well. Known as "happy talk" in the private sector, it is false comfort indeed. This emperor's-new-clothes approach to building public health systems will not work. The emergence of new infections is telling us we are naked, and pretending otherwise is dangerous and ludicrous.

Study Questions

1. How do new genetic diagnostic techniques help in the battle against trade-related infections? Give two examples of working international laboratory networks based on these technologies.
2. What are the five steps in field epidemiologic investigations?
3. Explain what an epidemic curve is. How is it useful in epidemic investigation? Give one example from the previous chapters.

Chapter 8

Preventing Global Outbreaks

Returning to our pyramid, we reach the top, or tertiary, level – preventing a local outbreak from becoming internationally dispersed. Just as initial efforts to detect and contain an outbreak rely on local regional and national health systems, attempts to prevent that outbreak from becoming an international pandemic also depend on global systems that regulate the major cross-border conduits of disease – trade, transportation and travel. Historically, the movement of humans, animals and goods has largely been controlled at a national level. But as global exchanges have proliferated, the importance of international legal rules has increased. The World Health Organization's International Health Regulations provide a framework for controlling the movement of people and goods in the event of concerns about international disease transmission. Also governing international trade are the agreements under the World Trade Organization (WTO), covering everything from food safety standards to patent protections for prescription drugs. This chapter will explore the aspects of these international rules that are most critical to controlling emerging infections.

Regulating the global express can be disruptive in many ways. It inconveniences travelers. There are enormous ripple effects when travel or trade is halted, or more commonly, when people or products are delayed to allow for testing or inspection. But when pathogens are zipping from place to place by air, sea or land, moved by humans, vehicles, or goods, they also can cause enormous damage to both health and economies. Although safety measures such as inspections or embargos may be merited, the disruptions present a challenge for business and industry, for whom predictability is central to success. For the most part, an effective public health system enables a community to go about its business without the threat of sudden cataclysmic health crises, such as epidemics. But microbes and Mother Nature are not always predictable, as we have seen. Crises do occur. Then, what happens among communities, among public health authorities, national governments and international organizations?

Regulating the flow of persons and goods traditionally has been an action between two economies, at port level or at national level. This occurs either when a country grounds its own traffic and prohibits it from leaving the country, or when a second country prohibits incoming traffic. But these restrictions often have been put into place in response to disease on a haphazard basis. Sometimes the motivation for stopping traffic may masquerade as a health concern, but actually be motivated by an economic or political interest. Regardless of the motivation, embargoes and quarantines can have enormous repercussions. When trade in a given product is stopped by an importing country, particularly when it is done abruptly, the exporting, producing country feels great economic pain. When Guatemala lost the

US market for raspberries due to a series of *Cyclospora* outbreaks in the US in the mid-1990s, the number of raspberry growers in Guatemala dropped from 85 to three (Calvin 2003). When trade in British beef was halted due to BSE and new variant Creutzfeldt-Jakob disease, the damage to that industry was more than $100 billion (Cunningham 2003). In addition to the immediate business lost during an embargo, there are the ill-defined future losses of the trading relationship, for postponement of deal-making for future trade, and the potential for one country's suppliers to be replaced by another's for an extended time. The estimated costs of lost business due to travel warnings and restrictions during the SARS epidemic figure in the tens of billions of dollars (World Bank Group 2003).

Given these high stakes, the international trading regimes seek to provide coherent frameworks that are consistently applied across countries and circumstances to achieve some measure of predictability and objective application. To this end, they rely on standards typically set by various international bodies and founded in "science." But the characterization of that science for trade purposes is vulnerable to various influences. Some contend that it is often guided by the interests of the wealthy countries and corporations that dominate research, policy making and trade in these arenas. Consequently, the resulting international rules, while perhaps well intended, may be influenced by the power dynamics at play during their creation. Much has been written about the power politics that many feel are embedded in the conception, negotiation, design and operation of the global trading regimes. But this is not the focus here. In this chapter, we will discuss the health-based regulatory systems for global trade and travel. We are looking to see how they work, have worked or could work to help prevent global epidemics of infectious diseases. Are they the potential tools and levers of a new global public health? Do they or could they provide effective alerts about emerging infections? How are they used to protect traffic? How do the "brakes" work?

Regulating International Travel – WHO and the International Health Regulations

While efforts to curb the international spread of disease via travel have taken on new urgency in recent years with the emergence of SARS and avian influenza, they are by no means new. The spread of disease to geographically dispersed areas via travel, immigration and indeed, the slave trade, reaches back centuries (Morse 1995). In the mid-1800s, as transportation advances and industrialization accelerated global commerce, the major trading nations began a series of so-called International Sanitary Conferences. Initial discussions focused on blocking the spread of plague, cholera and yellow fever, primarily by developing common quarantine standards among European trading partners (World Health Organization Regional Committee for the Western Pacific 1998). In the ensuing decades, international public health's emphasis would in part shift away from quarantine measures, focusing instead on improving individual nations' overall health systems and technical competencies for detecting and addressing disease. That focus was highlighted in 1948, with the creation of the World Health Organization, with its mission of "the attainment by all people of the highest possible level of health."

Strengthening disease prevention, surveillance and control on local and national levels remain core strategies for controlling international outbreaks, as do quarantines and other national measures for halting traffic. But in addition to these efforts, recent international events have underscored the need to retool WHO's primary legally binding mechanism for addressing actual or potential international disease spread – the International Health Regulations. As the fast-moving SARS outbreak made clear, in a world where people can circle the globe in less than a day, and the spread of a disease routinely outpaces its detection, the need for more proactive multilateral and international oversight has become critical. In such instances, border control approaches such as quarantine do not work as stand-alone strategies, and also may be introduced in inappropriate contexts. With these realities as a backdrop, WHO has been reshaping its role in the event of international outbreaks.

The International Health Regulations were first passed by the World Health Assembly in 1951 as the International Sanitary Regulations (ISR), and then renamed in 1969. As a United Nations specialized agency, WHO represents and serves virtually all of the world's countries. (The World Trade Organization, by contrast, includes only countries that have agreed to be bound by its treaties.) The IHR are generally considered to be legally binding international agreements for the countries that are parties and therefore constitute legal obligations for each of those countries. In recent decades, the International Health Regulations have been very limited in their scope and application. This has been in large part because until recently, the Regulations were outdated and consequently mostly irrelevant to the challenges of modern infectious disease prevention and control efforts. One major limitation was that the obligatory reporting by member countries to WHO of outbreaks had been limited to six and eventually just three diseases: yellow fever, plague and cholera.

In 1995, the World Health Assembly adopted a resolution to revise the regulations (WHA Resolution 48.7: "Revision and Updating of the International Health Regulations") and a multiyear process began to update the IHR. Before that, there had been relatively little change to the rules for some 30 years (other than to delete three diseases which they had previously covered – smallpox, relapsing fever and typhus). While a number of theories have been advanced regarding these decades of stagnation amidst a world of change, the fundamental reason is that after some significant advances in prevention and treatment, the world grew complacent about fighting infectious disease. Antibiotics, oral rehydration salts and vaccination made the three diseases covered in the IHR less feared. This complacency was accompanied by a general feeling post World War II that the battle against infectious disease had basically been won. The advent of antibiotics, improved standards of hygiene, clean water and waste disposal in much (although by no means all) of the world's peoples, and the "magic bullets" of vaccines against smallpox and polio all suggested that humankind had won the war with the microbes. If only that were true.

With the advent of HIV/AIDS in the early 1980s, the world became gripped by a new, unknown and fatal pandemic threat. This brought about efforts by some to close borders, require blood tests or "AIDS-free" certificates for admission, or restrict travel by people with HIV/AIDS. Cuba instituted compulsory testing and involuntary hospitalization of those with HIV. At the same time an unprecedented global effort to tackle the new disease (despite its stigma) was launched by the WHO and the Global Program on AIDS. AIDS and tuberculosis were seriously considered for addition to the list of notifiable diseases under the IHR regime in the 1980s. Some advocated including the diseases to enable border restrictions on the entry of potentially infected people, while others hoped that such a move would help protect people with HIV and tuberculosis. Discussions swirled as the Global Program on AIDS raised unprecedented funds for its program and launched global summits to bring together researchers, government, AIDS patients, and advocates in a potent mix for the media. In the end, the IHR were not permanently altered for HIV, but the appreciation of the threat of new human infections was heightened. The age of the pandemic was not over.

At the end of the 1980s and in the early 1990s several events spurred renewed interest in revising the IHR. In the battle against HIV/AIDS, donor fatigue, frustration, and internal infighting were taking their toll. The Global Program on AIDS was outgrowing its home within the WHO. The Institute of Medicine and others were beginning to outline the case that the emergence of HIV/AIDS was not a unique, solitary accident of history. It began to be seen as a harbinger for the reawakening of the threat of emerging infections to the increasingly global human community.

In 1991, cholera appeared in Latin America after a 50-year absence from the hemisphere. A large outbreak in Peru quickly extended throughout the region and severe trade embargos against a range of Peruvian products crippled an already poor national economy. Everything from fish products to cotton sundries was embargoed by trading partners under the guise of preventing extension of cholera into their territories. However, the epidemic marched on, extending up and down the coastline of Latin America and into the Andes. The punishing embargoes against Peru only served to deepen the country's misery. The Pan American Health Organization has estimated the economic cost in just nine months rose to $770 million (World Health Organization 1998) and most consider this estimate conservative. In 1994, an eruption of bubonic and pneumonic plague burst forth in India, originating in the city of Surat. Panic was widespread, with diamond workers abandoning the mines in Surat, and people desperately fleeing the affected areas. Air India jets were refused permission to enter the airspace of some other countries. Travel into India virtually halted. Broad trade embargoes were again put into place. The toll for the emergence of disease was mounting: nearly a billion dollars for Peru, several billion dollars for India. In each of these costly outbreaks, the prophetic Institute of Medicine 1992 report on the factors of emergence were at play: the demographic pressure of urbanization coupled with inadequate investment in public health infrastructure in both outbreaks conspired to create a fragile foundation for public safety. All it took for Peru was the introduction of cholera, suspected to have come from the ballast of a Chinese freighter discharged into harbor waters, and for India the packed underground quarters of the diamond mining industry, and the balance was tipped.

Meanwhile, the Global Program on AIDS evolved into a new, independent entity (UNAIDS), and WHO elected a new Director General who set a reorganization in motion, including a new cluster of programs dedicated to the surveillance, prevention, and control of infectious diseases. At the same time, WHO adopted a new strategy of international collaboration, as witnessed with the establishment of the Global Outbreak Alert and Response Network (GOARN – see Chapter 7). In the push toward international coordination, the International Health Regulations stood out as a possible tool. But the IHR were badly in need of revision.

The 10-year revision process, completed in May 2005, was complex both technically and politically. Revising the original structure of the IHR posed at least four major challenges: (1) the limited scope of disease covered by the Regulations, (2) the delay of critical disease notifications by countries due to lagging diagnoses and concerns about potential travel and trade repercussions, (3) the limited number of sources that were considered legitimate for reporting disease outbreaks, and (4) the limited resources available for addressing outbreaks. The revised Regulations, which take effect two years after their adoption by the World Health Assembly, or in May 2007, address most of these concerns.

Rather than relying only on a specific disease diagnosis, the requirement for notifying outbreaks to WHO for countries under the new Regulations is triggered primarily by the presence of indicators of a potential public health emergency that may affect other countries. An algorithm, or "decision instrument" has been developed to help determine if such a situation exists; this is shown in Figure 8.1.

In addition, to assist countries in deciding whether to make a notification to WHO, the new Regulations include a list of certain diseases which, if detected in a country, would specifically require the country to use the factors in the algorithm to see if reporting is necessary. These diseases include those with the demonstrated ability to seriously impact public health and to spread rapidly internationally, such as cholera and yellow fever. The Regulations also include a very short list of diseases, such as smallpox or SARS, which are considered potentially so serious that even one case in a country must be reported to WHO. Under the regulations, WHO may consider sources of disease reports other than official notifications (media reports or confidential contacts, for instance), and if they appear legitimate, attempt to confirm them with member states (Article 9). The Regulations also require member states to develop the capacity to prevent, detect, report and respond to outbreaks of any of the diseases considered notifiable under the conditions above (Article 5). Some members may be eligible for technical or financial assistance in meeting those criteria. Upon adoption of the revised Regulations, WHO Director-General Dr. Lee Jong-wook commented, "These new regulations recognize that diseases do not respect national boundaries. They are urgently needed to help limit the threats to public health" (WHO 2005).

Travel Advisories

Along with spurring the revision of the IHR, the recent international epidemics prompted WHO to make use of travel advisories, a sometimes controversial measure that warns off travelers from areas where they may be exposed to infectious

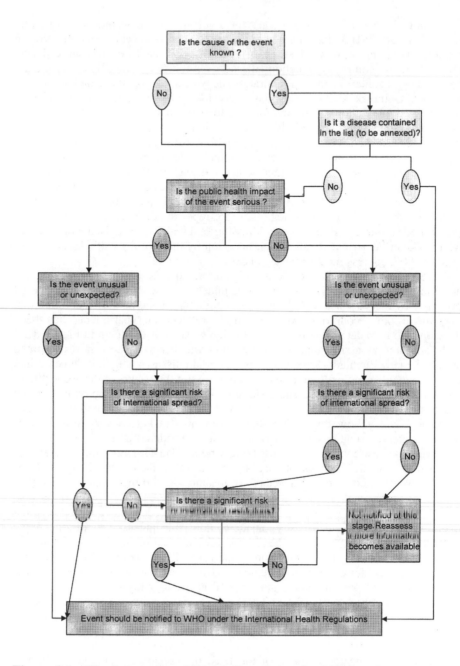

**Figure 8.1   The International Health Regulations' public health emergency
              decision algorithm**

Source: WHO International Health Regulations (2005).

disease. While the advisories are non-binding recommendations, their issuance carries considerable weight. The most striking example was the SARS outbreak. As SARS began to appear in growing number of countries around the globe, the role of air travel in its transmission became clear to all. WHO, struggling to address the new, unknown and highly mortal agent, set up three expert panels that communicated electronically with one another: biomedical laboratory researchers working to identify and describe the new agent, epidemiologists working to define the nature of the disease and its transmission, and a panel of expert policy advisors. As the crisis deepened, the Director-General of WHO consulted with her close circle of cabinet level advisors within the organization and determined that the situation called for international travel advisories.

The first advisory, issued on April 2, 2003, named the Hong Kong administrative district and Guangdong Province in the People's Republic of China as areas where travelers should postpone all but essential travel. On April 23 this advice was extended to include Toronto, Canada, and Beijing and Shanxi Province in China. Daily consultations were held to determine when and how the travel advisories would be revised or lifted in certain locations. The criteria for travel advisories were (1) the magnitude of the epidemic in terms of existing and new cases, (2) the extent of local transmission and (3) the export of cases from that territory to other areas of the globe (World Health Organization 2003).

Cases from Toronto were under investigation in the Philippines at the time of the advisory issued for the Canadian city. Mel Lastman, then mayor of Toronto, was furious. "They've never issued an advisory like this before in their history ... I've never been so angry in my life." The CBC news quotes the mayor as "sputtering" (CBC News Online 2003). Within Toronto, the epidemic was centered in hospitals and among health care workers, not in the general community. In issuing the advisory, WHO stated, "a small number of persons with SARS, now in other countries in the world, appear to have acquired the infection while in Toronto" (World Health Organization 2003). Tourists and business travelers canceled plans to visit Toronto and a major medical meeting that had been planned for months was canceled.

In Hong Kong, public health and law enforcement authorities partnered in ongoing attempts to limit the outbreak. Authorities in both Hong Kong and Singapore enacted stringent measures to prevent ill persons from traveling. In airports, passengers boarding flights were screened for temperature and if they were feverish, they were not allowed to travel until SARS had been ruled out. The domestic enforcement of these "stop travel" lists probably hastened the lifting of travel advisories against Hong Kong. They also prevented citizens under quarantine from fleeing the territory and potentially spreading the epidemic even more widely.

Travel advisories are standard practice for governments seeking to inform their citizens about risks of traveling internationally. The Centers for Disease Control issue advisories for US citizens about disease risks present in potential travel destinations, and the US Department of State issues advisories about other risks, such as security risks, that citizens traveling abroad may encounter. But the issuing of advisories by WHO warning travelers away from particular destinations is an unusual measure that carries potentially large consequences. Clearly the travel advisories were costly to the areas that were included. The tension between timely travel alerts and potential loss of tourist dollars is evident from SARS. It is a delicate balance between the global risk of introduction of a highly mortal new infection and the local risk of lost revenue through recommendations to avoid travel.

The International Convention on Civil Aviation

The other treaty that governs international travel, the International Convention on Civil Aviation (1944), makes only passing reference to infectious disease outbreaks. This treaty, which regulates air travel by people and freight, begins by explicitly reinforcing the sovereignty of states as a central principle in the agreement. Article 14 commits member states "to take effective measures to prevent the spread by means of air navigation of cholera, smallpox, yellow fever, plague" and in the event of disease incidents to consult with "agencies concerned with international regulations relating to sanitary measures applicable to aircraft." Article 35 authorizes states to ban certain cargo from their states "for reasons of public order and safety." The treaty asks its signatory states to notify the treaty's secretariat, the International Civil Aviation Organization (ICAO), when there are changes in practice. Nothing in the treaty puts conditions on the abilities of states to limit air traffic within their territorial airspace. And the treaty is silent on the issuance of travel advisories by international organizations such as WHO.

Regulating International Trade: The World Trade Organization

The primary vehicles for addressing health matters as they relate to internationally traded goods are the World Trade Organization agreements. Under these agreements member nations can regulate which products and services cross their borders to ensure they are safely produced and disease-free. But the primary aim of the WTO agreements are to reduce – not erect – trade barriers. The WTO, created in 1995, evolved out of the General Agreement on Tariffs and Trade (GATT), which had been established nearly 50 years earlier after World War II. Historically trade sanctions and embargoes had been used in political fighting among countries. After the war, nations longed for a peaceful means of settling disputes, both political and economic. At the same time, newly industrialized countries were churning out products and ready to trade. In 1944 they assembled an unprecedented agreement to frame their trading in the future. The Bretton Woods Accord mapped out plans for an international monetary system comprising the International Monetary Fund (IMF), the World Bank and an International Trade Organization (ITO). Ultimately, an agreement on the details of the trade organization proved elusive, in part because of a battery of objections raised by the US. Meanwhile, eager to get on with the business of trading, 23 of the 50 participants in the ITO talks in 1947 signed the GATT, formulated to liberalize trade by creating an even playing field for international commerce. The initial focus was on reducing tariffs, thus enabling a freer flow of trade across borders.

After the GATT was in place, subsequent "trade rounds" followed over the years, taking on new trade issues in addition to tariffs. The Kennedy Round, which took place between 1964–76, also addressed "dumping," or the practice of unloading goods at below-market value to create inroads in a new market. The Tokyo Round (1973–79) took on "non-tariff barriers," such as domestic subsidies. For instance, the agreements set concrete targets for member countries to reduce farm or steel production subsidies which, according to the view of free trade advocates, disadvantage non-subsidized producers in the global marketplace. And finally, the Uruguay Round (1986–94) revisited the need for establishing an organization to oversee the ever-more complex issues entailed in international trade, among them those associated with international investment and services. The end result was the WTO, founded in 1995 as the secretariat to implement the GATT.

The WTO primarily provides a forum for negotiations and enforces agreements signed by member countries. Secondarily the organization offers technical assistance to help members understand and comply with the agreements. Unlike most international organizations, the WTO has considerable enforcement clout. The source of that power is its dispute resolution system, which enables it to authorize millions of dollars in trade sanctions against members who are found to have violated agreements. Proponents of the WTO say it promotes peace and prosperity by minimizing trade-related conflicts, encouraging universal, scientifically based standards and advocating equal access to the global marketplace. Critics contend that the organization, dominated by the major trading economies, is not as equitable as its mission suggests. For detractors, the global trade agreements represent the worst of globalization, and serve the corporate interests of transnational companies rather than the interests of the public. Figure 8.2 represents its structure.

The Agreements

The General Agreement on Tariffs and Trade actually is a series of separate agreements under a common framework. While the agreements cover different products and aspects of production, they all emphasize similar themes designed to reduce obstacles to trade. They are (1) transparency, or the "degree to which trade policies and practices, and the process by which they are established, are open and predictable" (WTO glossary); (2) equivalency, or accepting trading partners' practices as equivalent assuming they achieve the same safety standards; and (3) the use whenever possible of scientifically based international standards. All of the agreements are in a continuous process of discussion, negotiation and implementation. Although there are set goals and targets for the loosening of trade barriers, and member countries are earnest in their efforts to reach these, the biannual working group meetings, held in Geneva, allow discussion, clarification and in some cases modifications. They also allow members to raise particular trade concerns that have not been satisfactorily resolved in bilateral discussions. For each agreement, WTO has a secretariat, which typically is a group of up to a dozen employees tasked to help implement that agreement among WTO member countries.

While the agreements aim above all to minimize obstacles to trade, members are allowed broad exceptions to limit trade in certain goods in the interests of protecting

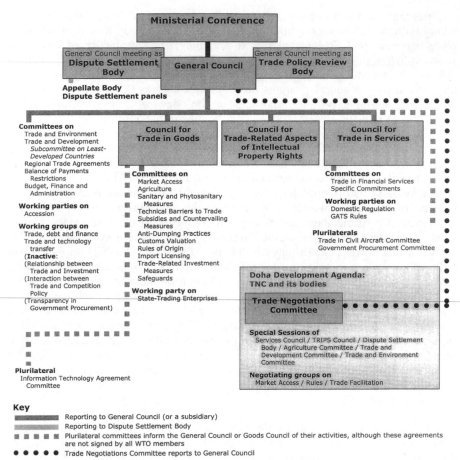

Key

▬▬▬▬ Reporting to General Council (or a subsidiary)

▬▬▬▬ Reporting to Dispute Settlement Body

■ ■ ■ ■ ■ Plurilateral committees inform the General Council or Goods Council of their activities, although these agreements are not signed by all WTO members

● ● ● ● ● Trade Negotiations Committee reports to General Council

The General Council also meets as the Trade Policy Review Body and Dispute Settlement Body

Figure 8.2 WTO organization chart
Source: http://www.wto.org/english/thewto_e/whatis_e/tif_e/org2_e.htm.

the health and welfare of their populations (article I and article XX). The GATT specifies that such protection must be non-discriminatory – in other words, it is impermissible to restrict imports of a dangerous product from one country without restricting it from all trading partners and, in fact, from domestic producers. These non-discrimination provisions are at the core of most disputes involving WTO agreements and account for the emphasis on science-based regulations.

There are four agreements within the GATT with major health implications for the peoples of the world: the Agreement on Technical Barriers to Trade (TBT), the Agreement on Sanitary and Phystosanitary Measures (SPS), the Trade-Related Aspects of Intellectual Property Rights Agreement (TRIPS), and the General

Agreement on Trade in Services (GATS). This discussion will focus only on the aspects of the agreements that are most pertinent to preventing, detecting, controlling and treating the problems of emergent infections. There are a clearly myriad other significant issues in the agreements related to human health that fall outside of the scope of the immediate problem of infectious disease.

Table 8.1 shows how the agreements basically relate to the emergence, amplification, control and economic consequences of infectious disease.

Table 8.1   World Trade Organization agreements: potential links to disease emergence

Agreement	Manner of action	Nexus with emergence paradigm
GATT	Commitment to targets for reduction of tariffs may necessitate enhanced efficiency of domestic production.	May encourage enterprises to "gear up" to enter global market place, or to consolidate. Intensified production can in turn lead to conditions that promote infectious diseases.
TBT (notifications: Articles 2.2, 2.10; 5.4, 5.7; Annex 3 L)	Requires notifications of trade change due to concerns with human health.	Potential detection, tracking of "stealth" infections in biologicals.
SPS (notifications: Annex B, 6)	Requires notifications of trade change due to concerns with human health.	Potential detection, tracking of zoonotic, food-related infections.
TRIPS	Protects intellectual property of new products such as pharmaceuticals, but allows compulsory licensing of products/processes for competitors in the event of a public health emergency.	Issues of innovation in pharmaceutical development of appropriate treatments for new infections. Issues of access to new treatments.
GATS	Provisions include "consumption abroad," or traveling to a member country to receive medical services (a.k.a. "medical tourism").	Potential for xenotransplants and nosocomial transmission of disease from hospitals in one country to those in another.

TBT and SPS Agreements   The Technical Barriers to Trade (TBT) and Sanitary and Phytosanitary (SPS) agreements address processes and standards for traded products. The TBT agreement covers a vast array of products, including pharmaceutical and biological products that are of potential importance, as we have seen, in the emergence of new infections. But the SPS covers most potential vehicles for microbe "hitchhiking," – that is, products from farms and fields. Both agreements aim to reduce discrimination among trading countries by setting common standards to be applied across the board. While member countries support these intentions, disputes arise when the standards are regarded in some cases as watering down domestic safety protections, and in others as setting the bar too high or serving as another means of discrimination. We will examine some of the key aspects of these agreements as they relate to health.

The Agreement on Technical Barriers to Trade   During the GATT negotiations a working group concluded that the largest barriers to trade were not tariffs but the technical requirements for product manufacture. In 1980, the Technical Barriers to Trade (TBT) agreement was designed to minimize such barriers. The TBT agreement basically covers technical processes and packaging, labeling and marketing practices for everything but agricultural products. Among the products included in the agreement are pharmaceuticals and biological products such as blood derivatives.

Two central elements of the TBT are "equivalence" and "conformity assessment". Establishing equivalence means accepting that trading partners' production practices result in a product that meets certain mutually, or ideally, internationally accepted technical regulations or standards – for instance certain safety requirements. Conformity assessment means establishing that the processes to ensure those standards are met are comparable. For example, with pharmaceuticals, a variety of sampling and test procedures are used to assure purity and detect potential chemical contamination in processing. Under the TBT, designated governmental agencies perform conformity assessments to determine whether the practices employed by a particular manufacturer produce pharmaceuticals that meet the specified safety requirements. The keys aspects of conformity assessment are accepting that a variety of methods may be employed to meet a common requirement, and applying the same assessment process to all potential suppliers, regardless of their country of origin, to determine if they meet that requirement. The TBT working group has also elaborated a "Code of Good Practice" to describe the best way to pursue these goals in the implementation of the agreement among its member states. The Code largely deals with the use of international standards whenever possible and how to assure transparency in the way national authorities put them into place. The Code is silent on any practices regarding collaboration with public health nationally or internationally.

The Agreement on Application of Sanitary and Phytosanitary Measures   The Sanitary and Phytosanitary Agreement (SPS), which covers agricultural products, is central to infectious disease control. "Sanitary" refers to human and animal health and "phytosanitary" to plant health. As with all of the agreements, the aim of the SPS is to reduce obstacles to trade while allowing members to limit trade in particular products they deem it risky to their population or territory (provisions 5.1, 5.7). The 1994 agreement governs matters such as pesticide use, additives, and microbial contamination. Some of the key issues that have been under discussion as the SPS agreement is implemented provide insights into how the agreement works, and how it could work better, for the control of emergent infections in trade. These areas include transparency, equivalency, and the use of international standards.

In SPS terms, *transparency* means trading economies make their rules and regulations regarding food safety apparent and obvious to their trading partners. In other words, in order to allow smooth commerce, there should be as few surprises as possible, and when the policies governing imports are changed, or when trade is limited or stopped, the member must notify the WTO. But under the SPS, transparency does not require disclosures about disease occurrence. Should it, could it? Would it be appropriate for the WTO as a trade organization to include the timely disclosure of emergent infectious disease threats by its members? Members would understandably be reluctant to report potential contamination of plant or animal products to trade authorities because of the potential economic repercussions. An alternative strategy may be for trade agreements to (1) encourage timely disclosure of infectious disease threats to national and international public health authorities, and (2) create incentives for making such notifications within the WTO's dispute resolution process by ensuring the products of members who report such outbreaks do not experience unwarranted discrimination.

Under the SPS *equivalency* provision, as with the TBT, member countries can designate trading partners' food production processes as "equivalent," thus eliminating the requirement for additional scrutiny at the border. In essence, equivalency establishes that trading partners with different production, inspection and sanitation standards can produce goods that are comparably safe. If one member rejects another's standards as insufficient, they can be required to prove that the rejection is based on valid health concerns and if they fail to do so, can face costly sanctions. The focus on equivalency is, in part, an effort to facilitate poor countries' participation in global commerce. Critics contend the danger is that systems that are declared equivalent in the interests of promoting freer trade are in fact not as safe, or alternatively, change after equivalency has been declared (Silverglade 2000; *Public Citizen* 2003). Technically, members are required to report any changes, but realistically, there is no guarantee that this happens. To date, equivalency has been determined without systematic consultation of domestic or international public health authorities. While this may be appropriate in some cases, the determination of equivalency represents an opportunity for additional input from public health.

Another source of tension between member countries in WTO, particularly in relation to the SPS agreement, is the emphasis on using *international standards* whenever possible. Developing countries feel they are unable to enter the global marketplace because of excessive sanitary requirements put into place for developed country markets and internationalized to apply to all countries. Under the SPS, the recognized sources for these standards are international organizations addressing food, plant and animal safety – respectively the Codex Alimentarius ("Food Law") Commission (run jointly by the World Health Organization and Food and Agriculture Organization of the United Nations), the International Plant Protection Commission (IPPC) and the Office Internationale de Épizootiques (OIE).

These organizations send representatives to all working group meetings. The World Health Organization also participates as an observer organization.

Notifications   The WTO agreements themselves cannot be easily amended. All member governments have passed them and they are binding on those members. But under both the SPS and TBT agreements, countries can change their own policies, or limit imports based on health, safety, environmental protection or national security concerns. When they do so, they are required to file a "notification" with the appropriate secretariat at the WTO. Additionally, in cases where an international standard does not exist for a particular technical regulation or safety practice, or a member country wishes to use a regulation that differs from the international standard, members are required to file notifications detailing what regulation or standard they will apply. The notifications may be "urgent" or more routine, and countries are encouraged to file them first in draft form for comment by their trading partners, and then again after they are finalized. The notifications list the affected products and trading partners; the nature of the change in import policy, such as an embargo of goods, or new inspection requirements; the duration of the changes; and the international guidelines under which the decision was taken.

Between 1995 and 2004, members filed 6,098 notifications under the TBT agreement (Figure 8.3). More than a third (2,240) were filed in response to measures taken for "the protection of human health/safety."

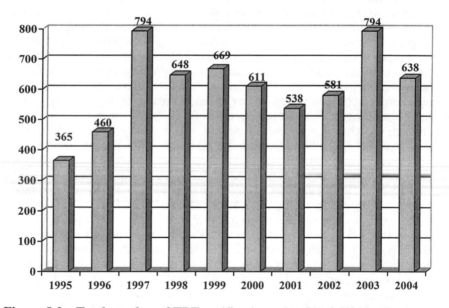

Figure 8.3   Total number of TBT notifications circulated (1995–2004)
Note: The TBT secretariat received 6098 notifications of technical regulations and conformity assessment procedures from 1995–2004.
Source: WTO 2005, http://www.wto.org/english/tratop_e/tbt_e/tbt_specialmeeting_note_21march05_e.doc.

The emergence of HIV in globally traded blood products occurred in the early 1980s, years before the current TBT agreement was in force. If a similar event happens in the future in human biological products, it would presumably become the subject of TBT notifications when it was detected, and countries would seek to protect themselves through trade restriction. But it is not at all clear whether such a problem, if detected, would be communicated to WHO or other public health authority in a timely way. Such communication is not discussed in the text of the agreement. While the protection of human health is the most frequently cited reason for changing import policy among WTO member countries, it is not clear (and in fact highly unlikely) that even in those notifying countries public health authorities would be part of the dialogue and decision making leading up to notification.

Under the SPS agreement, members had filed some 4,163 notifications, not including corrections, additions and revisions, by 2005; the number of notifications rose 42 percent from 2003 to 2004, when members filed 617 (World Trade Organization 2005). To date, the nature of those notifications has not been systematically analyzed. However, we conducted a review in 2002 that showed the notifications filed by the secretariat were increasing every year since the notification system began in 1995 and that notifications were most often filed by countries that were more affluent, as measured by their gross national products. A similar analysis conducted between January 2003 and June 2004 found that a majority of the notifications (nearly 63 percent) concerned food safety (Cash and Kastner 2004). At present the WTO secretariat does not maintain a database of the notifications. Such a database would not only allow more systematic analysis but also would make it easier to alert health authorities and all potential trading partners about safety concerns. As the system stands today, only the few trading partners directly involved in the notification are necessarily aware of the potential problem. The SPS secretariat is pursuing the development of a database that will allow them to search, sort, compile and analyze these notifications. They note that the US Department of Agriculture has been cataloguing the notifications but this database is "not public" and therein not accessible to the secretariat.

TRIPS   This agreement governs intellectual property and is a key in assuring the smooth functioning of global trade. Science and industry invest heavily in innovation in the conception, design, and improvement of the products that reach the marketplace. Corporations rely on selling these wares to recoup their investment in research and development. It is apparent that if competing industries in other countries were allowed to pirate these innovations with impunity the whole system would soon grind to a stop. Who would willingly ship a sparkling new innovation only to have it copied by another and sold at a cut rate? It is apparent that protections need to be put into place to prevent pirating but, as with most of the international regimes we are discussing, there is a balance to be achieved.

The TRIPS agreement describes patent protections not only for products and inventions (Section 5 Article 27, Article 31) of but also for proprietary information about products and inventions (Section 7). All WTO members must protect these intellectual properties. However there is a clause in the same agreement that recognizes the special needs and requirements of least developed country members

(Article 66). These poorest of poor countries ("least developed" means, among other things, a gross domestic product of less than $750 a year in United Nations terms) are allowed to request extensions for complying with those protections. In fact these countries received an extension in 2001 from 2006 until 2016 to implement TRIPS. The agreement expresses a commitment to allow them time to "create a sound and viable technological base" within their countries so they have the ability, for instance, to research and develop their own pharmaceuticals.

The HIV/AIDS epidemic brought this language to center stage for the global community. Developing countries had struggled for decades with the unaffordability of essential drugs prior to the AIDS epidemic, but the scope and gravity of this epidemic was unprecedented. When the epidemic began in the early 1980s, AIDS was considered a death sentence. There were no effective drugs to treat people with HIV/AIDS and they died within the first two years of becoming symptomatic with AIDS. This was uniformly the case, all over the world. However, effective antiretrovirals began to come onto the marketplace in the mid 1980s. The National Institutes of Health instituted unprecedented speed in their research program in part to find new medications. People with AIDS were allowed to seek "compassionate use" exceptions so they could access new and experimental drugs that might not yet have reached the marketplace. The community of people living with HIV and AIDS in the US and other developed countries organized and created their own communications networks and shared their collective expertise. Sometimes this sharing was lifesaving tips passed from one person to the other about how to access new and better drug regimes.

When the lifesaving drugs finally were ready for the global marketplace, they were cruelly unaffordable in the most affected countries because of patents held by the pharmaceutical companies. This seeded a sense of indignation among patients, their advocates, and health care providers that eventually reached a stage of full outrage in the poor countries that bore the brunt of the HIV epidemic. By 1990 Brazil had become the first country outside of North America, Cuba, and Europe to mandate state-provided medications for persons with AIDS. Other countries, especially those with the capacity to make quality pharmaceuticals themselves, vigorously made their case to the WTO. The Global Program on AIDS of the World Health Organization had been in negotiations with the pharmaceutical producers of AIDS drugs since the late 1980s without achieving significant price reductions for poor countries.

The resulting Doha declaration on the TRIPS agreement and public health was adopted at the Ministerial Meeting in Doha, Saudi Arabia, on November 14, 2001. It begins with the sentence, "We recognize the gravity of the public health problems afflicting many developing and least developed countries, especially those resulting from HIV/AIDS, tuberculosis, malaria, and other epidemics." Most importantly the ministers affirmed in clause 5: " b) Each member has the right to grant compulsory licenses and the freedom to determine the grounds upon which such licenses are granted, and c) Each member has the right to determine what constitutes a national emergency or other circumstances of extreme urgency, it being understood that public health crises, including those relating to HIV/AIDS, tuberculosis, malaria and other epidemics can represent a national emergency or other circumstances of extreme urgency." In other words, in the event of a crisis, countries can use compulsory licensing, which is licensing a product for production in their country that is patented by another individual or company without the permission of that person or company.

So does it work? Little systematic study has been published on this question. One such study by Oliveira and others reviewed national legislation in 11 countries in Latin America and the Caribbean to determine whether the TRIPS provisions made a difference (Oliveira, Bermudez et al. 2004). The report is mixed (see Table 8.2). While all countries except Panama had legislated to permit compulsory licensing, other major provisions of TRIPS that would serve public health had not been codified.

The barriers described by this study and others to fully implementing Public Health friendly TRIPS provisions include: (1) the lack of necessary legal and administrative systems to allow for the provisions to be used, (2) risks of bilateral and multilateral commercial sanctions by trading partners in response to changes in national legislation, (3) limited local manufacturing capability for pharmaceuticals, (4) difficulties with technology transfer, i.e., acquiring the technical expertise necessary to create successful production capacity, (5) the high-risk investment required in the competitive global pharmaceutical marketplace. Oliveira, Bermudez et al. also note that the US and particularly Canada have frequently used compulsory licensing, while opposing its use for lesser developed countries. They surmise that more technical assistance is needed for the TRIPS agreement to be implemented while safeguarding public health.

Table 8.2   Countries by WTO entry date and year patent legislation was modified

Country	Date of entry into WTO	Year IPR legislation modified
Argentina	1 January 1995	1996
Bolivia	12 September 1995	2000
Brazil	1 January 1995	1996
Columbia	30 April 1995	2000
Ecuador	21 January 1995	2000
Honduras	1 January 1995	1999
Mexico	1 January 1995	1999
Panama	6 September 1997	1996; amended 1997
Peru	1 January 1995	2000
Domincan Republic	9 March1995	2000
Venezuela	1 January 1995	2000

Note: IPR=Intellectual property rights.
Source: Oliveira, Bermudez et al. 2004.

Modes of heath services covered by GATS

Mode 1 Cross-border supply   Health services provided from the territory of one Member State in the territory of another Member State. This is usually via interactive audio, visual and data communication. The patient therefore has the opportunity to consult with physicians in a different country, as do local doctors. Typical examples include Internet consultation, diagnosis, treatment and medical education. This form of supply can bring care to under-served areas, but can be capital-intensive and divert resources from other equally pressing needs.

Mode 2 Consumption abroad   This usually covers incidents when patients seek treatment abroad or are abroad when they need treatment. This can generate foreign exchange, but equally can crowd out local patients and act as a drain on resources when their treatment is subsidized by the sending government.

Mode 3 Foreign commercial presence   Health services supplied in one Member State, through commercial presence in the territory of another Member State. This covers the opening up of the health sector to foreign companies, allowing them to invest in health operations, health management and health insurance. It is argued that, on the one hand, FDI can make new services available, contribute to driving up quality and create employment opportunities. On the downside, it can help create a two-tier health system and an internal brain-drain – and thus exacerbate inequity of health provision.

Mode 4 Movement of natural persons (individuals rather than companies). The temporary movement of a commercial provider of services (for example, a doctor) from their own country to another country to provide his or her service under contract or as a member of staff transferred to a different country. This is one of the most contentious areas for health, as there is concern that it will increase the brain-drain of health personnel from poor to rich countries. However, GATS is concerned only with health professionals working in other countries on a temporary basis. Brain-drain refers to the emigration of educated, qualified, and skilled people from poorer countries to richer countries. WHO's Human Resources for Health Initiative aims to increase individual countries' pools of qualified health staff.

Source: World Health Organization, General Agreement on Trade in Services (GATS).

GATS   The Global Agreement on Trade in Services is a relatively new area in the history of global trade. The original GATT was limited to trading products; that is, things. Services trade was considered too difficult to regulate. Curiously, in this context, software is actually considered a service rather than a product. Coincident with the burgeoning global trade in software the GATS negotiations moved forward and, as a result, health sector services have become an area of growing interest and concern. This has enormous implications for how public systems are run. While GATS implies that countries will progressively remove barriers to trade in services within their economies, the actual sectors to be affected are not specified. Thus in practice while 90 percent of countries liberalized tourism services and 70 percent included financial and telecommunication services, fewer than 40 percent offered commitments in their health or education service sectors. The box below shows the categories of health services that WTO member countries can open to the global market. Interestingly, the United States has offered only hospital services for liberalization (Conzaniga 2002).

Unsurprisingly, the negotiations involving health services have attracted the attention of the World Health Organization. The WHO has focused initial efforts on countries that are in the process of joining the WTO and therefore are considering whether to join the GATS agreement. Countries that sign GATS can decide which aspects of their health sector they want to liberalize. They might, for instance, decide that the cross-border supply of medical record transcription is acceptable, while allowing private entities from other economies to establish hospitals in their country is not. In essence, negotiations about health services are complex and potentially risky for countries where services are publicly funded, run by government and highly regulated. The chief concern is that establishing a private market for health care can erode services that traditionally have been provided by the government. Since there is not an overwhelming obligation to liberalize the sector, WHO is advising countries on specific issues to consider before making such commitments ("10 Steps before making commitments in health services under the GATS"). The maintenance of strong health systems for all health issues is of key importance. The process of examining accreditation and licensing of health personnel and institutions, which is under study by the WTO working group on Professional Services (which is now called Domestic Regulation), may address this in its discussions of "accountancy" which is the WTO term for creating equivalency across professional licensing entities. One point made in WTO working papers is that opening trade is through liberalization of trade barriers, not through deregulation (World Trade Organization Council for Trade in Services 1999).

Another Playing Field: Regional Trade Agreements

As in any contest, when one approach fails, another possible path to success is to change the rules. For WTO member countries, the equivalent of rule-changing is forging regional trade agreements, which can in effect result in reinstating most-favored nation relations that the WTO agreements prohibit. Regional and bilateral trade agreements have proliferated since the founding of the WTO; more than 100 are in effect. Basically regional and bilateral trade agreements may be made among WTO member nations if they satisfy two conditions: (1) they are more liberal in opening trade than the pertinent GATT provisions and (2) they do not constitute discriminatory trade against other nations that are not signatories to the agreement. By establishing more liberal trade conditions such as lower tariffs, the regional trade agreements essentially establish signatories of the regional agreements as favored trading partners. Meanwhile, there has been little systematic, or indeed unsystematic, review of the regional agreements to determine if they violate WTO provisions.

Politics and Power

While the World Trade Organization's primary mandate is to minimize trade obstacles and limit discrimination, inevitably the interests of some nations, and indeed powers within those nations, are better represented than others. Among the continuing challenges facing the WTO is finding ways to address these inequities. Below, we examine two issues – the forces that go into defining the science that is held out as the objective basis of policies that exclude particular products and practices, and the daunting proposition of attempting to establish equitable relationships among nations with vastly disparate resources.

The Role of Science – The Reinvention of Evidence?

Trade and travel, the ties that bring countries together, have always been subject to politics. Diplomatic relationships historically have determined the welcome one country extends to the people and goods of another country. Adding to the complexity of these dynamics is the emergence of new human infections that may or may not warrant extra protections against goods and people crossing borders. In an international trade regime in which the overarching goals are to reduce barriers and discriminatory treatment and provide some measure of predictability, science is becoming the explicit litmus test for decision making. International guidelines are formulated and member countries can use such guidelines and standards to justify the actions they take.

In general these international guidelines are the product of an elaborate system of expert consultation. Experts convene to discuss the issue, the evidence, and what standards should be put into place to assure safety or quality. There is an international standards setting body, the International Organization for Standardization (ISO). However the most relevant rules for trade and travel are embodied in the Codex Alimentarius Commission (run jointly by the World Health Organization and Food and Agriculture Organization of the UN), the International Plant Protection Commission (IPPC), the standards of the Office Internationale de Épizootiques (OIE, World Organization for Animal Health), the International Atomic Energy Agency convention and rules and the World Health Organization's International Health Regulations. While this science-based approach has great potential, it is not necessarily as agnostic as it appears.

Public versus private   A great deal of scientific work is carried out in industry. In pharmaceutical companies the search for new medications is unending, and in food science the work to create better products with longer shelf life and other marketable characteristics is similarly intense. In fact, in food and agriculture the majority of scientific research is carried out with industry investment. In the public arena, science is funded by government, private foundations or industry. It is driven by the intellectual curiosity of researchers as well as the identified needs of government agencies such as the National Institutes of Health (NIH), the US Department of Agriculture, the Environmental Protection Agency, and the National Science Foundation.

Although the two worlds of scientific enterprise are more similar than they are different, there are two key differences. In industry, investment in science is tightly tied to productive output that will benefit the enterprise in an immediate and tangible way. This is understandable because managers within enterprise need to justify this expenditure to their Board of Directors and shareholders explicitly. Disclosure of results beyond the company is not required or necessarily desirable. Consequently, evidence that will not benefit the funding industry is less likely to be made public. And scientific discoveries that may have public health benefits may be kept secret for competitive reasons. Much of what actually is learned remains proprietary – science that is owned by the company that created and funded it. The public side of science is not as closely tied to creation or improvement of goods and services. The "shareholder" in this scenario is the public, which funds the enterprise. That public and its representatives in Congress do question the directions taken by the NIH and other agencies. The agencies present the work of science in a way that will document the wisdom of the expenditures made.

Risk analysis   In using science to justify their actions in the international trade, whether it is a ban on certain products or a new policy, member nations employ a "risk analysis." While the basic concept is straightforward, a number of the steps require judgment calls and policy choices based on conflicting information and competing interests. Generally, a risk analysis involves identifying a hazard, assessing the actual risk from the hazard based on the exposure level, and then determining how to respond to and communicate that risk. But even the international authorities named within the WTO agreements do not have a single approach to risk analysis. There is controversy over what such analyses should include and must include to be considered an adequate basis for decision making. In fact, the OIE and the Codex Alimentarius groups, two key technical advisor groups to the SPS agreement deliberations, use different models. The Codex group uses the US National Academy of Science model and the OIE uses the "Covello-Merkhofer" model. Table 8.3 contrasts the two models.

In response to growing concerns and disputes about the emergence of antimicrobial resistance due to trade, the Office Internationale de Épizootiques, one of the agencies that sets standards for the SPS, published guidelines for performing the risk assessment (Vose, Acar et al. 2001). In doing so, the OIE working group essentially put into place the "rules of evidence" in the ongoing storm over antimicrobial resistance in food animals and humans. Risk analysis poses particular challenges for poor countries with limited technical resources. Proving that their standards are just, or other countries' regulations are excessive, can become an expensive proposition when risk analysis is required.

In the realm of emerging infections, risk assessment becomes even more complex. If the identified hazard is the potential emergence of entirely new human

Table 8.3   Comparison of the components of risk assessment

Components of risk assessment model	
Codex Alimentarius	**OIE**
Hazard identification	Risk release assessment
Hazard characterization	Exposure assessment
Exposure assessment	Consequence assessment
Risk characterization	Risk estimate

Note: The US National Academy of Science model is used by the Codex Ailmentarius and the Covello-Merkhofer model is used by the Office International des Épizooties (OIE).
Source: Vose, Acar et al. 2001.

pathogens, then the process of risk assessment in the early stages can be only theoretical. It was not possible to know the hazard posed by the emergence of prions until the human cases had occurred, some ten years after the occurrence of widespread "mad cow" disease. So really formal risk assessment in this case is less useful in that it must await the accumulation of evidence to be weighed.

The precautionary principle: controversial safety   In the case when risks are largely unknown, some advocate using what is known as the precautionary principle (PP). This approach is the ultimate prevention strategy – if there appears to be a risk, why take it? Recall the Chapter 4 discussion of "mad cow" disease and variant Creutzfeldt-Jakob Disease (vCJD) that measures such as the first offal ban in beef production were taken before the actual risk of human disease was known. In essence, this approach says that if there is a scientifically plausible (but not proven) risk, then exposure should be avoided. The precautionary principle generally is not accepted as a substitute for risk analysis in WTO deliberations. But in some cases, such as asbestos, a cancer-causing element in some materials, this seems to be the case (Goldstein and Carruth 2004 p. 491). Its use also is advocated in considering issues where evidence of risk is lacking, such as electromagnetic fields (Comba and Pasetto 2004).

The implications are clear for emerging infections. The acceptance of the precautionary principle in trade dealings would not require the experience with the infection that is included in the formulation of a risk assessment. On the other hand, its use could allow countries to more liberally close their borders to goods unnecessarily, which would cripple international trade and national economies.

The Rich and the Poor – Who is at the Table?

For detractors, the global trade agreements represent the worst of globalization, and serve the corporate interests of transnational companies rather than the interests of the public. WTO is not a United Nations organization; it is an international membership organization. While all countries participate in UN organizations such as WHO, not all countries participate in the WTO. Some economies, such as Hong Kong and Taipei, are recognized as independent entities in WTO whereas they are not in the UN system. Although the WTO has nearly 150 member countries, clearly most of the negotiation of GATT and its agreements was carried out between a limited number of active market economies that were engaged in international trade in the 1990s, when most of the agreements were drafted. Moreover, critics contend that delegates of those nations were disproportionately influenced by the interests of powerful multinational corporations seeking to further dominate international trade (McCrea 1997; Lang 1999). As a result, the interests of less developed and powerful economies have been underrepresented. Even today, the poorest countries cannot afford to send delegates to Geneva to participate in the working group meetings where concerns about the agreements are discussed and new policies are drafted.

These criticisms sparked the notorious protests when the WTO held its ministerial conference in Seattle, Washington, in 1999. Those in turn led to the 2001 conference in Doha, Qatar, that focused on concerns of least developing countries, particularly the challenges of implementing the terms of WTO agreements, such as sanitary requirements, without sufficient resources and technical expertise. The resulting Doha Declaration included "special and differential treatment" provisions that allow developing countries extra time to reach standards set by the agreements and to phase out supports such as export subsidies. The declaration also featured a commitment to provide more technical assistance for developing countries, an issue that also would be central in the 2003 ministerial conference in Cancún, Mexico.

Delegates in the corridors of WTO working group meetings generally hold one of three views regarding developing countries' participation. They can be (roughly) paraphrased as follows:

1. Limiting trading discussions to those nations that are trading most actively is appropriate since they have the most important stake.
2. Now that the rules are set, it is appropriate to bring in other member countries but they must play by the set rules without exceptions, since any substandard health or sanitary practices would be dangerous.
3. Global trade is potentially an important force in international economic development and as many countries as possible should be included in trade with whatever accommodation needed to ensure inclusivity.

Since the Seattle protests and the Doha conference, there have been some strides toward inclusivity. The wealthy countries have become aware that for the survival of the trade regime it is imperative to provide opportunities for poor countries to engage in the potential benefits of trade. A variety of measures and mechanisms have been set up to assure this, including a Global Trust Fund, financed by member states. Technical assistance has been offered by wealthy members through the SPS working group to enhance the implementation of the agreement. The Food and Agriculture Organization has funded participation in negotiations. However all involved concede the efforts fall short of the needs in this area. Among the remaining challenges is addressing the reality that most developing countries lack the resources to participate as equal partners. Only a third of the least developed countries, for instance, can afford to station a representative in Geneva full time, much less fund a costly dispute should an issue arise, or pay for the infrastructure (such as sanitation facilities or regulation system) necessary to meet the agreements' safety standards. In 2000, the United Nations Development Programme noted that the participation of African member states was particularly slim: the average delegation from the Organization for Economic Co-operation and Development (OECD) states, which are largely from Europe and the US, was eight representatives, whereas many of the African states had no consistent representation at working group sessions (Brown 2000).

WTO, WHO and Science

So in reviewing this rather complex thicket of international acronyms and organizations we learn the following:

1. The travel of humans and freight poses a moderate "onboard" risk, and a more important risk to receiving populations.
2. Border controls and frontier closures are no longer seen as effective as a sole strategy.
3. The SARS epidemic reignited interest in travel advisories as a tool for limiting transmission and it apparently worked.
4. The global trading regime and the agreements relevant to public health have many provisions relevant to the control of emergent infections.
5. The structural flaw of the WTO as an Geneva-based organization dominated by wealthy trading states is a limitation in its ability to deal with this global problem of emergence.
6. Science is promoted in trade regimes as a basis for decision making on trade flows.
7. The public/private information gulf impedes the use of science and the evidence base for science itself is controversial.

So, as we think about how to enhance the safety of the global express for the populations of the globe, we have many elements to take into account. This consideration and some options will be presented in Chapter 9.

Study Questions

1. If infections travel in trade and travel, why are authorities reluctant to stop travel and restrict trade when threats occur?

2. Explain what notifications are under the Technical Barriers to Trade and the Sanitary and Phytosanitary Agreements of the World Trade Organization. What is the principal reason cited by member countries for filing such notifications?
3. Explain why "risk analysis" evidence may be problematic for newly emergent infectious diseases. What is the alternative policy used to restrict trade?

Chapter 9

The Future of the Global Express: Promise or Peril for People?

The emergence of new human infections and the globalization of commerce are not threats; they are realities that will mold the way the people of the world live their lives and conduct business in the decades to come. The question is whether we will successfully tackle the challenge of this potent mix or suffer the misery of ever more virulent pandemics. The inexorable increase in the human population, recently projected to reach nine billion by the year 2050, will continue to contribute to "planetary overload," to quote epidemiologist Anthony J. McMichael (McMichael 1993). The underpinnings necessary for safe human habitation – clean water and sanitation – have never been universally available. The access to the global food supply and the adequacy of that supply has likewise never been assured in modern history. A central question raised by the emergence of new human infections in a "transnationalized" world is whether global safety and the security of populations are increasingly at risk. Does the globalization of commerce and travel fundamentally amplify risk of infection when that globalization is overlaid on an inadequate sanitary infrastructure?

Important to consider is that the surface area of the planet is 500 million square miles, with 70 percent underwater. So the ever-increasing human population must survive on a set amount of space. Human density ranges from the vast empty steppes of Mongolia, with 4.3 people per square mile, to the shoulder-to-shoulder lowlands of Bangladesh, with 2,200 people per square mile. Likewise on a continental basis the range is broad: from nine people per square mile in Australia to 203 people per square mile in Asia. The amazing mobility of people and goods today has essentially served to connect once far-distant populations. Physical distance no longer separates the poorest and most crowded areas of the world from the wealthiest and least crowded areas of the world in any meaningful way. In fact, the transnational production chains of many major food conglomerates literally bring produce from one setting onto the table of another.

Geographers have described globalized travel, trade and, to some extent, communications as the "collapse of space." This is a useful concept. The world is growing smaller in terms of actual separation of people and places. But the hypothesis of this book is not only that space is telescoping, but also that the attendant processes of international open trade efforts and consolidation are creating a new ecology of infectious diseases. This new ecology is producing emergent infections as well as stirring up some with which we are already familiar. This has been well demonstrated in the preceding chapters. So, the answer to our first question is yes, there clearly is increased risk with modern age globalization.

Consolidation – For Better or for Worse

Earlier chapters have described how international trade acts as a driver in this dynamic – for instance, how global agreements to lower protective tariffs and other competitive factors pressure industry to maximize efficiency by consolidating processing. The consolidation of feedlots and slaughter houses then contributes to the emergence and spread of new infections, such as *Escherichia coli* O157:H7. Similarly, in Southeast Asia, the combination of intensified poultry practices and inadequate sanitary systems gave rise to epidemics of virulent bird flu that remain stubbornly out of control. These infections in flocks of chickens and ducks pose an ongoing threat to the human population. The epidemics continue to smolder, and with that smoldering the "stew" of these RNA viruses continues to percolate. The potential for a new human flu is ever present. Global trade agreements are only one of many forces that push industry to consolidate: maximizing return, position in the global market and meeting market demand are certainly others that figure in the equation. Chapter 4 explored how scaling up production to satisfy global market needs also can entail risk. When the blood derivatives market blossomed in the early 1980s it unwittingly led to broad geographic transmission of HIV-1, a virus that was not, in itself, very effective in its contagion. The virus' infection rate through sexual contact is 10 in 10,000, or 0.1 percent (Varghese, Maher et al. 2002); but when carried in blood, or derivatives used in transfusion, that rate leaps to 9,000 out of 10,000, or 90 percent (Donegan, Stuart et al. 1990). These highly infective products made their way around the globe. Bigger and more efficient is the hallmark of consolidation in industry. However, as we have seen, it can also be risky, and when outbreaks occur, public health systems must scramble to cope and contain the threat.

Whither Health?

"Health" as a voice was not heard in deliberations around the global trade agreements. It is rarely heard in national discussions about trade or commerce. Health authorities are consulted, albeit not routinely, in deliberations about product safety and recall decisions in the US. The fragmentation of the regulatory system at our own national level has been amply documented here. It is an operational fact of bureaucratic life that is proving to be dangerous for the population's health. The systems need to be rationalized and strengthened. In particular, the epidemiologic competence of the Centers for Disease Control (CDC) is an underutilized resource in these processes. As we observed in the case of imported mangoes that were contaminated with pathogens (when they were sprayed with pesticide used to satisfy rules prohibiting insects on produce) (Jones and Schaffner 2003), shifting regulations do not always adequately consider all the potential public health implications.

Internationally other countries have also run their agencies on parallel rather than converging lines. Health ministries are rarely consulted about economic development activities. In fact on one of my visits to a Southeast Asian country my group actually introduced the Minister of Health to her counterpart in the Ministry of Science and Technology for the first time, although they had both been in their respective posts for over a year. My Business School colleagues who consult with corporations on foreign direct investment decisions suggest that site visits to consider such investments rarely, if ever, involve consultation with health authorities. And yet, as we have seen, the soundness of the public health infrastructure at the local level is one of the most important determinants in whether an emergent disease threat is controlled or becomes an epidemic. The costs in human suffering, lives and economic impact can be enormous. The local workforce and local production are put at risk. The costs mount when infections enter the global express, as we have seen. So the way we do business needs to change. Health authorities need to learn to communicate efficiently and effectively with their counterparts in ministries of commerce and economic development. Probably more importantly, business leaders considering foreign direct investment decisions would be wise to include explicit consultation on health aspects of the venture, both in country and with experts at home.

The lack of an ongoing health committee at the World Trade Organization (WTO) is baffling. The WTO has an environmental working group that reaches across all of the trade agreements, attends to their negotiation and performance and monitors relevant disputes. The environmental group focuses on conservation as well as "green protectionism," or the use of conservation concerns to close markets. A similar working group on health is essential. To develop successful strategies for combating emerging infections, it is imperative that global health concerns become an integral part of the global trade deliberative process. As Chapter 8 outlined, when member economies file urgent notifications indicating they are imposing trade restrictions, the reason cited most often for those measures is health concerns. No one systematically reviews these thousands of notifications filed with the Technical Barriers to Trade (TBT) and Sanitary and Phytosanitary (SPS) committees to scout for public health alerts. A globally tainted product could cause untold trade restrictions before it came to the attention of the World Health Organization or even the attention of the health authorities within the country placing the restrictions. The World Health Organization, meanwhile, has established a Department of Ethics, Trade, Human Rights and Health Law that monitors trade agreements and works to address related health considerations.

Level One: Steps toward Prevention

Together, health and trade officials, and individuals from the public and private sectors, can more effectively address the significant challenges set forth above. Where to begin? At the bottom of the pyramid. As outlined earlier, the pyramid of prevention illustrates the progression of emergent infection from its point of origin, into a local epidemic, and then finally an international pandemic. Key to preventing the initial emergence are clean water and sanitation. Another prevention tool at this level is the availability of antibiotics and vaccines. Figure 9.1 suggests how the prevention pyramid can be interpreted in terms of these remedies.

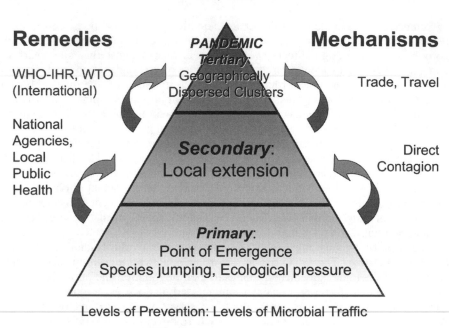

Figure 9.1   The remedies pyramid

Access to the Basics: Prospects

Since one cannot fabricate reliable product without clean water and sanitation, it makes sense to start here. What are the prospects for the world's peoples, animals and crops to have access to clean water and sanitary services? Unfathomably, water access has been an area of controversy. Progress was made in the 1990s towards the goal of universal access. Still, as of 2002, more than a billion people did not have access to clean water and nearly 2.6 billion did not have adequate sanitation (World Health Organization 2000; UNICEF and World Health Organization 2002). Urban coverage remains higher than rural access (World Health Organization 2000).

The inability to provide all of the world's citizens with purified water has been carefully examined by evolutionary microbiologists and found to be linked to the severity of waterborne infections. In fact in the 50 years since clean water systems have been put into place in many countries, the microbes causing diarrhea in those locations have been confined to the less lethal strains. This suggests three points: (1) pure water systems have a major impact on human health by preventing the most lethal forms of diarrheal disease such as classic cholera, (2) severe forms of diarrheal disease persist in areas with impure water, and (3) in the absence of successful decontamination, products that are produced or processed using such water will bring the risk of such diseases along with them when they are transported. So with the worldwide locomotion of persons and goods, what has historically been a local problem is now very much a global problem. While this reality presents an opportunity to bring more pressure to bear on efforts to ensure clean water worldwide, it also presents a danger, and that is focusing those efforts chiefly on the commercial sector – for instance, providing clean water primarily to those farms cultivating export crops. When the matter came up at a conference in 2001, an official from the Pan American Health Organization stressed the importance of providing such public goods to everyone. That is to say, not just to have clean water to irrigate green onions cultivated for export from Mexico, but also to provide it for the people who live and work where such cultivation takes place. This is a real concern. Access to water and sanitation is most effective and probably also most efficient when generalized as a public good to entire communities.

The Search for Magic Bullets – Technology to the Rescue

Another tactic targeting the foundation of the pyramid, or emergence, is fostering the development of and widespread access to bug-fighting drugs. Technology will not replace the need for clean water, sanitation and adequate public health infrastructure. However, while not a stand-alone solution, vaccines and antimicrobials are powerful tools for fighting infectious diseases. Vaccines historically have been astoundingly successful as magic bullets. Childhood illnesses such as measles, mumps and rubella (German measles) have declined to near extinction in wealthy countries through aggressive vaccination campaigns. In fact, just in March 2005, rubella was successfully eliminated from the US. Smallpox, once a deadly scourge, has been eradicated, living on only in (hopefully secure) laboratory freezers. Polio has been eliminated except in areas of political and social turmoil.

The tools for creating new vaccines are more sophisticated and capable than ever before. Science can easily sequence the genetic make-up of bacteria and viruses, and can characterize the protein structures that promote the immune response. New technology has allowed the creation of vaccine in human cell systems (as we did for rabies vaccine), which greatly reduces the problems of side effects and complications of vaccination. "Reverse engineering" allows the genetic manipulation of the whole immune process in the laboratory by recreating pathogens and their vaccines. Given all this, all of our new infections should be a year away from vaccine elimination, but sadly Mother Nature is not cooperating.

Take the efforts to develop an HIV vaccine. As soon as the virus causing HIV was described in the 1980s, the search for a vaccine began. HIV, as we have seen, is a highly mutable RNA virus. That is to say, it is evolving within its hosts at a fairly rapid rate. As such it is a moving target for vaccine development. In fact, despite more than a decade of work, a recent review notes that the following challenges persist:

1) the inability of current designs to elicit effective neutralizing antibodies against circulating stains of HIV 2) the inability of current designs to prevent HIV from establishing persistent infections 3) the extensive global variability of HIV 4) the lack of understanding regarding the mechanisms of protection in the most effective vaccine animal model system – the attenuated approach and 5) the lack of understanding of which HIV antigens induce protective immunity and which immune effector mechanisms are responsible.

(Klausner, Fauci et al. 2003 p. 2036)

In other words, top scientists are admitting that after millions of dollars and years of work an effective vaccine against HIV remains elusive. There are sound biological reasons for the trouble at the bench. As epidemiologist Paul M. Ewald notes, the virus is very capable of making "evolutionary end-runs" around the defenses of a host against it. By simply changing one component of the complex protein binding mechanism used by HIV, a variant strain can frustrate the immune defenses of a host. So today's vaccine targets may not be effective tomorrow as HIV continues to evolve within its hosts. This does not make the vaccine challenge insurmountable, but it makes a timely solution questionable.

Recently I asked the graduate students in my Emerging Infections course to evaluate the prospects of drugs and vaccines as "magic bullet" solutions to the ongoing challenges of emerging infections in a globalized world. Surprisingly of the 40 students writing on the question, not a single one expressed confidence in this technological fix, despite the fact that the course included several sessions and generous readings on vaccine development. One student put it particularly pessimistically, stating "today's magic bullets are tomorrow's bio-bullets," referring to the biological warfare risk of smallpox. By 1980, the unparalleled global smallpox vaccination effort had eradicated the highly lethal, disabling and disfiguring disease. However, the retention of stock of the virus by the former USSR, UK and US created a risk. Smallpox is now considered a major potential biological weapon (Henderson, Inglesby et al. 1999). The political disintegration of the Soviet Union placed the security of those virus stocks at risk of distribution or sale to groups bent on bioterrorism.

Even without such doomsday thinking, most health authorities are skeptical of solving the problem of emerging infections with magic bullets alone. On the one hand, continued and ever-increasing global use of antibiotics in animal feeds and human treatment are rendering the old antibiotics less and less effective with agents such as *Salmonella*. On the other hand, the pharmaceutical industry is not investing in research and development of new antibiotics intensively because (1) they may become useless in a short time due to the emergence of resistance, (2) the market may be primarily in less affluent countries where purchasing power is not great, (3) intellectual property issues such as patent protections can come under fire if a public health emergency develops, and a company may not recoup its investment and requisite profit. Pharmaceuticals look for lucrative markets for their products. Dr. David L. Heymann, WHO's Executive Director, Communicable Diseases, told my Emerging Infections class in 2004 that the approximately 250 million doses of influenza vaccine created each year is used only in wealthy countries. And even with public as well as private dollars going towards flu vaccine, the profits from vaccine manufacture are marginal compared to those from wealthy countries on new arthritis, pain or sexual enhancement drugs. One wonders about the core mission of making pharmaceuticals – is it in the interest of enhancing health or making money? We will return to the significant clash between business and public health values later in this chapter.

Level Two: Disease Diffusion at the Local Level

As we have discussed, after emergence occurs, the next level of prevention is avoiding a local epidemic. Once the emergence of a new disease has been noted in a population, there is an urgent need for care of the individual cases, diagnosis of the disease and investigation and containment of the outbreak. While the science of how to carry out these tasks is known, as we saw in Chapter 7, the resources to do so are not uniformly available.

Creating the Safety Net

As Chapter 8 noted, the new International Health Regulations for the first time articulate a positive obligation on the part of all member states to create epidemiologic capacity within their borders (World Health Organization 2005 Article 5, Section 1). In fact, this was one of the most controversial points in the draft regulations. For years, the international community has pretended that such capacity exists or simply parachuted in to save the day when local authorities are overwhelmed. This new approach implies something much more affirmative – that member states will create this capacity. But significant resource challenges make it difficult, if not impossible, for poor and middle income countries to achieve this standard. This resource issue is multifaceted, but by no means hopeless. The traditional means of building capacity is clearly not adequate to the challenges at hand. There is an enormous mismatch in the scale of work to be done to assure safety and the volume and pace of mobility in the modern world with its attendant risk of dispersion of new microbes. In the 1980s, Development Bank lending to poor and middle income countries often required governments to reduce their public work force in social services, which were regarded as inefficiently run, not to mention unprofitable sectors (this process was called "structural adjustment"). While many of those systems were largely inadequate, the services that remained or replaced them after this process are in many cases worse. In light of the profound risks that many populations face today in terms of disease emergence, additional urgent investment is required to bring services up to an adequate level.

There are sound economic and development arguments for investment in public health infrastructure and services. As noted by Jeffrey Sachs, director of The Earth Institute at Columbia University and Special Advisor to UN Secretary-General Kofi Annan on the Millennium Development Goals, "The more one looks at it, the more one sees that the question isn't whether the rich can afford to help the poor, but whether they can afford not to" (Sachs 2005 p. 288). Sachs makes a persuasive long-term argument for such investment. I believe that the global express as described in the preceding chapters provides additional evidence. There has been an ongoing policy dialogue about financing "global public goods" (Smith, Beaglehole et al. 2003; Smith, Woodward et al. 2004); the additional concerns of safety raised by the global express reinforce the need for this investment.

Level Three: International Pandemics

Who will assure the safety of these populations in poor and middle income countries? Beyond the humanitarian concerns that have always made this an important question, increasingly there are international health implications to consider. More and more, the populations in poor and middle income countries are being brought into production chains for food and biological products that circle the globe – consequently their health problems are essentially the world's health problems. As I will discuss later, part of the solution to this problem is more involvement on the part of businesses that benefit from globalization in building the necessary infrastructure to provide these populations with safe drinking water, sanitation and disease surveillance and control. But given that current infrastructure building for local surveillance and control is lagging in time and inadequate in scale, it is critical to explore other strategies to achieve early disease detection in areas of highest risk for emergent diseases. One path is transborder collaboration; some of the cooperative research projects currently underway offer considerable promise.

Upscaling Systems

In processing food and biological products, consolidation presents risks for disease emergence, but in surveillance of emerging infections, quite the opposite is true – the more consolidation, the better. The current system for laboratory surveillance is fragmented into clinical laboratories, public health laboratories and research laboratories scattered around the world. In addition to the inevitable communications problems among these systems, there are missing pieces in resource-poor settings where laboratory diagnostics are literally and figuratively out of reach. Given the reality of the global express, the world cannot afford to have incomplete and halting diagnosis of emergent disease threats. The scale of the systems in place is nowhere near the commensurate challenge.

Visionaries such as epidemiologist Scott Layne and his colleagues have been designing and promoting scaled-up systems for the modern age. As they recognize, for threats such as influenza, the concept of a global laboratory is increasingly critical (Layne, Beugelsdijk et al. 2001). For such a system to be realized, the current, non-cooperative approach to the study and surveillance of influenza virus must be dismantled and rebuilt as a strong global system that employs epidemiology, robotics, and supercomputing to carry out rapid, high-volume analysis and study of emergent viruses. This approach is eminently reasonable for influenza and likely has utility for other rapidly mutating RNA viruses as well. The concept is to carry out high-throughput (that is, high-volume) processing of information from a network of testing laboratories and to track the direction of genetic drift as it is occurring across geographic areas. This would provide early warning, where none now exists, of new influenza threats.

The beginnings of this kind of international cooperation were evident during the SARS crisis. When the SARS epidemic emerged, we witnessed an unprecedented marshaling of scientific resources by the world community to tackle the new infection. This was a new way of doing business on the part of national governments, international agencies and, perhaps most importantly, the scientific research community. In a global effort to decipher SARS, scientists joined together and shared information over electronic secure networks in real time. The cooperative network linking laboratories in search of the genetic code of the new pathogen was unprecedented. Business as usual in the research science enterprise is much more fragmented, non-transparent and less responsive to events. The product of this collaboration was the discovery of the SARS genome in a month's time. This new strategy is quite similar to that being called for in the HIV vaccine enterprise. This kind of collaborative intensive research in the public sector will prove increasingly important as infectious diseases continue to emerge.

The Last Cohort

The many collaborative research projects underway in related fields suggest potentially fruitful opportunities for addressing emergent infections. One example is the "last cohort" concept that is currently being applied to cancer research (Potter 2004). The term "last" refers to the fact that the effort would synthesize current science and therein be a best and final version of a technique to garner maximum scientific insight. Cohort refers to a cohort study, a tool commonly used in environmental health and in cancer studies. These studies also have been used to a more limited degree with HIV/AIDS. A prospective cohort study entails following a group of people ("cohort") through time and examining their exposures and disease outcomes to determine what, if any, associations exist between particular exposures and development of disease. Case control studies, which look retrospectively at the exposures of people who have developed disease (see Chapter 7), are typically used for faster-acting infections. However the case control study relies on strong local competence in epidemiologic investigation in the public sector and, as discussed, that competence is still under construction in many target areas of the region.

So the cohort offers an alternative. There is no reason that acute infections cannot be added on to large cohort studies that are in place or about to be put into place for cancer. By following a million individuals forward in time with periodic examinations and blood draws, science could begin to isolate new infectious agents that might not yet be clinically apparent. It would also allow for rapid, targeted public health outbreak investigation and control to be mounted sooner, rather than later, to assure the health of the people.

Another benefit of linking the international scientific discovery mission with the surveillance and safety mission is that it enhances public health's professional capacity. In other words, connecting global practitioners and researchers in public health to the broader ongoing discussion of innovation in health and safety enhances their effectiveness and prestige at home. Over and over again the global AIDS effort has produced this side benefit as the work to prevent, understand, and treat AIDS has spanned borders and professions. The collective genius of scientists and health care workers all around the world has been mobilized to create one of the most diverse communities of science ever seen. The SARS response showed that promoting such open and ongoing transparent collaboration pays off with spectacular growth in new knowledge.

Fortuitously, the target sites of the large ongoing collaborative research into cancer and environmental health are also the most populous regions of the globe with the most fragile infrastructures – and consequently the most likely places for new infectious disease emergence from animal sources, as we have seen with SARS and with influenza. This could be our opportunity to learn how the "macro" factors of travel, commerce, technological and environmental change correlate with the emergence of infections. Given that the pace of emergence in these regions has been increasing, and is at this point occurring on a regular basis every two to three years, monitoring a large population prospectively for a decade would be the very best way to catalogue the incidence of infections in the population and also measure the impacts on individuals of a variety of changes such as frequency of travel, changes in diet, levels of air pollution, and changes in ambient temperature.

At this point such cohort studies are the most reliable and realistic way to gain insight into the pre-jump dynamics between individuals and microbes. Even in the absence of large cohort studies important information could be gleaned retrospectively from looking at specific emergent events and testing other changes that correlated in time for their relationship with that emergence. Doing this after the fact is difficult, but not futile. In fact much of this work is ongoing in the wake of SARS and in the face of avian influenza.

Modeling: If We Can Count It We Can Fix It

Learning more about emergence and transmission through cohort and other studies would provide part of what is needed to create the "last model" of disease emergence and transmission. If we can actually measure emergence and transmission in terms of time, magnitude and distance, we can actually begin to systematically describe, understand and ultimately prevent progression up the Pyramid of Prevention.

The right side of the pyramid illustrates modes of disease emergence and transmission – species jumping, direction contagion, trade and travel. The graphic also illustrates a new reality for science: the entire process from emergence to pandemic is quantifiable. We can create a transmission model mathematically from the base to the peak of the pyramid – the last model. The tools and information sets required to build this model already exist – they just have not been pieced together yet. Components of the last model are in large datasets kept by a variety of institutions and agencies. Modeling tools are with university researchers in mathematics, biological and microbiological sciences, demography, medicine, epidemiology, economics and geography, to name just a few.

Computer models that can forecast the range and pace of transmission of a new infection are rapidly coming on line. Efforts to understand disease transmission in populations through mathematical modeling began in the 20th century, and have continued to fascinate scientists. Disease modeling as a discipline is becoming more and more accurate and sophisticated in using mathematics to chart the progress of infectious diseases in populations (Anderson and May 1991). The computer gives us the capability to quickly carry out complex calculations and run millions of scenarios. This ability is reshaping our thinking about how science can foretell the future direction of many systems: climate systems, logistic and trade systems, transportation systems. The "system" by which new microbial threats travel the world is a ready target for this kind of work.

In 2004, a group headed by Lars Hufnagel at the Max Planck Institute in Germany published an important new step. They linked up the traditional "SEIR (Susceptible, Exposed, Infected, Recovered)" model for infectious diseases (a calculation that predicts infection rates based on the portion of people in a population who are susceptible to infection, exposed, infectious, or recovered and immune) with a model of global aviation travel (Hufnagel, Brockmann et al. 2004). Using data from the early days of the recent SARS outbreak, they applied their model to predict which countries would experience what level of SARS cases. They then looked back at the SARS epidemic to see how accurately the model reflected reality. The model did not perform perfectly. There are a number of reasons for this, including poor data quality on disease occurrence and false assumptions within the design of the model. But their efforts are an example of where science needs to go to understand the interaction of the global express and the emergence and transmission of microbial disease. The ability to predict how and where diseases might spread by identifying those places that are most likely to receive visitors or vector goods from the region where the disease originated could guide placement of safety systems such as surveillance and epidemiologic control.

Picking up the Tab: The Cost of Doing Business

Ultimately, approaches such as cohort studies in high impact areas and sophisticated computer modeling of disease patterns are adjunct strategies. They do not replace the need for strong local safety nets. Somehow the cost of local safety needs to become a cost of doing business. This begins to touch on the vigorous and as yet incomplete discussion of "global governance" – the notion that in an increasingly interconnected world, private sector participation is critical in efforts to tackle global problems such as poverty, hunger and environmental degradation. While this initiative has entranced the educated elite in the public sector of developed countries, it has not yet adequately penetrated the board room. However, there is a parallel conversation going on in some board rooms that may be building towards a similar future vision.

The problem with public health is that it is "public." The protection of people's health is broadly seen as a government responsibility and not a business enterprise. Everyone desires safe water, sanitary protection, security from infectious diseases, and safety from bioterror attacks. The thought of basic necessities such as water becoming a commercial product is, to many people, reprehensible. The attempt to privatize water as a commodity and buy and sell it in poor and middle income countries has been largely a failure. Not only is it morally and ethically repugnant (and unsafe from a population health perspective) to make access to water dependent on purchasing power, it is also largely unaffordable. The processing and distribution of water and maintenance of water systems require large scales to be efficient; consequently limiting the scale to the size of the moneyed class reduces efficiency and becomes prohibitively costly. This is not to say the efforts to privatize water markets and make them profitable will be abandoned any time soon. Making money is a powerful incentive.

Although business typically is not called upon to build and maintain the infrastructure of safe water and sanitation, commercial entities in industries such as agriculture, slaughtering, and processing certainly make good use of this infrastructure in production. And, as we have seen, in some parts of the globe that infrastructure is lacking and the resulting products, while generally cheaper, are also sometimes more dangerous from a disease standpoint. From this perspective, it seems to make sense that industry would help to improve those systems upon which it relies.

Some public/private partnership models exist, but few link public sectors in poor countries with transnational commercial concerns. This is an area of inquiry: with all of the wheel-spinning discourse around governance, the central point is how to bring poor and middle income public sectors to the same table with the companies that potentially have a hand in creating the global risk of infection with their transnational operations. The corporations that are raising the wage in-country also are placing the entire global marketplace (as well as their own corporate operations) at risk by failing to include in the bargain the basics of water and sanitation and the timely detection and treatment and control of infectious diseases. The time for these discussions to begin is when the venture is put in place. In the US, communities often seek from corporations who locate within them mitigation for systems that are overburdened by their new presence, such as schools, roads or sewers. Local authorities in poor and middle income countries should have the same opportunity to discuss the stress that incoming operations place on fragile local public health infrastructure. This has been overall good business practice in the US, assuring the mutual benefit between populations and the businesses in their communities. The risks of the global express suggest that this is also good business practice around the world.

What globalization creates is an efficient system for originating and disseminating novel infections via travel and trade. At the same time, it often isolates the interested parties – the disempowered populations of producing countries and, thousands of miles away, the powerful safety-obsessed populations of the major consumer markets. There are clearly bridges of awareness, understanding and insight to be built that can bring these two constituencies closer together. When such self-interests are understood and articulated it will help change the way business is carried out.

Values Clash

One of the challenges of generating a conversation between the private and the public sectors is an inherent values clash. This disconnect, as mentioned earlier, is particularly apparent in issues around the mission of pharmaceutical firms, but it also pervades all other discussions of global health and welfare. My first encounter with this conflict was in the Empty Quarter of the Yemen Arab Republic, where I was working for a short while as a medical consultant with Yemen Hunt Oil

Company. In the early 1980s, Yemen had very few physicians. Most of us held at least three consulting positions with the numerous expatriate corporations. Texas-based Yemen Hunt had a contract with the government to explore for oil in the Empty Quarter, the governorates of Al Jawf and Ma'rib, in the vast reaches of scrub and rippled brown sand dunes. Just across the border in what was then South Yemen, British Petroleum was on the same quest.

The Texans had a can-do attitude, with a Wild West approach that seemed to work well with their Yemeni counterparts, who found them amusing. The work was not easy; the rig was reachable only by truck (with very large tires) or by helicopter. The first time I went to the rig, the manager reassured me that they only hired Bedouin drivers who knew the desert like their back yard. And besides, "if he gets lost it will be such a shaming thing; he would have to commit suicide." This remark was not as reassuring to me as it seemed to be to the manager.

The rig was a huge drill and platform, with a community of 50–60 workers who rotated every several weeks. The work was difficult and dangerous; most rigs lost a life a year at that time from industrial accidents. Yemen Hunt had just begun hiring Indian physicians rather than male British nurses, at a great saving to the company. The manager crowed, "I can get two Indian doctors for what I was paying for one British nurse!" A condition of my working with this effort was to visit the rig, meet the physician and see what he knew and did not know. I found a very polite well-dressed man, sitting in an almost entirely bare room, which was his clinic. He told me he that was waiting for his equipment and medications. He had been waiting for two months. In fact, he had not ordered any equipment and medications. Nor had management, which had been waiting for the doctor to indicate what he wanted. Clearly communication was not optimal.

On quizzing my new colleague I learned that he was not familiar with cardiopulmonary resuscitation (CPR). So I arranged for him to come back to the capital with me, and for a British nurse in residence in Sana'a to take his place (bringing along some basic supplies for the clinic), while we did some tutorial on first aid and CPR. By the third day of our tutorial, it had become clear to me that there was a large gap in knowledge and experience between us. Early the following morning, the radio crackled with a distress call from the rig. A worker from the Philippines had collapsed with crushing substernal chest pain. The British nurse was calm, but firm; we needed to get the man off the rig and into a cardiac care unit as soon as physically possible.

After conferring through the remaining dark hours by radio with the nurse, the manager and I and a lifepack lifted off at dawn's first light in a Yemeni army helicopter. As we soared across the gray sand dotted with hobbled camels, I steeled myself for the worst, and hoped for the best. I also lectured my manager extensively (one might call it a harangue) on the importance of a skill base in medicine. "You would not hire accountants from a foreign country just because they were cheaper," I shouted over the chopper. "No, I sure wouldn't," he replied. "Well, medicine is the same way...it's not an area where you should economize!!" He nodded, concerned.

The worker was successfully transported to Sada'a's hospital, placed in cardiac care, and survived his heart attack. He was not happy because he was the source of support for his family in the Philippines and his cardiac condition prevented him from returning to such a remote and difficult worksite. The company reverted to its former policy of hiring male nurses for the rig clinics.

My reflections over the intervening 20 years have clarified a number of points about this dramatic event, which to me epitomizes the conflict in values that I have seen over and over again in working with colleagues in the private sector. First, it was not the intent of management to place their workers on the rig in jeopardy. They were simply saving money. Their lack of appreciation of the skills required to provide care on their rigs was authentic. There were few guidelines for "how to employ foreign workers in the middle of the desert" available to them. Certainly information was not shared between the two rigs in sight of each other – BP and Yemen Hunt. These rigs and their respective companies were so competitive that efforts were made to conceal the instrument panel from possible long-distance prying eyes so that the drill's depth would remain secret. So sharing across industry on critical health-related issues was not the practice.

Secondly, a piece of the problem was the mystification of medicine. Historically, the profession has not been the most transparent or user-friendly. In my thirty years of practice, I have developed a whole lexicon from translating the Latin and Greek-based terminology of medicine into words that my patients and others can understand. To some extent, the reluctance of our profession to be consumer-oriented has come back to haunt us as physicians. By eschewing advertisement for decades as the society around us became more and more information-based, we in health and medicine are behind in explaining what we do, and what qualities and skills are necessary to do it well.

Thirdly, in operating outside of the US, Yemen Hunt, as any company, is not necessarily required to follow health and safety rules in force in the US. They make an agreement with the national government to follow the customary practice in that country. In the case of Yemen, which had very few doctors, there was no licensure and little health and safety regulation. The lack of stringency would be viewed as a boon by both partners – the government and business – since both undervalued the importance of health and safety.

Medical competence is not at all the sole province of the developed world, and India clearly has many highly competent scientists and physicians. However, in the case in Yemen, the physician hired was out of his depth. Issues of competence and safety are complex. Today, more and more medical work is being outsourced to India, from remote radiology readings on CT and X-rays from US hospitals, to testing of laboratory (blood) samples from the UK and Middle East. Despite the 4,000 extra miles, the cost of testing is 40 percent less overall (Kennedy 2005). Laboratories and physician groups in the source countries are protesting and raising the issue of quality, but cynics see their financial motivations first and it is doubtful that the hospital industry will reverse the outsourcing trend.

The Business Case

As my experiences in Yemen highlighted, businesses, by definition, exist to serve the bottom line. But as the foregoing chapters have demonstrated, global business also needs to include public health, especially freedom from emerging infectious disease, as a core value. It is clear to even the most casual observer that HIV/AIDS is a profound epidemic, that SARS threatened the modern transportation systems in a very central way, and that avian flu could exact a death toll far exceeding that of the influenza pandemic of 1918 – and that we need to marshal all our resources to fight these threats.

There are many ways of securing "armslength" investment from profit for infrastructure building or disease fighting in producer economies, all of which can be rationalized as a requisite cost of doing business, if not from a corporate responsibility perspective. One terrific example has been the business service organization Rotary International's role in the drive against polio. More than one million Rotarians have participated in the "polio plus" campaign, raising money and actually working directly on vaccine administration. More than $3 billion has been invested globally in the eradication effort. Resources raised in wealthy countries help underwrite vaccination campaigns in poor countries, where local Rotary clubs help with implementation. For instance, when a Health Ministry carries out vaccination programs with Rotary dollars, local Rotary clubs get involved and help assure that the funding goes where intended. This is one venue for public/private collaboration: the voluntary sector, where corporate priorities become secondary to private "service above self," and great achievements result.

But the investment required from business not just money, it is also information sharing. Most food manufacturers, for instance, meticulously track their products from farm to table. That data lays out essentially the same pathways that that public health investigators must recreate when they conduct a traceback (see Chapter 7) to discover the source of foodborne disease outbreaks. When seeds are found to be contaminated with *Salmonella*, and public health investigators begin to go back up the chain, sometimes they are recreating (at public expense) something that is already known – basically the food distributor's marketing plan. As they test and query the product, the distributor of the product, and the central importer of the seeds, someone within the chain of sourcing, processing, importation, distribution and sales knows exactly where the seeds involved originated. Someone knows exactly where the individual batch of seeds had been exported and sold. It is their business, literally, to know.

To know and to tell are two entirely different things for corporate enterprise. Beyond good citizenship and altruism, it is hard to imagine any financial reward for a company in disclosing its role in marketing and distributing a tainted product. On the other hand, in the US there are compelling reasons not to disclose. Disclosure entails potential legal exposure for the corporate entity. If I am the distributor of beef that you can prove gave your relative a deadly disease such as new variant Creutzfeldt-Jakob disease, you might be motivated to seek compensation for the damage my business has inadvertently done to you and your loved ones.

The private sector is not insensitive to the need to share information on critical issues of safety. In 2001 the American Meat Association declared food safety a "non-competitive" issue. This, in the face of the Bovine Spongiform Encephalopathy (BSE) crisis, means that corporations share more freely information on safety concerns and new technologies to address them. It is not considered a proprietary secret how to keep the consumer safe. This is an important step, given that similar cooperation could have saved many people from exposure to tainted factor VIII blood product in the early 1980s. If viral deactivation processes had been shared across the pharmaceutical industry in a timely way, many of these exposures could have been prevented.

Success Stories

There has been some heartening recognition of the potential role of public/private partnering in HIV/AIDS. In Southern Africa, for instance, some firms have begun actively promoting counseling and testing and the provision of antiretrovirals to their workforce. Sadly the concern to prevent HIV/AIDS infection has been less well generalized and the vision of vigorous corporate engagement in prevention of infection remains a vision.

But those whose business or geographic location put them at ground zero of this epidemic "get it." They are the first wave, and they see and understand the urgency and centrality of addressing such threats. At the World Economic Forum annual meeting in Davos, Switzerland, in 2005, David Arkless, Senior Vice President of Manpower (a global human resources firm), framed the argument for concern for the HIV/AIDS epidemic this way: "It is perhaps somewhat inconvenient that the countries most impacted by HIV/AIDS represent the future workforce of the world. Manpower's research into the future 'world of work' predicts an absolute necessity for corporations to move sites of operations from the G-8 to a variety of global locations ..." He went on to exhort his business colleagues, "We need to get the issue of HIV/AIDS out of the CSR 'box'[1] and place it firmly in the 'economic imperative' arena" (Arkless 2005).

In 1994, we began to promote the involvement of business in the HIV/AIDS epidemic in the Asia Pacific. At the time there was an enormous opportunity to prevent the widespread transmission of HIV/AIDS into the region through prevention. The Thai Business Coalition on AIDS (TBCA) had been formed in Bangkok, with initial success. I worked with funding from USAID to bring business and public health together during the Yokohama International AIDS Conference. We dubbed the effort the "Asia Pacific Alliance against AIDS" and organized a meeting of 75 public health and business people in the 100 degree weather of Yokohama AIG insurance, Levi Strauss, Hong Kong Shanghai Banking, Green Cross and a number of other businesses were represented. The concept was to present the work that TBCA had begun and try to promote business interests in prevention. The core of the arguments are summarized in our 1996 Lancet article, "A Role for Businesses in HIV prevention in Asia" (Kimball and Thant 1996). The Boeing Company sponsored a second conference in Vancouver, British Columbia.

The arguments that were successful in arousing business interest were: (1) compassion and corporate responsibility, (2) expense of the epidemic if prevention was not successful, and (3) the business consequences of that failure. The first point, compassion and corporate responsibility, was a very hard sell for AIDS. HIV/AIDS

---

1 He contends that HIV/AIDS is relegated to the Corporate Social Responsibility (CSR) box, a safe and secure place to park any marginally difficult corporate or social issue.

was and remains a highly stigmatized disease. Throughout the late 1980s and early 1990s it was (incorrectly) characterized as a disease spawned by promiscuous homosexuals. The leadership in the US administration at the time either was silent or morally condemning of the victims. This media representation had impacts far beyond the borders of the US. Most of the companies we spoke with in Japan, Hong Kong, China and Thailand had real misgivings about becoming identified with something so stigmatized.

The second and third points were more successful but necessitated a great deal of research. We cobbled together work from a variety of researchers on the past, current and projected economic impact of AIDS. We attempted to specify our discussion of consequences for the businesses we were talking to as much as possible. For example, the Boeing support was in part a product of the ability to explain how Boeing wing assembly contractors in China would be adding cost to product if they lost their trained work force and had to replace it.

Thus, making the business case involved appealing not only to our own value system but also to those of the companies we were attempting to woo into the effort. This is a key strategy for conveying the risks of transnational business practices – showing the links between emerging infections and practices such as consolidation, processing short-cuts, and far-flung travel and product distribution. Most business managers will be concerned about the human impacts in theoretical terms – and about the immediate impacts to their business in practical terms. The second non-theoretical concern can spawn active, creative solutions.

Most economic studies of epidemics such as SARS have used macroeconomic models that do not allow the specification of costs to particular kinds of businesses. Most businesses do not understand the risks to their enterprise well enough to commission scenarios that will inform them. The information gap between private and public is so vast that publicly generated scenarios by economists may appear so disjointed from the reality within the corporation that they are not seen as useful. What businesses do understand is the impact when the emergence of new infections compromises their enterprises. The beef industry has been reeling since 2000 when countries began to actively embargo British beef. In 2004, the US beef industry lost its entire Asian market after the diagnosis of BSE in one American cow. The export market to Asia includes the following countries that embargoed American beef: Japan (37 percent market share), Korea (24 percent), Taiwan and Hong Kong (4 percent) (Baumes and Ramsey 2005). The impact reverberates up the entire supply chain in the production of beef, changing the price of feed, on up to cattle.

The impact of SARS, while somewhat more transitory than that of BSE, was also substantial in terms of major dislocation of travel and tourist business. Tens of billions of dollars have been lost throughout Southeast Asia, China and Canada, with ripple effects to their travel and trading partner economies as well. What is remarkable about the globalized estimates for each of the cases discussed is how large the numbers are. While this is impressive, probably more impressive to business is the impact on their own earnings.

If change is going to occur, the business case must be made. As we have seen, business has a major influence upon how bilateral and multilateral trade agreements are implemented. Business is a major actor in assuring the safety of food products from "farm to fork," or the safety of biological products from one bloodstream to another. Business and private enterprise represent the major concentration of capital required to carry out the scientific, programmatic and infrastructure development so necessary to assuring safety of the global express.

The Way Forward

When I speak with business leaders, they always ask, "What do you want us to do?" The model of modern capitalist enterprise was built in the 20th century and is not suited to meet the challenge presented by the emergence of new infections in the 21st century and beyond. Today's model of public health systems, developed in the 19th and 20th centuries, also is far outstripped by the scope of the challenge. What is needed is serious, cooperative, creative thinking and problem solving at every level of both the private and public sector. Each partner will need to do things differently than their history and organizational culture has thus far motivated them to do. But the exact "what" that business can do, or consumers can do, will be answered in the collaborative sharing of global intellectual capital. The paths will become clearer, the priorities straightforward and the strategies to get from point A to point B evident once the need to have an effective global safety net is accepted.

The phrase "public/private partnership" has been bandied about for over a decade. This broad term covers a multitude of sins or achievements, depending on one's perspective. To tackle the challenge of emerging infections, the collusion of private and public interests should include the following goals:

- The promotion of and investment in basic infrastructure of clean water and adequate sanitation in the world.
- The promotion of and investment in public health surveillance control and intervention systems for human infectious diseases.
- The promotion of and investment in veterinary public health surveillance control and intervention systems for zoonotic diseases.
- The assurance of adequate investment in research and testing of changes in processing of biological materials and in the processing of commodities for the global marketplace. This would include the consolidation of processing sites.
- The promotion of and resource investment in transparency and information sharing about infectious diseases and product safety.

This charge would distinguish this effort from the long range public/private partnerships that have been put in place by the National Institutes of Health and industry to generate capital for biotech research leading to pharmaceutical or vaccine innovation, for example. This public/private partnering would center on the concept of safety now and in the future for the burgeoning mobile, man-made, microbial-friendly, eco-space that spans the globe.

Creating Incentives

Just as we have described the brakes on the global express, there are other levers and gears that can guide its progress and direct it in ways that will benefit today's and tomorrow's global population. Increasing government oversight of the practices of enterprise is one avenue. But civic systems are particularly weak in poor and middle income producer countries, and prospects for their reinforcement are dim. So, is there a way to create incentives for good corporate behavior?

Historically, corporate social responsibility has offered the appeal of the high regard of customers and peers. But as businesses become increasingly transnational the community from which high regard is valued becomes more distant. So we are back to the bottom line, a concept that spans borders and cultures. We can all agree upon what numbers mean. The fixation on the bottom line suggests that tax incentives or insurance and underwriting discounts for safety in corporate activities might be effective. The huge insurance conglomerate AIG offered some incentives for workplace AIDS-prevention activities in collaboration with the Thai Business Coalition in the mid-1990s that were well-received by business. Insurers and banks represent transgenerational business ventures – they intend to be in business for decades, and consequently they are natural stakeholders in initiatives to promote global safety. In contrast to businesses operating on the short-term cycles of Wall Street earnings reports, such long-lasting ventures are more able to take a position and make an investment in the future because it is more clearly in their corporate strategic interest (albeit long-term) to do so.

But some economists, such as Joseph Stiglitz, warn of a side effect of the bottom line fixation. Some have become so entranced that they have, like numerologists of medieval times, ascribed wisdom to numbers and to the marketplace. Labeling these as "market fundamentalists," this Nobel Laureate suggests this misplaced faith in the unseen hand is one of the core problems inhibiting proactive thinking about the future of humanity on the globe (Stiglitz 2003). The bottom line argument is one that is heard often in the hallways of working meetings of the World Trade Organization, and other such venues where business interests meet government delegations. Gratefully it also is an argument that is losing its cachet as the reality of a future bereft of direction based on scientific evidence and intellect becomes evident. In making the case for public, not-for-profit *and* private support for scientific innovation in the service of poor countries, Sachs warns that "market forces alone will not suffice"(Sachs 2005 p. 367).

Organizationally this effort to create incentives and build new alliances will be challenging. Corporations and governments are motivated to act at times of crisis or immediately after the crisis, but as crises fade so too does the motivation to act – until the next crisis. Government and corporate revenues rise and fall and with them their appetite for new ventures outside their core activities. Thus this kind of initiative will necessitate long-range strategic planning to mitigate the bumps in the road.

Purists on the public health side see this appeal to business as selling out. They ask, "Why should we pitch to those people who are so basely motivated and create the problems in the first place through their greed?" Jared Diamond refers to this criticism in his recent book *Collapse: How Societies Choose to Fail or Succeed*. But public health is not religion, it is not doctrinal. In fact it is supported by the public dollar because it is practical and of value to the people it protects. Helping public health realize its mission requires realistic and practical approaches that will succeed. One can be as doctrinaire as one chooses on one's own dime. Public health, especially in the modern era of extreme challenge can only succeed when all of the resources for population protection are successfully mobilized and engaged. There is a great deal of real work to be done.

In his book *Agendas, Alternatives, and Public Policies*, first published in 1984, political scientist John Kingdon theorized that the greatest opportunities for significant change arise when the "three streams" that run through policy decisions converge – problems, policies and political forces (Kingdon 1995). Any of these elements alone stands less of a chance to provoke action. Various constituencies or media attention may raise the profile of a problem, such as unsafe rendering practices, but without an available solution or political will, the attention will likely wane and the problem will go unattended. Similarly, a policy to provide safe water worldwide may fail to gain traction unless the problems of unsafe water appear sufficiently pressing to mobilize the global community. Finally, even if there is general agreement that the problem of international disease transmission could be limited with a policy of international disease reporting, that solution may not be put into place unless there are political forces to make it happen. Today, we have just the kind of window of opportunity that Kingdon describes to make inroads on these issues at the nexus of health and trade. The recent SARS and avian influenza pandemics leave little doubt that the problem is substantial. The ongoing revision of the International Health Regulations and the World Trade Organization agreements present an opportunity for policy makers to take action. And a practical policy solution is at hand: public/business partnerships.

Flagging Down the Global Express

The global express is barreling down the tracks. Public health is off to the side, waving a flag, trying to introduce caution. It is time for public health to move into the conductor's position with the other engineers of the global express: politics, industry, commerce, and travel, to name but a few. There needs to be a reordering of the global conversation. As the drumbeat of new human infections is telling us, this needs to happen very, very quickly. Yesterday may not have been soon enough.

Study Questions

1. Clinical trials are underway in the United States for a vaccine against the H5N1 virus (bird flu). If a pandemic begins, what are the obstacles to deploying this vaccine to control the epidemic?
2. Outline three immediate goals that may mitigate the risk of the conflagration of an emergent infectious disease that could be addressed through public/private cooperation.
3. How would you create regulations or incentives to perfect the global public safety net? What would your top priority be?

References

Chapter One

Arcal, Y. and M. Maetz (2000). "Trends in world and agricultural trade", *Multilateral Trade Negotiations on Agriculture: A Resource Manual*, Food and Agriculture Organization of the United Nations.

Ewald, P. M. (1996). *Evolution of Infectious Disease*, Oxford University Press.

Huang, S. W. (2004). "An overview of global trade patterns in fruits and vegetables", *Global Trade Patterns in Fruits and Vegetables*, United States Department of Agriculture Economic Research Service.

Kimball, A., K. Taneda, et al. (2005, in press). "An evidence base for international health regulations: quantitative measurement of the impacts of epidemic disease on global trade", *Revue scientifique et technique*.

Koivusalo, M. (2003). "Assessing health policy implications of WTO agreements", *Health Impacts of Globalization: Towards Global Governance*, K. Lee, Palgrave Macmillan.

Lederberg, J., R. E. Shope, et al. (eds) (1992). *Emerging Infections: Microbial Threats to Health in the United States*, Institute of Medicine, National Academy Press.

McMichael, A. (1993). *Planetary Overload: Global Environmental Change and the Health of the Human Species*, Cambridge University Press.

UNICEF and World Health Organization (2002). *Meeting the MDG Drinking Water and Sanitation Target: A Mid-term Assessment of Progress*.

United Nations Development Programme (2002). *Human Development Report 2002: Deepening Democracy in a Fragmented World*.

Wilson, M. E. (2003). "The traveller and emerging infections: sentinel, courier, transmitter", *Journal of Applied Microbiology* **94 Suppl**: 1S-11S.

World Tourism Organization (2005). "Short-term tourism data 2004, international tourism: arrivals, receipts and expenditure", *WTO World Tourism Barometer* 3(1).

World Trade Organization (2004). *World Trade Report 2004: Trade and Trade Policy Developments*.

World Trade Organization Committee on Sanitary and Phytosanitary Measures (2003), *Summary of the meeting held on 24–25 June 2003*.

Chapter 2

BC Centre for Disease Control (2002). *Food poisoning outbreak: Listeria Monocytogenes, soft ripened cheese, Switzerland.*

Bell, B. P., M. Goldoft, et al. (1994). "A multistate outbreak of Escherichia coli O157:H7 – associated bloody diarrhea and hemolytic uremic syndrome from hamburgers. The Washington experience", *Journal of the American Medical Association*, **272**(17): 1349–53.

Besser, R. E., P. M. Griffin, et al. (1999). "Escherichia coli O157:H7 gastroenteritis and the hemolytic uremic syndrome: an emerging infectious disease", *Annual Review of Medicine* **50**: 355–67.

Calvin, L. (2003). "Produce, food safety and international trade: response to U.S. foodborne illness outbreaks associated with imported produce", Chapter 5 in J. C. Buzby (ed.) *International Trade and Food Safety: Economic Theory and Case Studies*, Economic Research Service, US Department of Agriculture.

Centers for Disease Control and Prevention (1985). "Listeriosis outbreak associated with Mexican-style cheese – California", *MMWR Morbidity and Mortality Weekly Report* **34**(24): 357–9.

Centers for Disease Control and Prevention (1997). "Multidrug-resistant Salmonella serotype Typhimurium – United States, 1996", *MMWR Morbidity and Mortality Weekly Report* **46**(14): 308–10.

Centers for Disease Control and Prevention (2002). "Outbreak of multidrug-resistant Salmonella Newport – United States, January–April 2002", *MMWR Morbity and Mortality Weekly Report* **51**(25): 545–8.

Centers for Disease Control and Prevention (2004). "Outbreak of Salmonella serotype Enteritidis infections associated with raw almonds – United States and Canada, 2003–2004", *MMWR Morbidity and Mortality Weekly Report* **53**(22): 484–7.

Centers for Disease Control and Prevention (2005). "Escherichia coli O157:H7 infections associated with ground beef from a U.S. military installation – Okinawa, Japan, February 2004", *MMWR Morbidity and Mortality Weekly Report* **54**(2): 40–2.

Chalk, P. (2004). "The bio-terrorist threat to agricultural livestock and produce", *The Office of Science and Technology Policy Blue Ribbon Panel on the Threat of Biological Terrorism Directed Against Livestock*, RAND Corporation.

Codex Alimentarius Commission (2002). *Risk Profile for Enterohemorragic E. Coli Including the Identification of the Commodities of Concern, Including Sprouts, Ground Beef and Pork.*

Food and Nutrition Board, Institute of Medicine, et al. (2003). *Scientific Criteria to Ensure Safe Food.*

Glynn, M. K., C. Bopp, et al. (1998). "Emergence of multidrug-resistant Salmonella enterica serotype typhimurium DT104 infections in the United States", *New England Journal of Medicine* **338**(19): 1333–8.

Gupta, A., J. Fontana, et al. (2003). "Emergence of multidrug-resistant Salmonella enterica serotype Newport infections resistant to expanded-spectrum cephalosporins in the United States", *Journal of Infectious Diseases* **188**(11): 1707–16.

Hart, M. and B. Sutton (1997). *Economic Development, Food Safety, and Sustainable Export Market Access: The Case of Snow Peas from Guatemala*, Guatemala, Centre for Trade Policy and Law/International Commercial Diplomacy Project.

Hennessy, T. W., C. W. Hedberg, et al. (1996). "A national outbreak of Salmonella enteritidis infections from ice cream. The Investigation Team", *New England Journal of Medicine* **334**(20): 1281–6.

Herwaldt, B. L. (2000). "Cyclospora cayetanensis: a review, focusing on the outbreaks of cyclosporiasis in the 1990s", *Clinical Infectious Diseases* **31**(4): 1040–57.

Ho, A. Y., A. S. Lopez, et al. (2002). "Outbreak of cyclosporiasis associated with imported raspberries, Philadelphia, Pennsylvania, 2000", *Emerging Infectious Diseases* **8**(8): 783–8.

Horby, P. W., S. J. O'Brien, et al. (2003). "A national outbreak of multi-resistant Salmonella enterica serovar Typhimurium definitive phage type (DT) 104 associated with consumption of lettuce", *Epidemiology and Infection* **130**(2): 169–78.

Huang, P., J. T. Weber, et al. (1995). "The first reported outbreak of diarrheal illness associated with Cyclospora in the United States", *Annals of Internal Medicine* **123**(6): 409–14.

Jones, T. F. and W. Schaffner (2003). "Salmonella in imported mangos: shoeleather and contemporary epidemiologic techniques together meet the challenge", *Clinical Infectious Diseases* **37**(12): 1591–2.

Lang, T. (1999). "Diet, health and globalization: five key questions", *Proceedings of the Nutrition Society* **58**(2): 335–43.

McLauchlin (2004). "Listeria monocytogenes and listeriosis: a review of hazard characterisation for use in microbiological risk assessment of foods", *International Journal of Food Microbiology* **92**(1), April: 15–33.

Martin, L. J., M. Fyfe, et al. (2004). "Increased burden of illness associated with antimicrobial-resistant Salmonella enterica serotype typhimurium infections", *Journal of Infectious Diseases* **189**(3): 377–84.

Ortega, Y. R., C. R. Sterling, et al. (1993). "Cyclospora species – a new protozoan pathogen of humans", *New England Journal of Medicine* **328**(18): 1308–12.

Osterholm, M. T. (1997). "Cyclosporiasis and raspberries – lessons for the future", *New England Journal of Medicine* **336**(22): 1597–9.

Ostroff, S. (1998). *Testimony on the Safety of Food Imports to the Senate Committee on Governmental Affairs*, US Department of Health and Human Services.

Powell, D. (2000). "Risk-based regulatory responses in global food trade: Guatemalan raspberry imports into the U.S. and Canada, 1996–1998", *Risk and Regulation*, B. Doern, University of Toronto, pp. 131–5.

Riley, L. W., R. S. Remis, et al. (1983). "Hemorrhagic colitis associated with a rare Escherichia coli serotype", *New England Journal of Medicine* **308**(12): 681–5.

Ryser, E. T. and E. H. Marth (1988). "Behavior of Listeria monocytogenes during manufacture and ripening of Cheddar cheese", *Journal of Food Protection* **50**: 7–13.

Shea, K. M. (2004). "Nontherapeutic use of antimicrobial agents in animal agriculture: implications for pediatrics", *Pediatrics* **114**(3): 862–8.

Shields, J. M. and B. H. Olson (2003). "Cyclospora cayetanensis: a review of an emerging parasitic coccidian", *International Journal of Parasitology* **33**(4): 371–91.

Sivapalasingam, S., E. Barrett, et al. (2003). "A multistate outbreak of Salmonella enterica serotype Newport infection linked to mango consumption: impact of water-dip disinfestation technology", *Clinical Infectious Diseases* **37**(12): 1585–90.

Smolinski, M. S., M. A. Hamburg, et al. (eds) (2003). *Microbial Threats to Health: Emergence, Detection, and Response*, Institute of Medicine.

State of Utah Department of Agriculture and Food (1998). *Radishes, Not Beef, to Blame for 1996 Japan E. coli Outbreak*.

Taormina, P. J., L. R. Beuchat, et al. (1999). "Infections associated with eating seed sprouts: an international concern", *Emerging Infectious Diseases* **5**(5): 626–34.

Threlfall, E. J. (2002). "Antimicrobial drug resistance in Salmonella: problems and perspectives in food- and water-borne infections", *FEMS Microbiology Reviews* **26**(2): 141–8.

US Food & Drug Administration Center for Food Safety & Applied Nutrition (2003). *Quantitative Assessment of Relative Risk to Public Health from Foodborne Listeria Monocytogenes among Selected Categories of Ready-to-Eat Foods*.

US General Accounting Office (2004). *Antibiotic Resistance: Federal Agencies Need to Better Focus Efforts to Address Risk to Humans from Antibiotic Use in Animals*.

Varma, J. K., K. D. Greene, et al. (2003). "An outbreak of Escherichia coli O157 infection following exposure to a contaminated building", *Journal of the American Medical Association* **290**(20): 2709–12.

Villar, R. G., M. D. Macek, et al. (1999). "Investigation of multidrug-resistant Salmonella serotype typhimurium DT104 infections linked to raw-milk cheese in Washington State, *Journal of the American Medical Association* **281**(19): 1811–6.

Wells, J. G., B. R. Davis, et al. (1983). "Laboratory investigation of hemorrhagic colitis outbreaks associated with a rare Escherichia coli serotype", *Journal of Clinical Microbiology* **18**(3): 512–20.

World Trade Organization (2004). *World Trade Report 2004: Trade and Trade Policy Developments*.

Chapter 3

Breiman, R. F., M. R. Evans, et al. (2003). "Role of China in the quest to define and control severe acute respiratory syndrome", *Emerging Infectious Diseases* **9**(9): 1037–41.

Capua, I. and D. J. Alexander (2002). "Avian influenza and human health", *Acta Tropica* **83**(1): 1–6.

Centers for Disease Control and Prevention (2005). "Threat to Public Health from Influenza A(H2N2) is Low", available at CDC website.

Centers for Disease Control and Prevention (2005). *Information About Influenza Pandemics*, http://www.cdc.gov.

Centers for Disease Control and Prevention (1995). "Exposure of passengers and

flight crew to Mycobacterium tuberculosis on commercial aircraft, 1992–1995",
MMWR Morbidity and Mortality Weekly Report **44**(8): 137–40.

Claas, E. C., A. D. Osterhaus, et al. (1998). "Human influenza A H5N1 virus related
to a highly pathogenic avian influenza virus", *Lancet* **351**(9101): 472–7.

Food and Agriculture Organization of the United Nations (2004). *Avian Influenza:
Stop the Risk for Humans and Animals at Source.*

Fritz, C. L., D. T. Dennis, et al. (1996). "Surveillance for pneumonic plague in the
United States during an international emergency: a model for control of imported
emerging diseases", *Emerging Infectious Diseases* **2**(1): 30–6.

Gamblin, S. J., L. F. Haire, et al. (2004). "The structure and receptor binding
properties of the 1918 influenza hemagglutinin", *Science* **303**(5665): 1838–42.

Glezen, W. P. (1996). "Emerging infections: pandemic influenza", *Epidemiology
Reviews* **18**(1): 64–76.

Hai-yan, L., Y. Kang-zhen, et al. (2004). "Isolation and characterisation of H5N1
and H9N2 influenza viruses from pigs in China", *Chinese Journal of Preventive
Veterinary Medicine* **26**(1).

Horimoto, T. and Y. Kawaoka (2001). "Pandemic threat posed by avian influenza A
viruses", *Clinical Microbiology Reviews* **14**(1): 129–49.

Kaiser Commission on Medicaid and the Uninsured (2004). *The Cost of Care for
the Uninsured: What Do We Spend, Who Pays, and What Would Full Coverage
Add to Medical Spending?*, Washington, D.C., Kaiser Foundation.

Leder, K. and D. Newman (2005). "Respiratory infections during air travel",
Internal Medicine Journal **35**(1): 50–5.

Lederberg, J., R. E. Shope, et al. (eds) (1992). *Emerging Infections: Microbial
Threats to Health in the United States*, Institute of Medicine, National Academy
Press.

Lee, L. (2004). "The current state of public health in China", *Annual Review of
Public Health* **25**: 327–39.

Mandell, G., J. Bennett, et al. (2000). *Principles and Practice of Infectious
Diseases*, Churchill Livingstone, pp. 1823–34.

Mangili, A. and M. A. Gendreau (2005). "Transmission of infectious diseases
during commercial air travel", *Lancet* **365**(9463): 989–96.

Miller, J. M., T. W. Tam, et al. (2000). "Cruise ships: high-risk passengers and the
global spread of new influenza viruses", *Clinical Infectious Diseases* **31**(2):
433–8.

Moser, M. R., T. R. Bender, et al. (1979). "An outbreak of influenza aboard a
commercial airliner", *American Journal of Epidemiology* **110**(1): 1–6.

Naik, G. and J. Hookway (2005). "Demand, Cost for Avian-Flu Drug Could Leave
Neediest With Least", *Wall Street Journal*, 18 May, p. 1.

Ninomiya, A., A. Takada, et al. (2002). "Seroepidemiological evidence of avian H4,
H5, and H9 influenza A virus transmission to pigs in southeastern China",
Veterinary Microbiology **88**(2): 107–14.

Olsen, S. J., H. L. Chang, et al. (2003). "Transmission of the severe acute respiratory
syndrome on aircraft", *New England Journal of Medicine* **349**(25): 2416–22.

Reuters (2003). "Bird Flu Spreads in Europe, Human Health Concerns", *ProMED-
mail*, 18 April.

Schlagenhauf, P., M. Funk, et al. (2004). "Focus on cruise ship travel", *Journal of Travel Medicine* **11**(3): 191–3.

Schuettler, D. (2005). "Bird flu experts urge wider duck cull in Vietnam", *Reuters*, 19 April.

Shortridge, K. F. (2003). "Severe acute respiratory syndrome and influenza: virus incursions from southern China", *American Journal of Respiratory and Critical Care Medicine* **168**(12): 1416–20.

Shortridge, K. F., J. S. Peiris, et al. (2003). "The next influenza pandemic: lessons from Hong Kong", *Journal of Applied Microbiology* **94 Suppl**: 70S–79S.

Smolinski, M. S., M. A. Hamburg, et al. (eds) (2003). *Microbial Threats to Health: Emergence, Detection, and Response*, Institute of Medicine.

Stephenson, I., K. G. Nicholson, et al. (2004). "Confronting the avian influenza threat: vaccine development for a potential pandemic", *Lancet Infectious Diseases* **4**(8): 499–509.

Swayne, D. E. and D. J. King (2003). "Avian influenza and Newcastle disease", *Journal of the American Veterinary Medicine Association* **222**(11): 1534–40.

Uyeki, T. M., S. B. Zane, et al. (2003. "Large summertime influenza A outbreak among tourists in Alaska and the Yukon Territory", *Clinical Infectious Diseases* **36**(9): 1095–102.

Vietnam News Brief Service (2004). "Viet Nam: deaths of 5 children attributed to avian influenza H5 virus", 10 September.

Widdowson, M. A., E. H. Cramer, et al. (2004). "Outbreaks of acute gastroenteritis on cruise ships and on land: identification of a predominant circulating strain of norovirus – United States, 2002", *Journal of Infectious Diseases* **190**(1): 27–36.

World Health Organization, *WHO Global Influenza Programme*.

World Health Organization (2005). *Cumulative Number of Confirmed Human Cases of Avian Influenza A/(H5N1) since 28 January 2004*.

World Health Organization (2004). "Avian influenza – update: implications of H5N1 infections in pigs in China", 25 August.

Chapter 4

Alper, T., D. A. Haig, et al. (1966). "The exceptionally small size of the scrapie agent", *Biochemical and Biophysical Research Communications* **22**(3): 278–84.

Beisel, C. E. and D. M. Morens (2004). "Variant Creutzfeldt-Jakob disease and the acquired and transmissible spongiform encephalopathies", *Clinical Infectious Diseases* **38**(5): 697–704.

Centers for Disease Control and Prevention (1982). "Update on acquired immune deficiency syndrome (AIDS) among patients with hemophilia A", *MMWR Morbidity and Mortality Weekly Report* **31**(48): 644–6, 652.

Ghani, A. C., N. M. Ferguson, et al. (2003). "Factors determining the pattern of the variant Creutzfeldt-Jakob disease (vCJD) epidemic in the UK", *Proceedings of the Royal Society of London, Series B (Biological)* **270**(1516): 689–98.

Hillier, C. E. and R. L. Salmon (2000). "Is there evidence for exogenous risk factors in the aetiology and spread of Creutzfeldt-Jakob disease?", *Quarterly Journal of Medicine* **93**(9): 617–31.

Institute of Medicine (1995). "HIV and the blood supply: an analysis of crisis decisionmaking", *Committee to Study HIV Transmission Through Blood and Blood Products*, eds L. Leveton, H. Sox and M. Stoto, Washington, D.C., Institute of Medicine, National Academy Press.

Krever Commission (1997). *Commission of Inquiry on the Blood System in Canada.*

Supervie, V. and D. Costagliola (2004). "The unrecognised French BSE epidemic", *Veterinary Research* **35**(3): 349–62.

Varghese, B., J. E. Maher, et al. (2002). "Reducing the risk of sexual HIV transmission: quantifying the per-act risk for HIV on the basis of choice of partner, sex act, and condom use", *Sexually Transmitted Diseases* **29**(1): 38–43.

Volkow, P. and C. Del Rio (2005). "Paid donation and plasma trade: unrecognized forces that drive the AIDS epidemic in developing countries", *International Journal of STD and AIDS* **16**(1): 5–8.

Wells, G. A., A. C. Scott, et al. (1987). "A novel progressive spongiform encephalopathy in cattle", *Veterinary Record* **121**(18): 419–20.

Chapter 5

Bolton, J. R., Undersecretary for Arms Control and International Security (2002). *The US Position on the Biological Weapons Convention: Combating the BW Threat*, Tokyo America Center, Tokyo, Japan, US Department of State.

British Medical Association (2004). *Biotechnology, Weapons and Humanity.*

Centers for Disease Control and Prevention (2003). "Nicotine poisoning after ingestion of contaminated ground beef – Michigan, 2003", *MMWR Morbidity and Mortality Weekly Report* **52**(18): 413–6.

Chaffee, M., C. Conway-Welch, et al. (2001). "Bioterrorism in the United States: take it seriously", *American Journal of Nursing* **101**(11): 59, 61.

Chalk, P. (2004a). "The bio-terrorist threat to agricultural livestock and produce", *The Office of Science and Technology Policy Blue Ribbon Panel on the Threat of Biological Terrorism Directed Against Livestock*, RAND Corporation.

Chalk, P. (2004b). *Hitting America's Soft Underbelly: The Potential Threat of Deliberate Biological Attacks Against the US Agricultural and Food Industry*, RAND National Defense Institute.

Christopher, G. W., T. J. Cieslak, et al. (1997). "Biological warfare. A historical perspective", *Journal of the American Medical Association* **278**(5): 412–7.

Council of State and Territorial Epidemiologists (2004). *National Assessment of Epidemiologic Capacity: Findings and Recommendations.*

Cupp, O. S., D. E. Walker, et al. (2004). "Agroterrorism in the US: key security challenge for the 21st century", *Biosecurity and Bioterrorism* **2**(2): 97–105.

Franz, D. R. (2004). "Threats and Risks to US Agriculture: An Overview", *The Office of Science and Technology Policy Blue Ribbon Panel on the Threat of Biological Terrorism Directed Against Livestock*, RAND Corporation.

Gips, M. (2003). "The first link in the food chain", *Security Management Online*, Security Management Magazine.

Inglesby, T. V., R. Grossman, et al. (2001). "A plague on your city: observations from TOPOFF", *Clinical Infectious Diseases* **32**(3): 436–45.

Institute of Medicine (2001). *Biological Threats and Terrorism: Assessing the Science and Response Capabilities*, National Academy Press.

Knobler, S., A. Mahmoud, et al. (eds) (2001). *Biological Threats and Terrorism: Assessing the Science and Response Capabilities*, Institute of Medicine.

North Atlantic Treaty Organization (1992). *NATO Handbook on the Medical Aspects of NBC Defensive Operations*, AMedP-6(B), Part II, Biological.

O'Toole, T., M. Mair, et al. (2002). "Shining light on 'Dark Winter'", *Clinical Infectious Diseases* **34**(7): 972–83.

Office of the Surgeon General (1997). "Medical aspects of chemical and biological warfare", *Textbook of Military Medicine*, eds F. R. Sidell, E. T. Takafuji and D. R. Franz, TMM Publications. Part I.

Pear, R. (2004). "US Health Chief, Stepping Down, Issues Warning", *The New York Times*, December 4th.

Potter, W. C. (2004). *Prospects for International Cooperation on Biological Security*. PIR Center Conference, Moscow.

Stith Butler, A., A. Panzer, et al. (eds) (2003). *Preparing for the Psychological Consequences of Terrorism: A Public Health Strategy*, Institute of Medicine.

Turnbull, W., and P. Abhayaratne (2003). *2002 WMD Terrorism Chronology: Incidents Involving Sub-National Actors and Chemical, Biological, Radiological, and Nuclear Materials*, Monterey Institute of International Studies.

US Food and Drug Administration (2004). "Agencies team up to protect food supply", *FDA Consumer* **38**(2): 28-9.

US General Accounting Office (2003). *Bioterrorism: A Threat to Agriculture and the Food Supply*.

US Government Accountability Office (2005). *Homeland Security: Much Is Being Done to Protect Agriculture from a Terrorist Attack, but Important Challenges Remain*.

Venkatesh, S. and Z. A. Memish (2003). "Bioterrorism – a new challenge for public health", *International Journal of Antimicrobial Agents* **21**(2): 200–6.

World Health Organization (2004). *Public Health Response to Biological and Chemical Weapons: WHO Guidance*.

Chapter 6

Animal Health Institute (2002). *Antibiotic Use in Animals: The Facts*, http://www.ahi.org/mediaCenter/mediaKit/antibUseAnimals.asp.

Boneva, R. S. and T. M. Folks (2004). "Xenotransplantation and risks of zoonotic infections", *Annals of Medicine* **36**(7): 504–17.

Centers for Disease Control and Prevention (1993). "Creutzfeldt-Jakob disease in patients who received a cadaveric dura mater graft – Spain, 1985–1992", *MMWR Morbidity and Mortality Weekly Report* **42**(28): 560–3.

Centers for Disease Control and Prevention (2003). "Update: Creutzfeldt-Jakob disease associated with cadaveric dura mater grafts – Japan, 1979–2003", *MMWR Morbidity and Mortality Weekly Report* **52**(48): 1179–81.

Centers for Disease Control and Prevention (2005). *Recent Avian Influenza Outbreaks in Asia*, May.

Dowell, S. F., C. G. Whitney, et al. (2003). "Seasonal patterns of invasive pneumococcal disease", *Emerging Infectious Diseases* **9**(5): 573–9.

Ewald, P. M. (1996). *Evolution of Infectious Diseases*, Oxford University Press.

Fidler, D. P. (1999). "Legal challenges posed by the use of antimicrobials in food animal production", *Microbes and Infection* **1**(1): 29–38.

Fishman, J. A. and C. Patience (2004). "Xenotransplantation: infectious risk revisited", *American Journal of Transplant* **4**(9): 1383–90.

Food and Agriculture Organization of the United Nations (2004). *Avian Influenza: Stop the Risk for Humans and Animals at Source*.

Lancaster, J. (2004). "Surgeries, side trips for 'medical tourists'", *The Washington Post*, A1, October 21st.

Levy, S. B. (2002). "The 2000 Garrod lecture. Factors impacting on the problem of antibiotic resistance", *Journal of Antimicrobial Chemotherapy* **49**(1): 25–30.

Sipress, A. (2005). "Bird flu adds new danger to bloody game: cockfighting among Asian customs that put humans at risk", *The Washington Post*, A16, April 14th.

Slingenbergh, J. I., M. Gilbert, et al. (2004). "Ecological sources of zoonotic diseases", *Revue scientifique et technique* **23**(2): 467–81.

US General Accounting Office (2004). *Antibiotic Resistance: Federal Agencies Need to Better Focus Efforts to Address Risk to Humans from Antibiotic Use in Animals*.

Witte, W. (2000). "Selective pressure by antibiotic use in livestock", *International Journal of Antimicrobial Agents* **16 Suppl 1**: S19–24.

World Health Organization (2001). *Use of Antimicrobials Outside Human Medicine*, WHO.

World Health Organization (2002). *Implementation Workshop on the WHO Global Strategy for Containment of Antimicrobial Resistance*, WHO.

Chapter 7

Barcos, L. O. (2001). "Recent developments in animal identification and the traceability of animal products in international trade", *Revue scientifique et technique* **20**(2): 640–51.

Caporale, V., A. Giovannini, et al. (2001). "Importance of the traceability of animals and animal products in epidemiology", *Revue scientifique et technique* **20**(2): 372–8.

Centers for Disease Control and Prevention (2005). "Escherichia coli O157:H7 infections associated with ground beef from a U.S. military installation – Okinawa, Japan, February 2004", *MMWR Morbidity and Mortality Weekly Report* **54**(2): 40–2.

Jones, T. F., B. Imhoff, et al. (2004). "Limitations to successful investigation and reporting of foodborne outbreaks: an analysis of foodborne disease outbreaks in FoodNet catchment areas, 1998–1999", *Clinical Infectious Diseases* **38 Suppl 3**: S297–302.

Killalea, D., L. R. Ward, et al. (1996). "International epidemiological and microbiological study of outbreak of Salmonella agona infection from a ready to eat savoury snack – I: England and Wales and the United States", *British Medical Journal* **313**(7065): 1105–7.

Lober, W. B., B. T. Karras, et al. (2002). "Roundtable on bioterrorism detection: information system-based surveillance", *Journal of the American Medical Informatics Association* **9**(2): 105–115.

Mahon, B. E., A. Ponka, et al. (1997). "An international outbreak of Salmonella infections caused by alfalfa sprouts grown from contaminated seeds", *Journal of Infectious Diseases* **175**(4): 876–82.

Pettitt, R. G. (2001). "Traceability in the food animal industry and supermarket chains", *Revue scientifique et technique* **20**(2): 584–97.

US Food and Drug Administration (2004). *Fact Sheet on FDA's New Food Bioterrorism Regulation: Establishment and Maintenance of Records*.

US General Accounting Office (1999). "Emerging Infectious Diseases: National Surveillance System Could Be Strengthened", *Testimony before the Subcommittee on Public Health, Committee on Health, Education, Labor and Pensions*, US Senate.

US Government Accountability Office (2004a). *Food Safety: USDA and FDA Need to Better Ensure Prompt and Complete Recalls of Potentially Unsafe Food*.

US Government Accountability Office (2004b). *Infectious Diseases: Review of State and Federal Disease Surveillance Efforts*.

Van Pelt, W., D. J. Mevius, et al. (2004). "A large increase of Salmonella infections in 2003 in the Netherlands: hot summer or side effect of the avian influenza outbreak?", *Euro Surveillance* **9**(7).

Werber, D., J. Dreesman, et al. (2005). "International outbreak of Salmonella Oranienburg due to German chocolate", *BMC Infectious Diseases* **5**(1): 7.

Chapter 8

Brown, M. (2000). *Administrator, UNDP, Address to Ministers of Trade of Least Developed Countries, Bangkok, Thailand*.

Calvin, L. (2003). "Produce, food safety, and international trade: response to US foodborne illness outbreaks associated with imported produce", Chapter 5 in J. C. Buzby (ed.) *International Trade and Food Safety: Economic Theory and Case Studies*, Economic Research Service, US Department of Agriculture.

Cash, J. and J. Kastner (2004). *SPS Notifications Tool*, Kansas State University.

CBC News Online (2003). "Toronto mayor rails against WHO warning", April 24th.

Comba, P. and R. Pasetto (2004). "The precautionary principle: scientific evidence and decision processes", *Epidemiologia e preventzione* **28**(1): 41–5.

Conzaniga, A. (2002). "GATS and trade in health services" in N. Drager and C. Viera, *Trade in Health Services*, World Health Organization.

Cunningham, E. P. (2003). *After BSE – A Future for the European Livestock Sector*, European Association for Animal Production, Wageningen Academic Publishers.

Goldstein, B. and R. S. Carruth (2004). "The precautionary principle and/or risk assessment in World Trade Organization decisions: a possible role for risk perception", *Risk Analysis* **24**(2): 491–9.

Lang, T. (1999). "Diet, health and globalization: five key questions", *Proceedings of the Nutrition Society* **58**(2): 335–43.

McCrea, D. (1997). "Codex Alimentarius – in the consumer interest?", *Consumer Policy Review* **7**(4): 132–8.

Morse, S. S. (1995). "Factors in the emergence of infectious diseases", *Emerging Infectious Diseases* **1**(1): 7–15.

Oliveira, M. A., J. A. Bermudez, et al. (2004). "Has the implementation of the TRIPS Agreement in Latin America and the Caribbean produced intellectual property legislation that favours public health?", *Bulletin of the World Health Organization* **82**(11): 815–21.

Public Citizen (2003). "The WTO comes to dinner: US implementation of trade rules bypasses food safety requirements", July.

Silverglade, B. A. (2000). "The WTO agreement on sanitary and phytosanitary measures: weakening food safety regulations to facilitate trade?", *Food and Drug Law Journal* **55**(4): 517–24.

Vose, D., J. Acar, et al. (2001). "Antimicrobial resistance: risk analysis methodology for the potential impact on public health of antimicrobial resistant bacteria of animal origin", *Revue scientifique et technique* **20**(3): 811–27.

World Bank Group (2003). *World Bank Responds to SARS*.

World Health Organization (1998). *Global Infectious Disease Surveillance*.

World Health Organization (2003). *WHO Extends its SARS-related Travel Advice to Beijing and Shanxi Province in China and to Toronto, Canada*.

World Health Organization (2005). *International Health Regulations*.

World Health Organization Regional Committee for the Western Pacific (1998). *Fifty Years of WHO in the Western Pacific Region*.

World Trade Organization (2005). *Review of the Operation and Implementation of the SPS Agreement*.

World Trade Organization Committee on Technical Barriers to Trade (2005). *Transparency Requirements and Procedures*.

World Trade Organization Council for Trade in Services (1999). "Article VI.4 of the GATS: Disciplines on domestic regulation applicable to all services", Note by the Secretariat, 1 March 1999.

Chapter 9

Anderson, R. M. and R. M. May (1991). *Infectious Diseases of Humans: Dynamics and Control*, Oxford, Oxford University Press.

Arkless, D. (2005). *Report on Business and HIV/AIDS*, World Economic Forum, Davos, Switzerland.

Baumes, H. and S. Ramsey (2005). "Mad cow loose in the United States?", *Global Insight*, http://www.globalinsight.com/Perspective/PerspectiveDetail724.htm.

Donegan, E., M. Stuart, et al. (1990). "Infection with human immunodeficiency virus type 1 (HIV-1) among recipients of antibody-positive blood donations", *Annals of Internal Medicine* **113**(10): 733–9.

Henderson, D. A., T. V. Inglesby, et al. (1999). "Smallpox as a biological weapon: medical and public health management. Working Group on Civilian Biodefense", *Journal of the American Medical Association* **281**(22): 2127–37.

Hufnagel, L., D. Brockmann, et al. (2004). "Forecast and control of epidemics in a globalized world", *Proceedings of the National Academy of Sciences of the USA* **101**(42): 15124–9.

Jones, T. F. and W. Schaffner (2003). "Salmonella in imported mangos: shoeleather and contemporary epidemiologic techniques together meet the challenge", *Clinical Infectious Diseases* **37**(12): 1591–2.

Kennedy, M. (2005). "India and its medical outsourcing industry" in *Marketplace*, National Public Radio, 5 April.

Kimball, A. M. and M. Thant (1996). "A role for businesses in HIV prevention in Asia", *Lancet* **347**(9016): 1670–2.

Kingdon, J. W. (1995). *Agendas, Alternatives, and Public Policies*, New York, Addison-Wesley Longman.

Klausner, R. D., A. S. Fauci, et al. (2003). "Medicine – the need for a global HIV vaccine enterprise", *Science* **300**(5628): 2036–9.

Layne, S. P., T. J. Beugelsdijk, et al. (2001). "A global lab against influenza", *Science* **293**(5536): 1729.

McMichael, A. (1993). *Planetary Overload: Global Environmental Change and the Health of the Human Species*, Cambridge University Press.

Potter, J. D. (2004). "Toward the last cohort", *Cancer Epidemiology Biomarkers and Prevention* **13**(6): 895–7.

Sachs, J. (2005). *The End of Poverty: Economic Possibilities for Our Time*, New York, Penguin Press.

Smith, R. D., R. Beaglehole, D. Woodward and N. Drager (2003). *Global Public Goods for Health: A Health, Economic and Public Health Perspective*. Oxford University Press.

Smith, R. D., D. Woodward, et al. (2004). "Communicable disease control: a 'global public good' perspective", *Health Policy and Planning* **19**(5): 271–8.

Stiglitz, J. E. (2003). *Globalization and Its Discontents*, W. W. Norton & Company.

UNICEF and World Health Organization (2002). *Meeting the MDG Drinking Water and Sanitation Target: A Mid-term Assessment of Progress*.

Varghese, B., J. E. Maher, et al. (2002). "Reducing the risk of sexual HIV transmission: quantifying the per-act risk for HIV on the basis of choice of partner, sex act, and condom use", *Sexually Transmitted Diseases* **29**(1): 38–43.

World Health Organization (2000). *Global Water Supply and Sanitation Assessment, 2000 Report*.

World Health Organization (2005). *International Health Regulations*.

Additional Resources

Commission on Macroeconomics and Health, from http://www.chm.org.

APEC considers creating financial intelligence units to fight terrorism, *Xinhua News Agency*.

"Nestle's Milk Collection: Enabling Market Access for smallholder Dairy Farms in Pakistan and China [not for quotation]."

(2002). "Independent evaluation of the Codex Alimentarius and other FAO-WHO work on food standards." *Wkly Epidemiol Rec* **77**(17): 138–9.

(2003). "Revision of the International Health Regulations." *Epidemiol Bull* **24**(4): 14–15.

(2004). "Chile calls on APEC to seek balance between trade, anti-terror. *Xinhua New Agency*.

(2004). "Federal Food Safety and Security System: Fundamental Restructuring is Needed to Address Fragmentation and Overlap." *Subcommittee on Civil Service and Agency Organization, Committee on Government Reform*.

(2004). "A new public health world order." *Lancet Infect Dis* **4**(8): 475.

(2004). Statement of Robert E. Brackett, Ph.D., Director, Center for Food Safety and Applied Nutrition, Food and Drug Administration. *Committee on Government Reform: Subcommittee on Civil Service and Agency Organization*.

(2004). Testimony by Dr Barbara J. Masters, Food Safety and Inspection Service Fiscal 2005 Appropriations: Agriculture and Related Agencies. *House Appropriations*.

Joint First FAO/OIE/WHO Expert Workshop on Non-human Antimicrobial Usage and Antimicrobial Resistance: Scientific assessment, Geneva.

Allos, B. M., M. R. Moore, et al. (2004). "Surveillance for sporadic foodborne disease in the 21st century: the FoodNet perspective." *Clin Infect Dis* **38 Suppl 3**: S115–20.

Alocilja, E. C. and S. M. Radke (2003). "Market analysis of biosensors for food safety." *Biosens Bioelectron* **18**(5–6): 841–6.

Altekruse, S. F., M. L. Cohen, et al. (1997). "Emerging foodborne disease." *Emerg Infect Dis* **3**(3): 285–93.

Anderson, A. D., J. M. Nelson, et al. (2003) "Public health consequences of use of antimicrobial agents in food animals in the United States." *Microb Drug Resist* **9**(4): 373–9.

Anderson, M. A. W. (2001). "The Economics of Quarantine and the SPS Agreement." 414.

Angulo, F. J. and P. M. Griffin (2000). "Changes in antimicrobial resistance in Salmonella enterica serovar typhimurium." *Emerg Infect Dis* **6**(4): 436–8.

Apostolakis, G. E. (2004). "How useful is quantitative risk assessment?" *Risk Anal* **24**(3): 515–20.

Bern, C., B. Hernandez, et al. (1999). "Epidemiologic studies of Cyclospora cayetanensis in Guatemala." *Emerg Infect Dis* **5**(6): 766–74.

Bertollini, R. and V. T. Gee (2004). "Working across sectors for public health." *Bull World Health Organ* **82**(5): 322.

Besser, R. E., S. M. Lett, et al. (1993). "An outbreak of diarrhea and hemolytic uremic syndrome from Escherichia coli O157:H7 in fresh-pressed apple cider." *Jama* **269**(17): 2217–20.

Bonanno, A. (1994). *From Columbus to ConAgra: the globalization of agriculture and food*, University Press of Kansas.

Broome, C. V., H. H. Horton, et al. (20030. "Statutory basis for public health reporting beyond specific diseases." *J Urban Health* **80**(2 Suppl 1): i14–22.

Brown, C. (2004). "Emerging zoonoses and pathogens of public health significance – an overview." *Rev Sci Tech* **23**(2): 435–42.

Bruemmer, B. (2003). "Food biosecurity." *J Am Diet Assoc* **103**(6): 687–91.

Busch, M. P., S. H. Kleinman, et al. (2003). "Current and emerging infectious risks of blood transfusions." *Jama* **289**(8): 959–62.

Buss, P. M. (2002). "Globalization and disease: in an unequal world, unequal health!" *Cad Saude Publica* **18**(6): 1783–8.

Butler, D. (1996). "Did UK 'dump' contaminate feed after ban?" *Nature* **381**(6583): 544–5.

Calvin, L., B. Avendaño, et al. (2004). *The Economics of Food Safety: The Case of Green Onions and Hepatitis A Outbreaks*. E. R. Service, USDA.

Capua, I. and S. Marangon (2003). "Vaccination in the control of avian influenza in the EU." *Vet Rec* **152**(9): 271.

Cardenas, V. M., M. C. Roces, et al. (2002). "Improving public health leadership through training in epidemiology and public health: the experience of TEPHINET. Training Programs in Epidemiology and Public Health Interventions Networks." *Am J Public Health* **92**(2): 196–7.

Caswell, J. A. (2000). "Economic approaches to measuring the significance of food safety in international trade." *Int J Food Microbiol* **62**(3): 261–6.

Center for Nonproliferation Studies (2004). The Biological and Toxin Weapons Convention: Negotiating Inspection and Enforcement Provisions, Monterey Institute.

Centers for Disease Control and Prevention (1993). "Update: multistate outbreak of Escherichia coli O157:H7 infections from hamburgers – western United States, 1992–1993." *MMWR Morb Mortal Wkly Rep* **42**(14): 258–63.

Centers for Disease Control and Prevention (1994). "Escherichia coli O157:H7 outbreak linked to home-cooked hamburger – California, July 1993." *MMWR Morb Mortal Wkly Rep* **43**(12): 213–16.

Centers for Disease Control and Prevention (1998). "Outbreak of cyclosporiasis – Ontario, Canada, May 1998." *MMWR Morb Mortal Wkly Rep* **47**(38): 806–9.

Centers for Disease Control and Prevention (2001). "HIV and AIDS – United States, 1981–2000." *MMWR Morb Mortal Wkly Rep* **50**(21): 430–34.

Centers for Disease Control and Prevention (2001). "Outbreak of listeriosis associated with homemade Mexican-style cheese – North Carolina, October 2000–January 2001." *MMWR Morb Mortal Wkly Rep* **50**(26): 560–62.

Centers for Disease Control and Prevention (2002). "Multistate outbreak of Escherichia coli O157:H7 infections associated with eating ground beef – United States, June–July 2002." *MMWR Morb Mortal Wkly Rep* **51**(29): 637–9.

Centers for Disease Control and Prevention (2002). "Outbreak of listeriosis – northeastern United States, 2002." *MMWR Morb Mortal Wkly Rep* **51**(42): 950–51.

Centers for Disease Control and Prevention (2004). "Outbreak of cyclosporiasis associated with snow peas – Pennsylvania, 2004." *MMWR Morb Mortal Wkly Rep* **53**(37): 876–8.

Centers for Disease Control and Prevention (2004). "Preliminary assessment of the effectiveness of the 2003-04 inactivated influenza vaccine – Colorado, December 2003." *MMWR Morb Mortal Wkly Rep* **53**(1): 8–11.

Centers for Disease Control and Prevention (2004). "Preliminary FoodNet data on the incidence of infection with pathogens transmitted commonly through food – selected sites, United States, 2003." *MMWR Morb Mortal Wkly Rep* **53**(16): 338–43.

Checa, N., J. Maguire, et al. (2003). "The new world disorder." *Harv Bus Rev* **81**(8): 070–9, 140.

Chen, J. (2004). "Challenges to developing countries after joining WTO: risk assessment of chemicals in food." *Toxicology* **198**(1–3): 3–7.

Clarke, S. C., R. D. Haigh, et al. (2002). "Enteropathogenic Escherichia coli infection: history and clinical aspects." *Br J Biomed Sci* **59**(2): 123–7.

Codex Alimentarius Commission (2004). Compatability of Data Reporting Formats Used by FAO/WHO International Risk Assessment Bodies. Bratislava, Slovakia.

Colebunders, R., R. Ryder, et al. (1991). "Seroconversion rate, mortality, and clinical manifestations associated with the receipt of a human immunodeficiency virus-affected blood transfusion in Kinshasa, Zaire." *J Infect Dis* 164(3): 450–6.

Collins, J. D. and P. G. Wall (2004). "Food safety and animal production systems: controlling zoonoses at farm level." *Rev Sci Tech* 23(2): 685–700.

Commission, C. A. (2003). *Risk Profile for Enterohemorragic E. Coli Including the Identification of the Commodities of Concern, Including Sprouts, Ground Beef and Pork*. Joint FAO/WHO Food Standards Programme, Orlando, USA.

Commission, K. (1997). Commission of Inquiry on the Blood System in Canada, Health Canada.

Cookson, B., A. P. Johnson, et al. (1995). "International inter- and intrahospital patient spread of a multiple antibiotic-resistant strain of Klebsiella pueumoniae." *J Infect Dis* **171**(2): 511–13.

Cortinois, A. A., S. Downey, et al. (2003). "Hospitals in a globalized world: a view from Canada." *Healthc Pap* 4(2): 14–32.

Cox, L. A., Jr. and D. A. Popken (2004). "Bayesian Monte Carlo incertainty analysis of human health risks from animal antimicrobial use in a dynamic model of emerging resistance." *Risk Anal* 24(5): 1153–64.

Crump, J. A., A. C. Sulka, et al. (2002). "An outbreak of Escherichia coli O157:H7 infections among visitors to a dairy farm." *N Engl J Med* **347**(8): 555–60.

Cuellar, S. (2002). *Marketing Fresh Fruit and Vegetable Imports in the United States: Status, Challenges and Opportunities*, Cornell University.

De Buyser, M. L., B. Dufour, et al. (2001). "Implication of milk and milk products in food-borne diseases in France and in different industrialised countries." *Int J Food Microbiol* **67**(1–2): 1–17.

Dentinger, C., L. Pasat, et al. (2004). "Injection practices in Romania: progress and challenges." *Infect Control Hosp Epidemiol* **25**(1): 30–35.

Diamond, J. (2004). *Collapse: How Societies Choose to Fail or Succeed*, Viking.

Donnelly, C. A., N. M. Ferguson, et al. (2002). "Implications of BSE infection screening data for the scale of the British BSE epidemic and current European infection levels." *Proc R Soc Lond Bio Sci* **269**(1506): 2179–90.

Dorozynski, A. (2000). "Sevn die in French listeria outbreak." *Bmj* **320**(7235): 601.

Doyle, R. (2003). "Trade globalization. It is nearly two centuries old and likely to continue." *Sci Am* **288**(6): 30.

Edwards, D. S., A. M. Johnston, et al. (1997). "Meat inspection: an overview of present practices and future trends." *Vet J* **154**(2): 135–47.

Fan, E. X. (2003). "SARS: Economic Impacts and Implications." *ERD Policy Brief*, Economics and Research Department, Asian Development Bank.

FAO/OIE?WHO Expert Workshop (2004). "Non-Human Antimicrobial Usage and Antimicrobial Resistance: Management Options." Oslo, Norway.

Farmer, P. (1999). *Infections and Inequalities*. Los Angeles, University of California Press.

Fauci, A. (April 28, 2005). Univer.

Feng, P. and S. Weagant (2002). "Diarrheagenic Escherichia coli." *Bacteriological Analytical Manual Online*.

Ferber, D. (2003). "Antibiotic resistance. WHO advises kicking the livestock antibiotic habit." *Science* **301**(5636): 1027.

Fernández de Larrinoa Arcal, Y., M. Maetz, et al. (2000). *Multilateral Trade Negotiations on Agriculture: A Resource Manual*.

Fidler, D. P. (1998). "Legal issues associated with antimicrobial drug resistance." *Emerg Infect Dis* **4**(2): 169–77.

Fidler, D. P. (2003). "Antimicrobial Resistance: A Challenge for Global Health Governance." *Health Impacts of Globalization: Towards Global Governance*. K. Lee, Palgrave Macmillan.

Fidler, D. P. (2004). "Germs, governance, and global public health in the wake of SARS." *J Clin Invest* **113**(6): 799–801.

Fisher, I. S. (2004). "Dramatic shifts in the epidemiology of Salmonella enterica serotype Enteritidis phage types in western Europe, 1998–2003 – results from the Enter-net international salmonella database." *Euro Surveill* **9**(11).

Fisher, I. S. (2004). "International trends in salmonella serotypes 1998–2003 – a surveillance report from the Enter-net international surveillance network." *Euro Surveill* **9**(11).

Fleck, F. (2003). "Conference warns of danger of re-emergence of smallpox as weapon of bioterror." *Bull World Health Organ* **81**(12): 917–18.

Folch, E., I. Hernandez, et al. (2003). "Infectious diseases, non-zero-sum thinking, and the developing world." *Am J Med Sci* **326**(2): 66–72.

Food and Agriculture Organization of the United Nations FAOSTAT.

Food and Agriculture Organization of the United Nations (2002). World agriculture: towards 2015/2030. Summary report.

Food and Agriculture Organization of the United Nations (2003). "Animal disease outbreaks hit global meat exports."

Food and Agriculture Organization of the United Nations (2004). Improving the quality and safety of fresh fruits and vegetables: a practical approach.

Food and Agriculture Organization of the United Nations (January 28, 2004). High geographic concentration of animals may have favored the spread of avian flu.

Frenzen, P. D. (2004). "Deaths due to unknown foodborne agents." *Emerg Infect Dis* **10**(9): 1536–43.

Gagnon, L. (2004). "Fujian flu more severe, but not unusual." *Cmaj* **170**(3): 325.

Gibbs, J. and S. Shaw (1995). "Implications of changes in GATT for the marketing strategies of British beef producers." *British Food Journal* **97**(1): 3–10.

Goodman, L. (2004). "Profits of public-private partnerships." *J Clin Invest* **114**(6): 742.

Gostin, L. O. (2004). "International infectious disease law: revision of the World Health Organization's International Health Regulations." *Jama* **291**(21): 2623–7.

Greenberg, A. E., P. Nguyen-Dinh, et al. (1988). "The association between malaria, blood transfusions and HIV seropositivity in a pediatric population in Kinshasa, Zaire." *Jama* **259**(4): 545–9.

Group, T. W. B. (2002). Water Supply and Sanitation.

Group, T. W. B. (2003). Improving Livelihoods on Fragile Lands, Chapter Four, World Development Report.

Gushulak, B. D. and D. W. MacPherson (2004). "Globalization of infectious diseases: the impact of migration." *Clin Infect Dis* 38(12): 1742–8.

Haas, G. J. (1995). "'Yakugai' AIDS and the Yokohama Xth international AIDS conference." *Common Factor* (no 10): 1, 22.

Haggett, P. (2000). *The Geographical Structure of Epidemics*, Oxford.

Harlow, S. D. (2004). "Science-based trade disputes: a new challenge in harmonizing the evidentiary systems of law and science." *Risk Anal* **24**(2): 443–7.

Health Canada (2003). Global Mercury – Post Exercise Report.

Health Canada (2003). The Naylor report on SARS and public health in Canada, Health Canada, Ottawa.

Health Protection Agency (2005). "Enter-Net: International surveillance network for the enteric infections Salmonella and VTEC O157." From http://www.hpa.org.uk/hpainter/enter-net_outbreaks.htm.

Henson, S. J., R. J. Loader, et al. (1999). *Impact of sanitary and phytosanitary measures on developing countries*. The University of Reading.

Hersh, B. S., F. Popovici, et al. (1993). "Risk factors for HIV infection among abandoned Romanian children." *Aids* **7**(12): 1617–24.

Herwaldt, B. L. and M. L. Ackers (1997). "An outbreak in 1996 of cyclosporiasis associated with imported raspberries. The Cyclospora Working Group." *N Engl J Med* **336**(22): 1548–56.

Heymann, D. L. (2002). *Food safety, and essential public health priority*. FAO/WHO Global Forum of Food Safety Regulators, Marrakesh, Morocco.

Horton, L. R. (2001). "Risk analysis and the law: international law, the World Trade Organization, Codex Alimentarius and national legislation." *Food Addit Contam* **18**(12): 1057–67.

Howse, R. (2004). "The WHO/WTO study on trade and public health: a critical assessment." *Risk Anal* **24**(2): 501–7.

Hueston, W. (2004). *The Science Driving North American BSE Policy*. International Association for Food Protection. Phoenix, Arizona.

Iezzoni, L. (1999). *Influenza 1918 The Worst Epidemic in American History*. New York, TV Books, L.L.C.

Ingham, G. (1999). "Capitalism, money and banking: a critique of recent historical sociology." *Br J Sociol* **50**(1): 76–96.

Institute of Food Science & Technology (1995). "Listeria monocytogenes in Cheese."

Institute of Medicine (2003). "Microbial Threats to Health: Emergence, Detection, and Response."

James, A. D. and J. Rushton (2002). "The economics of foot and mouth disease." *Rev Sci Tech* **21**(3): 637–44.

Jimba, M. and D. D. Joshi (2001). "Health promotion approach for the control of food-borne parasitic zoonoses in Nepal: emphasis on an environmental assessment." *Southeast Asian J Trop Med Public Health* **32 Suppl 2**: 229–35.

Jones, R. W. (2003). "Globalization and the distribution of income: the economic arguments." *Proc Natl Acad Sci USA* **100**(19): 1158–62.

Josefson, D. (2003). "Haemophilia patients launch action against Bayer over contaminated blood products." *Bmj* **326**(7402): 1286.

Joshi, D. D., M. Maharjan, et al. (2003). "Improving meat inspection and control in resource-poor communities: the Nepal example." *Acta-Trop* **87**(1): 119–27.

Joshi, D. D., P. M. Poudyal, et al. (2001). "Controlling Taenia solium in Nepal using the PRECEDE-PROCEED model." *Southeast Asian J Trop Med Public Health* **32 Suppl 2**: 94–7.

Katz, L. M. (2003). "A Comment from Dr. M. Katz of the Mississippi Valley Regional Blood Center." *ProMed-mail* Retrieved September 16, 2003, from http:www.promedmail.org/pls/askus/f?p=2400: 1000.

Kehl, S. C. (2002). "Role of the laboratory in the diagnosis of enterohemorrhagic Escherichia coli infections." *J Clin Microbiol* **40**(8): 2711–15.

Kelly, T. K., P. Chalk, et al. (2004). *The Office of Science and Technology Blue Ribbon Panel on the Threat of Biological Terrorism Directed Against Livestock*, RAND Corporation.

Kennedy, M., R. Villar, et al. (2004). "Hospitalizations and deaths due to Salmonella infections, FoodNet, 1996–1999." *Clin Infect Dis* **38 Suppl 3**: S142–8.

Kimball, A. M. and K. Taneda (2004). "A new method for assessing the impact of emerging infections on global trade." *Rev Sci Tech* **23**(3): 753–60.

Kirk, M. D., C. L. Little, et al. (2004). "An outbreak due to peanuts in their shell caused by Salmonella enterica serotypes Stanley and Newport-sharing molecular information to solve international outbreaks." *Epidemiol Infect* **132**(4): 571–7.

Kitching, R. P. (2000). "OIE List A disease as a constraint to international trade." *Ann N Y Acad Sci* **916**: 50–54.

Koopmans, M., H. Vennema, et al. (2003). "Early identification of common-source foodborne virus outbreaks in Europe." *Emerg Infect Dis* **9**(9): 1136–42.

Kouba, V. (2003). "Quantitative analysis of global veterinary human resources." *Rev Sci Tech* **22**(3): 899–908.

Lashley, F. R. (2003). "Factors contributing to the occurrence of emerging infectious diseases." *Biol Res Nurs* **4**(4): 258–67.

Lee, K. and P. Patel (2002). "Far from the maddening cows: The global dimensions of BSE and vCJD." *Health impacts of globalization: towards global governance.* K. Lee. London, Palgrave-Macmillan: 47–60.

LeJeune, J. T., T. E. Besser, et al. (2004). "Longitudinal study of fecal shedding of Escherichia coli O157:H7 in feedlot cattle: predominance of persistence of specific clonal types despite massive cattle population turnover." *Appl Environ Microbiol* **70**(1): 377–84.

Leslie, J. and M. Upton (1999). "The economic implications of greater global trade in livestock and livestock products." *Rev Sci Tech* **18**(2): 440–57.

Lightowlers, M. W. (1999). "Eradication of Taenia solium cysticercosis: a role for vaccination of pigs." *Int J Parasitol* **29**(6): 811–17.

Lopez, A. S., J. M. Bendik, et al. (2003). "Epidemiology of Cyclospora cayetanensis and other intestinal parasites in the community of Haiti." *J Clin Microbiol* **41**(5): 2047–54.

Louzoun, Y., S. Solomon, et al. (2003). "World-size global markets lead to economic instability." *Artif Life* **9**(4): 357–70.

Ludwig, B., F. B. Kraus, et al. (2003). "Viral zoonoses – a threat under control?" *Interviology* **46**(2): 71–8.

Lupien, J. R. (2002). "The precautionary principle and other non-tariff barriers to free and fair international food trade." *Crit Rev Food Sci Nutr* **42**(4): 403–15.

Malhotra, K. (2003). *Making Global Trade Work for People*, United Nations Development Programme, Earthscan Publication.

Mansfield, L. S. and A. A. Gajadhar (2004). "Cyclospora cayetanensis, a food- and waterborne coccidian parasite." *Vet Parasitol* **126**(1–2): 73–90.

Matthews, D. (2003). "BSE: a global update." *J Appl Microbiol* **94 Suppl**: 120S–125S.

McCrindle, C. M. E. "Trends in Veterinary Public Health Regulations: possible impacts on poor consumers and producers of livestock products [not for quotation]."

McDonald's Corporation (2003). *McDonald's Global Policy on Antibiotic Use in Food Animals.*

McKean, J. D. (2001). "The importance of traceability for public health and consumer protection." *Rev Sci Tech* **20**(2): 363–71.

McLauchlin, J., R. T. Mitchell, et al. (2004). "Listeria monocytogenes and listeriosis: a review of hazard characterisation for use in microbiological risk assessment of foods." *Int J Food Microbiol* **92**(1): 15–33.

McMurray, C. S. R. (2001). *Diseases of Globalization.* London, Earthscan Publication Ltd.

Mead, P. S. and P. M. Griffin (1998). "Escherichia coli O157:H7." *Lancet* **352**(9135): 1207–12.

Mead, P. S., L. Slutsker, et al. (1999). "Food-related illness and death in the United States." *Emerg Infect Dis* **5**(5): 607–25.

Meadows, M. (2004). "The FDA and the fight against terrorism." *FDA Consum* **38**(1): 20–27.

Mellon, M., C. Benbrook, et al. (2001). "Hogging It! Estimates of Antimicrobial Abuse in Livestock." Union of Concerned Scientists.

Memish, Z. A., S. Venkatesh, et al. (200.). "Impact of travel on international spread of antimicrobial resistance." *Int J Antimicrob Agents* **21**(2): 135–42.

Mermin, J. L. Hutwagner, et al. (2004). "Reptiles, amphibians, and human Salmonella infection: a population-based, case-control study." *Clin Infect Dis* **38 Suppl 3**: S253–61.

Michion, H., K. Araki, et al. (1999). "Massive outbreak of Escherichia coli O157:H7 infection in schoolchildren in Sakai City, Japan associated with consumption of white radish sprouts." *Am J Epidemiol* **150**(8): 787–96.

Molbak, K., P. S. Mead, et al. (2002). "Antimicrobial therapy in patients with Escherichia coli O157:H7 infection." *Jama* **288**(8): 1014–16.

Morens, D. M., G. K. Folkers, et al. (2004). "The challenge of emerging and re-emerging infectious diseases." *Nature* **430**(6996): 242–9.

Morgan, N. (2001). Repercussions of BSE in International Meat Trade, United Nations Food and Agricultural Organisation.

Morohashi, Y. (1997). "Controversial issues surrounding the case of HIV infections and AIDS through the use of unheated commercial blood products." *Jpn Hosp* **14**: 1–3.

National Center for Biotechnology Information (1999). "The Salmonella battle plan: how Salmonella gain entry into human intestinal cells to grow and divide."

National Food Safety System Project (2001). Multistate Foodborne Outbreak Investigations: Guidelines for Improving Coordination and Communication.

National Research Council Committee on Science and Technology for Countering Terrorism (2002). *Making the Nation Safer: The Role of Science and Technology in Countering Terrorism*. Washington DC, National Academies Press.

Nicholson, B., Associated Press (2004). "Veterinary Corps are Being Outfitted for Bioterror Attacks; Units Would also Fight Disease Outbreaks." *The Washington Post*.

Nishtar, S (2004). "Public private 'partnerships' in health – a global call to action." *Health Res Policy Syst* **2**(1): 5.

O'Brien, S. J. and G. K. Adak (2002). "Escherichia coli O157:H7 – piecing together the jigsaw puzzle." *N Engl J Med* **347**(8): 608–9.

Office International des Épizooties Bovine spongiform encephalopathy.

Office International des Épizooties (2004). "Number of reported cases of bovine spongiform encephalopathy (BSE) in farmed cattle worldwide (excluding the United Kingdom)."

Ogden, I. D., N. F. Hepburn, et al. (2002). "Long-term survival of Escherichia coli O157 on pasture following an outbreak associated with sheep at a scout camp." *Lett Appl Microbiol* **34**(2): 100–104.

Oldfield, E. C. (2003). "The road to resistance: antibiotics as growth promoters for animals." *Am J Gastroenterol* **98**(2): 499.

Olson, K. B. (1999). "Aum Shinrikyo: once and future threat?" *Emerg Infect Dis* **5**(4): 513–16.

Osterholm, M. T. (1999). "Lessons learned again: cyclosporiasis and raspberries." *Ann Intern Med* **130**(3): 233–4.

Osterholm, M. T. (2000). "Emerging infections – another warning." *N Engl J Med* **342**(17): 1280–81.

Otsuki, T. M. Sewadeh, et al. (2001). *A Race to the Top? A Case Study of Food Safety Standards and African Imports*, The World Bank Group.

Pearce, N. (2004). "The globalization of epidemiology: introductory remarks." *Int J Epidemiol* **33**(5): 127–31.

Pellerin, C. (2000). "The next target of bioterrorism: your food." *Environ Health Perspect* **108**(3): A126–9.

Pieniazek, N. J. and B. L. Herwaldt (1997). "Reevaluating the molecular taxonomy: is human-associated Cyclospora a mammalian Eimeria species?" *Emerg Infect Dis* **3**(3): 381–3.

Pierson, M. (2003). *Farm to Fork – Looking Forward*. International Center for Food Industry Excellence, Texas Tech University.

Polyak, M. (2004). "The Threat of Agroterrorism: Economics of Bioterrorism." *Georgetown Journal of International Affairs*.

Posfay-Barbe, K. M. and E. R. Wald (2004). "Listeriosis." *Pediatr Rev* **25**(5): 151–9.

Price-Smith, A. T. (2001). *Plagues and Politics*. New York, Palgrave.

Price-Smith, A. T. (2002). *The Health of Nations*. Massachusetts, The MIT Press.

Ray, D. (2002). "Impacts of Bio-terrorism on the US Agricultural Sector and Exports: A Hypothetical Case of FMD." *Bio-terrorism and Food Security: Issues and Challenges*. Fargo, North Dakota.

Rhodes, R. (1997). *Deadly Feasts*. New York, Simon and Schuster.

Ribot, E. M., R. K. Wierzba, et al. (2002). "Salmonella enterica serotype Typhimurium DT104 isolates from humans, United States, 1985, 1990, and 1995." *Emerg Infect Dis* **8**(4): 387–91.

Robinson, A. (2001). *Veterinary Public Health and the Control of Zoonoses in Developing Countries*. FAO/WHO/OIE Electronic Conference on Veterinary Public Health and Control of Zoonoses in Developing Countries.

Ross, T. and T. A. McMeekin (2003). "Modeling microbial growth within food safety risk assessments." *Risk Anal* **23**(1): 179–97.

Rother, L. (2004). "South America Seeks to Fill the World's Table." *The New York Times*.

Rweyemamu, M. M. and V. Astudillo (2002). "Global perspective for foot and mouth disease control." *Rev. Sci. Tech. Off. Int. Epiz.* **21**(3).

Saker, L., K. Lee, et al. (2004). "Globalization and infectious diseases: A review of the linkages." *Social, Economic and Behavioural Research, Special Topics No. 3*, World Health Organization.

Schmid, G. P., A. Buve, et al. (2004). "Transmission of HIV-1 infection in sub-Saharan Africa and effect of elimination of unsafe injections." *Lancet* **363**(9407): 482–8.

Scudamore, J. M. "The dynamics of SPS (animal health and food safety) regulations and impacts on domestic livestock markets in developing countries [not for quotation]."

Shaffer, E. R., H. Waitzkin, et al. (2005). "Global Trade and public health." *Am J Public Health* **95**(1): 23–34.

Shanm H., J. X. Wang, et al. (2002). "Blood banking in China." *Lancet* **360**(9347): 1770–75.

Shnayerson, M. and M. J. Plotkin (2002). *The Killers Within*. New York, Little, Brown and Company.

Simonsen, G. S., J. W. Tapsall, et al. (2004). "The antimicrobial resistance containment and surveillance appoach – a public health tool." *Bull World Health Organ* **82**(12): 928–34.

Sivapalasingam, S., C. R. Friedman, et al. (2004). "Fresh produce: a growing cause of outbreaks of foodborne illness in the United States, 1973 through 1997." *J Food Prot* **67**(10): 2342–53.

Sklair, L. (2001). *The Transnational Capitalist Class*, Oxford, Blackwell.

Slutsker, L., A. A. Ries, et al. (1997). "Escherichia coli O157:H7 diarrhea in the United States: clinical and epidemiologic features." *Ann Intern Med* **126**(7): 505–13.

Smith, R. D. (2004). "Foreign direct investment and trade in health services: a review of the literature." **59**: 2313–23.

Soave, R., B. L. Herwaldt, et al. (1998). "Cyclospora." *Infect Dis Clin North Am* **12**(1): 1–12.

Sobel, J., A. S. Khan, et al. (2002). "Threat of a biological terrorist attack on the US food supply: the CDC perspective." *Lancet* **359**(9309): 874–80.

Steinfeld, H. (2004). "The livestock revolution – a global veterinary mission." *Vet Parasitol* **125**(1–2): 19–41.

Sterling, C. R. and Y. R. Ortega (1999). "Cyclospora: an enigma worth unraveling." *Emerg Infect Dis* **5**(1): 48–53.

Steyerberg, E. W., S. E. Bleeker, et al. (2003). "Internal and external validation of predictive models: a simulation study of bias and precision in small samples." *J Clin Epidemiol* **56**(5): 441–7.

Supervie, V. and D. Costagliola (2004). "The unrecognised French BSE epidemic." *Vet Res* **35**(3): 349–62.

Suppan, S. (2004). Consumer International's Decision-Making in the Global Market: Codex Briefing Paper, Institute for Agriculture and Trade Policy.

Taubenberger, J. K. and S. P. Layne (2001). "Diagnosis of influenza virus: coming to grips with the molecular era." *Mol Diagn* **6**(4): 291–305.

Taylor, D. M. and S. L. Woodgate (2003). "Rendering practices and inactivation of transmissible spongiform encephalopathy agents." *Rev Sci Tech* **22**(1): 297–310.

Teunis, P., K. Takumi, et al. (2004). "Dose response for infection by Escherichia coli O157:H7 from outbreak data." *Risk Anal* **24**(2): 401–7.

Thiermann, A. (2004) "Adapting veterinary infrastructures to meet the challenges of globalisation and the requirements of the World Trade Organization Agreement on Sanitary and Phytosanitary Measures." *Rev Sci Tech* **23**(1): 109–14.

Threll, E. J., I. S. Fisher, et al. (2003). "Antimicrobial drug resistance in isolates of Salmonella enterica from cases of salmonellosis in humans in Europe in 2000: results of international multi-centre surveillance," *Euro Surveill* **8**(2): 41–5.

Torres, A., M. J. David, et al. (2002). "Risk management of international trade: emergency preparedness." *Rev Sci Tech* **21**(3): 493–8.

Townsend, P. G. D. (2002). *World Poverty*. Bristol UK, The Policy Press.

Trampuz, A., R. M. Prabhu, et al. (2004). "Avian influenza: a new pandemic threat?" *Mayo Clin Proc* **79**(4): 523–30; quiz 530.

U.S. Census Bureau (2002). Foreign Trade Statistics.

U.S. Department of Agriculture (2004). USDA Homeland Security Efforts.

U.S. Department of Agriculture, Food Safety and Inspection Service (2002). Colorado Firm Recalls Beef Trim and Ground Beef Products for Possible E. Coli. O157:H7.

U.S. Food and Drug Administration (2003). Import Program System Information.

U.S. General Accounting Office (2000). Food Safety Actions Needed by USDA and FDA to Ensure that Companies Promptly Carry Out Recalls.

U.S. General Accounting Office (2001). Food Safety: CDC is Working to Address Limitations in Several of Its Foodborne Disease Surveillance Systems.

U.S. General Accounting Office (2001). Global Health: Challenges to Improving Infectious Disease Surveillance Systems.

U.S. General Accounting Office (April 2004). Antibiotic Resistance: Federal Agencies Need to Better Focus Efforts to Address Risks to Humans from Antibiotic Use in Animals.

U.S. State Department Convention on the Prohibition of the Development, Production and Stockpiling of Bacteriological (Biological) and Toxin Weapons and on their Destruction.

USDA Foreign Agricultural Service (2001). "FDA Says No to Access for Guatemala Raspberries, Citing Health Concerns."

Van Voris, B. (1997). "Jack in the Box Ends E. Coli Suits." *The National Law Journal*.

Venkatesh, S. and Z. A. Memish (2003). "Bioterrorism – a new challenge for public health." *Int J Antimicrob Agents* **21**(2): 200–206.

Voelker, R. (2002). "Listeriosis outbreak prompts action – finally." *Jama* **288**(21): 2675–6.

Walther, B. A. and P. W. Ewald (2004). "Pathogen survival in the external environment and the evolution of virulence." *Bio Rev Camb Philos Soc* **79**(4): 849–69.

Watanabe, Y., K. Ozasa, et al. (1999). "Factory outbreak of Escherichia coli O157:H7 infection in Japan." *Emeg Infect Dis* **5**(3): 424–8.

Webster, R. G. (1997). "Influenza virus: transmission between species and relevance to emergence of the next human pandemic." *Arch Virol Suppl* **13**: 105–13.

Weinberg, P. D., J. Houmshell, et al. (2002). "Legal, financial, and public health consequences of HIV contamination of blood and blood products in the 1980s and 1990s." *Ann Intern Med* **136**(4): 312–19.

Weir, E., K. Dore, et al. (2004). "Enhanced surveillance for Salmonella Newport." *Cmaj* **171**(2): 127–8.

Williams, R. A. and K. M. Thompson (2004). "Integrated analysis: combining risk and economic assessments while preserving the separation of powers." *Risk Anal* **24**(6): 1613–23.

Wilson, D. W. and P. T. Beers (2001). "Global trade requirements and compliance with World Trade Organization agreements: the role of tracing animals and animal products." *Rev Sci Tech* **20**(2): 379–84.

Wilson, K. and M. N. Ricketts (2004). "The success of precaution? Managing the risk of transfusion transmission of variant Creutzfeldt-Jakob disease." *Transfusion* **44**(10): 1475–8.

Windsor, R. S. (2002). "Relating national veterinary services to the country's livestock industry: case studies from four countries – Great Britain, Botswana, Peru, and Vietnam." *Ann N Y Acad Sci* **969**: 39–47.

Wolf, D. G., D. Rekhtman, et al. (2004). "A summer outbreak of influenza A virus infection among young children." *Clin Infect Dis* **39**(4): 595–7.

World Bank Group (2002). Developing countries – Health, Nutrition – 2002.

World Health Organization. *WHO trade and health*, from http://www.who.int/trade/en/.

World Health Organization Drug Resistance.

World Health Organization (2001). Health Aspects of Biological and Chemical Weapons.

World Health Organization (2001). "WHO Global Strategy for Containment of Antimicrobial Resistance." **2**.

World Health Organization (2002). Food safety and foodborne illness.

World Health Organization (2002). Future Trends in Veterinary Public Health. *WHO Technical Report Series*. Geneva.

World Health Organization (May 23, 2005). World health assembly adopts to International Health Regulations: New rules govern national and international responses to disease outbreaks.

World Health Organization/World Trade Organization (2002). WTO Agreements and Public Health: A joint study by the WHO and the WTO Secretariat. Geneva, WHO/WTO.

World Trade Organization (1999). Technical Barriers to the Market Access of Developing Countries.

Zhu, T., B. T. Korber, et al. (1998). "An African HIV-1 sequence from 1959 and implications for the origin of the epidemic." *Nature* **391**(6667): 594–7.

Index